AF609285

JUMPING JACK

JUMPING JACK

GARRY JACK

WITH

ADAM HAWSE

First published in 2026 by Fair Play Publishing
PO Box 4101, Balgowlah Heights, NSW 2093, Australia

www.fairplaypublishing.com.au

ISBN: 978-1-923236-39-4
ISBN: 978-1-923236-40-0 (ePub)

© 2026 Garry Jack and Adam Hawse.
The moral rights of the authors have been asserted.

All rights reserved. Except as permitted under the *Australian Copyright Act 1968* (for example, a fair dealing for the purposes of study, research, criticism or review), no part of this book may be reproduced, stored in a retrieval system, communicated or transmitted in any form or by any means without prior written permission from the Publisher.

Cover design and typesetting by Leslie Priestley.

All photographs supplied by Garry Jack.

All inquiries should be made to the Publisher via hello@fairplaypublishing.com.au

A catalogue record of this book is available from the National Library of Australia.

CONTENTS

FOREWORD

There are two moments etched in my memory that told me Garry Jack was destined for greatness.

The first is when we were both playing in the under-18s for Wests Red Devils in Wollongong.

One day at training someone from first grade was talking to the juniors' officials. We were all naturally curious as to what was going on. Word got back that one of the team had been selected to play first grade with the men. Being full of myself as a footballer, I naturally presumed it was me.

However, to my great disappointment, it was Garry Jack.

It was unheard of for a player so young to be selected in first grade.

Garry's parents didn't allow him to play. History has proved that to be a great decision.

The second moment came in the same year.

I had the privilege of meeting Wests Red Devils' greatest player, Bob Fulton. I was introduced by Greg 'Scrubber' Brazier. I remember Scrubber pointing to Garry and saying, "This bloke will play for Australia."

He was right. Scrubber saw in Garry what many of us were only beginning to understand—raw, undeniable talent.

Outside of Garry's family, I doubt anyone followed his career as closely as I did. I was in awe of his ability, talent, skill and determination. He lived the dream I always had—representing both New South Wales and Australia—and he did it with distinction.

Garry Jack is, in my view, one of the greatest players the game has ever seen. It brings me immense joy to see his incredible career honoured and preserved in this book

Peter V'Landys, AM

Chairman, Australian Rugby League Commission

PROLOGUE

Some memories never fade. The sting of a hard tackle. The silence before a kick. I've lived a life shaped by those moments—some glorious, some painful—but all unforgettable.

I was just a kid from Wollongong with a dream. I didn't have much, but I had heart. Rugby league gave me a purpose, a place to belong, and a chance to prove myself. From my junior days at Wests Red Devils to my debut with the Western Suburbs Magpies in 1981, playing five premiership and three mid-week games for them, to the years I spent with the Balmain Tigers.

Every game was a chapter in a story I never imagined I'd get to write.

I played 244 first-grade games for Balmain, plus another 22 mid-week and pre-season competition appearances. That gave me 266 appearances in the top grade in all competitions.

That's not just a stat—it was a privilege and something which makes me feel very proud. That black and gold jersey became part of who I am.

I've stood on the biggest stages—17 State of Origin matches for New South Wales, and 22 Tests in a row for Australia.

I've felt the pride of singing the national anthem with my hand on my heart, and the weight of expectation that comes with representing your country.

The 1986 Kangaroo Tour, the 1988 World Cup, the Golden Boot Award... they were milestones, yes. But they were also moments that reminded me how far I'd come from that wide-eyed boy kicking a ball in the backyard in Figtree, Wollongong.

But it wasn't always easy. Injuries, setbacks, the pressure to perform—it takes a toll.

When the final whistle blew on my playing career, I faced a different kind of challenge: figuring out who I was without the game. That transition was tough. But it's also what led me to where I am now—working for the NRL to support young players in the pathways and participation teams in the Illawarra and South Coast area, with my managers Kyle Williams and Adam Bezzina. We help kids to find their path, and make sure they know they're a lot more than just players.

Thank you to Peter V'landys, NRL chief executive Andrew Abdo, Kyle and Adam for your continued support in this great game.

This book is my story. Not just the highlights, but the heartaches, the lessons learned, and the people who lifted me up when I couldn't stand on my own. It's about the power of sport to shape character, build resilience and create lifelong bonds. Because rugby league didn't just give me a career—it gave me a life. And I'm grateful for every moment.

I dedicate *Jumping Jack* to my family, especially my wife, Donna. My journey wouldn't have been possible without your love and support. Your love, patience and unwavering support have been my foundation. Through every high and low, I know that life won't break me with you beside me, reminding me of who I am.

To our family—Bill, Wendy, Kieren, Charlotte, Alfie, Clara, Hugo, Brandon, Rhys, Kat, Natalie, Mandy, Peter, Brenton, and Jenna. I love you all.

To my mum, dad and nan and pop who are no longer here—your love and support was unyielding. You all inspired me to "give my best" and to never give up on my dreams. This is also your story. Thank you for believing in me. I will pass our memories and lessons learned on to the next generation of Jacks.

To my teammates at Balmain, NSW, Australia, Western Suburbs, Sheffield and Salford. You were more than just players on the field. You were blood brothers in battle, friends off the pitch, and part of a bond that only sport can forge. Every tackle, every triumph, every heartbreaking loss—we shared it all. Thank you for your friendship and your loyalty. You will forever be in my heart.

To my author, Adam Hawse, thank you so much, Hack. You've done an amazing job pulling all my adventures together into a great story for everyone to enjoy. Our friendship has made this possible. Thank you, Adam. This book is for you as much as it is for me.

Regards,
'Jimmy' Jack

CHAPTER 1

THE DAY I DIED

JANUARY 22, 2021, was a typically sweaty mid-summer's day in the north-western suburbs of Sydney.

The temperature hovered around 40 degrees all afternoon, barely dropping as evening approached.

At the Jack household in Cherrybrook, it was business as usual. My wife Donna joined me in the backyard to admire the new fence we'd had put up that week. We spoke about getting the guy back to do some stairs.

Rupey, our pug, was scooting around in excited circles. It wouldn't be long before he would crash in the loungeroom, drowning the place with his snoring.

It was Friday, which meant I was scheduled for Brazilian jiu-jitsu training. Otherwise known as BJJ, it's a martial art and combat sport based on grappling, ground fighting and submission holds.

I trained three times a week at the Universal Combat Academy (UCA) at Castle Hill, where I earned my black belt. Overall, I had been training for 20 years, and introduced BJJ to my three sons Kieren, Rhys and Brandon. Rhys was the keenest and progressed through to black belt (at the time I was told we were the first father and son BJJ black belts in Australia, something that I am very proud of as a dad).

I was looking forward to class on this particular Friday evening. Since New Year's Day, I had been punching out some fast lap times down the road at Edward Bennett Park. In just two weeks, I had slashed three minutes off my three-kilometre run, from 29 minutes to 26 minutes.

I always felt running in my spare time was good for my BJJ. It gave me an edge over others in the class.

I arrived at the UCA just after 6 p.m. and the same old friendly faces were there to greet me.

Some people see Friday evenings as a great time to grab a schooner of cold beer at the pub after work. At this stage of my life, I see it as a chance to grab someone half my age and wrestle them to the floor.

The competitive fire still burns more than two decades after I last laced on a pair of footy boots. I like to challenge myself against men who are younger, fitter and stronger than this old fullback.

Leading the way at UCA was Simon Farnsworth. He's a fourth-degree black belt in Brazilian jiu-jitsu, which makes him a formidable fighter.

Simon is a top bloke. I have been training with him for 20 years. He's the instructor and when he says it's time to start training, everyone knuckles down.

Simon took us for our warm-up, and I wanted to show him what great nick I was in. We did five laps of the venue, and the pace was quick. That was fine by me. I pushed myself. The harder Simon took it out, the harder I went with him. We followed up the run with a series of dips, push-ups and crunches.

Even though it was getting late in the day, it was still very hot.

In between sets I could feel my heart beating quickly. I also had some short, shallow breaths. I reminded myself that this was nothing out of the ordinary. During my runs at Edward Bennett Park, I often felt the same way. I would just slow down and walk until my heartbeat settled.

I put it down to not being a young man anymore.

After our run, Simon stopped and spoke with the group. My heart was still racing. I was aware of it but not panicking. My only thought was to try and somehow slow the rate of beats before we started wrestling.

Simon finished speaking and it was time to get down to business. Each of us had to find a training partner. I paired up with Frank Gehret, another black belt in the group.

Frank and I made small talk, but I could still feel my heart pounding. I told myself to "walk it off", just like I would at Edward Bennett Park.

As I walked to Frank, getting my breath back, I felt better. It was time for jiu-jitsu. Frank approached and I crouched to face him.

Then my life changed in a split-second.

I collapsed backwards into a wall, giving out a sickening moan. I then slumped back on the matting at Frank's feet.

My heart had suffered a catastrophic failure—a cardiac arrest.

Simon ran straight over. He was shaking me, screaming "Gaz! Gaz!"

I was unconscious and my stricken body was fighting against itself. My fists and jaw were clenched tight as I convulsed and writhed in front of my shocked peers.

My heart, beating so fast only minutes earlier, had stopped completely. So had my breathing. My face and lips had gone from grey to blue.

By now, everyone inside the hall had stopped what they were doing. Students, mums, dads and kids were watching on in horror.

One of my training buddies, Dave Ward, thought I had fainted. Frank was asking me if I was okay. When there was no response, Simon said he was starting CPR.

His brother, Luke Farnsworth, called for an ambulance. Someone else grabbed the defibrillator, which proved unsuccessful in reviving my heart.

Simon started CPR on me. He did this with his typical focus and intensity. He wasn't going to let me go without pounding my sternum, using every bit of strength in his powerful 70-kilo frame.

My entire body was bouncing off the floor as Simon pumped out 100–120 compressions per minute.

Dave and Frank offered to take over, but Simon said he wasn't stopping until the ambulance arrived. He knew every extra minute it took to get my heart restarted was a 10% less chance of avoiding permanent brain damage and death.

While Simon hit me with everything he had, Frank and Dave were trying to keep my airways open.

After about six minutes, just as hopes were fading, there was a flash of hope. Simon felt a weak pulse. But then I slipped away for a second time. My lips went blue, and Simon started up again.

You don't become a fourth-dan Brazilian jiu-jitsu black belt without a lot of discipline and determination. Simon kept going. He's the fiercest competitor I've ever met.

After 10 minutes of CPR from Simon, the ambulance arrived. NSW Ambulance Inspector Kevin McSweeney led a team of four paramedics who took over. They threw another defibrillator on me, then rushed me to Westmead Hospital.

The three men who worked so hard to save my life shared a hug, not knowing if they would ever see me again.

Throughout all this, Donna had been called by Simon's son, Jake, to let her know what was happening. She was driven by Kevin McSweeney to Westmead Hospital, not knowing if her husband was alive or dead. It was agony for her. She was beside herself and in no state to drive.

Kevin told Donna that at one stage during the cardiac arrest, I had been trying to turn from my back to my belly to try and get up. He said that was a good sign because in his experience, most patients don't move at all.

Later that night at Westmead, with Donna keeping a bedside vigil, my condition improved. The nurses took out my breathing tubes so I could breathe on my own.

I had memories of my late mum watching over me as I lay in that hospital bed. The clock in front of me displayed JAN 22 (the date of January 22). My mum's name was Janice, and her date of birth was the 22nd (of June.)

Mum had passed away 11 years earlier from heart-related complications. I have no doubt my mum was there with me.

They say your life flashes before your eyes in those final moments before you die. Memories as a kid, your wedding day, the birth of your first child, etc.

As Simon fought to save my life, that didn't happen for me.

But I did have a vision of myself alone in a room that I couldn't escape.

All I can recall was being in a dark room, looking down on myself, with a shining light on me. And I kept falling over. Every time I got up, I'd fall over again and again.

I was saying to myself in this dream, "I can't stay here, I can't stay here." It was like an out-of-body experience where I was watching myself from the corner of a room.

That's the only recollection I have.

An angiogram showed the left circumflex artery to my heart was completely blocked. Everyone has four arteries taking blood to and from the heart. I was a ticking timebomb.

I required major surgery to rebuild the artery with two stents inserted. I was also put through an induced cardiac arrest—which terrified me—to ensure the electrics of my heart were working properly, before I could be released from hospital.

I have since learned so much about cardiac arrests. I didn't even realise they were different to heart attacks. Kevin McSweeney said to me, "You can survive a heart attack, but you won't survive a cardiac arrest, unless you have people around you who know what to do."

I became an ambassador for the Michael Hughes Foundation, a not-for-profit charity whose primary focus is to "Turn Bystanders into First Responders" in the event of cardiac arrest. I want to help others avoid my experience.

In the year leading up to January 2021, more than 33,000 Australians suffered a cardiac arrest.

Sadly, 90–95 percent of cardiac arrests are fatal. We need to improve this with better awareness of CPR. Performing CPR keeps the brain alive.

Simon has since admitted he thought I was "gone". In a magazine article, Insp. McSweeney said: "When Simon says he thinks Garry was gone, well that's because he was—he was dead."

Cardiac arrest can happen to anyone. I had no pain. I just collapsed. If I'd have died, I wouldn't have felt a thing.

I had unknowingly joined a very exclusive club, called the cardiac arrest survivors' club. I'm very glad to be in this club.

I now have three grandchildren: Alfie, and twins Hugo and Clara Jack. They are beautiful. There will be special times ahead with their pop.

It's all down to my guardian angel Simon Farnsworth. He saved my life.

Thank you to Simon, Luke, Dave, Frank, Jake and my BJJ family who I trained with for 20 years. I can never repay what you did for me.

CHAPTER 2

MY INSPIRATIONS

NONE of what I achieved in my career would have been possible without some very special people in my life.

I first met Donna Verhaeghe at, of all places, North Sydney Oval. It was round 7 of the 1982 NSW Rugby League season, and I was playing for Balmain against Norths.

Donna attended the game as a friend of Cathy Walsh, girlfriend of my Tigers' teammate Steve Roach (they would later marry).

Donna and Cathy were in their first year as trainee nurses at nearby Royal North Shore Hospital.

I was lucky that Cathy's surname began with a 'W' because it meant she worked alongside Donna. Rosters were filled in alphabetical order for trainee nurses. If she was Cathy Baker, for example, I may never have met Donna.

It was a modest first encounter. I thought Donna was very pretty, but we basically said hello to each other and that was it.

About a month later, we met again at popular theatre restaurant Dirty Dicks at St Leonards. All Donna's nursing friends were there... plus her boyfriend.

That relationship petered out (thankfully) and when we bumped into each other at another party a couple of weeks later, we exchanged phone numbers and agreed to catch up for dinner.

We went to a bar in Beattie Street, Balmain, where we talked about... sport.

But don't worry—I wasn't boring her with my footy stories. Instead, it was *Donna's* sports prowess that dominated conversation. She was a gun basketball player!

Donna represented NSW at both under-15 and open levels while at high school.

Things picked up from there. Donna accompanied me to the 1982 Dally M awards ceremony at St. George Leagues Club.

In early 1984, Donna went to the USA to visit a friend.

While she was away, I decided it would be a good time to visit her dad and ask for his blessing to have his daughter's hand in marriage.

I made two mistakes there. One, not telling Bill that I was paying him a visit. Two, I decided to do this on the day of a Balmain against Penrith game.

Billy lived on a farm in Bowral in the NSW Southern Highlands. I decided I would travel there first from our home in Wollongong, ask him the question, then drive to Penrith Park to face the Panthers at 3 p.m.

I arrived at Bill's house around 12 p.m. He wasn't home. There were no mobile phones back then, so I waited and waited, hoping he'd appear in the driveway.

I waited till 1.30 p.m. I had to get going. I'd budgeted 45 minutes of travel time to get to Penrith by 2.15 p.m. for warm-up.

The drive was slightly longer than expected.

I walked into our dressing room at 2.45 p.m., giving me a mere 15 minutes to get ready. Our coach Frank Stanton lived up to his 'Cranky Franky' nickname. He was not happy when I walked in.

I told him what had happened. "Okay—just get yourself ready."

We won 16–8. It was the only time I was ever late to a game.

I eventually received Bill's blessing and was waiting for Donna at Sydney Airport when she returned... an engagement ring in my pocket. I popped the question, and the answer was in the affirmative!

We married on November 2, 1985, in Bowral, which is where Donna grew up. We bought a house at Cordeaux Heights, a suburb of Wollongong, and lived there for three years. We then moved to Cherrybrook in north-western Sydney.

Our plan was to have kids while we were still in our 20s, so we could enjoy them—and maybe even take them to a few Tigers' games while I was still playing!

Kieren was the first to come along. He was born the day after we played a game against Cronulla at Leichhardt Oval in 1987.

We trailed 26–2 at halftime and were booed off the field by our own supporters. We made a huge comeback to level the scores, but the Sharks scored late to win 32–26.

All the excitement sent Donna into labour later that night!

I took her to Wollongong Hospital at about 3 a.m., and Kieren James Jack was born at 11 a.m. on June 28. It is still the greatest experience of my life seeing my first son being born, it was just amazing.

Rhys was next to arrive a couple of years later, then Brandon while we were living in the UK in 1994.

Kieren, Rhys and Brandon grew up in a footy family, and loved the Tigers, NSW and Kangaroos.

Every day after school there was something happening with at least one of the boys. There were training sessions for rugby league, Aussie Rules, golf, cricket—even Brazilian jiu-jitsu.

All of this was possible because of their mum, who drove them all over Sydney to help them follow their dreams.

They were never pushed into sport. I always heeded the lesson I learned as a 15-year-old, when I told my dad that I didn't want to play rugby league anymore.

That I wanted to play golf instead. He respected my wishes.

That's why when Kieren wanted to play Aussie Rules at 14—not rugby league—I was okay with it.

Kieren always showed a natural ability to kick a ball, either in the backyard, on the front lawn, or in the cul-de-sac.

When we went to England at the end of 1992, Kieren had to learn how to play soccer—because they're obsessed with it over there. He had no idea what to do.

He would play against a kid next-door named Chris and would get beaten 11–0!

Kieren worked hard at his game, until one day I heard a scream coming from the football pitch on the front lawn. I thought someone was hurt.

I raced outside, and thankfully, found no one injured. It was just Chris screaming his head off because Kieren had beaten him at soccer for the first time!

He has always shown this determination at whatever sport he played.

When Kieren began playing Aussie Rules, his coaches loved the way he competed for the ball, and his defence. No one tackled like him. He made the under-12s' NSW team in his first year. He was drafted by the Sydney Swans in the second-round picks as draft pick 75.

Kieren played 256 games at the top level, kicking 166 goals. He won a premiership with the Swans in 2012.

He's married to Charlotte, and they have three children.

Alfie was born on Boxing Day, 2022, then twins Clara Elizabeth and Hugo Matthew Jack came along on August 30, 2025.

We love them all so much. We are very proud grandparents.

Rhys showed a love for rugby league from a young age. When we were living in England, he and Kieren would put on their little Aussie footy jerseys and boots to take me on in the backyard.

Rhys was a very talented player. He played in the halves for the NSW Combined Catholic Colleges team. Also in that team were some names who had lengthy NRL careers—Kieran Foran, Jamie Buhrer and Jamal Idris.

Rhys was signed by Canterbury and was part of their under-20s' team that won the premiership in 2010.

A couple of years later, Rhys played for Balmain, who were a feeder team for the Wests Tigers.

Like me, Rhys found a love for Brazilian jiu-jitsu. He's progressed all the way to a black belt, which is a great achievement.

He is now called upon by rugby league teams to teach the art of grappling in defence, which is so important in the modern game.

Rhys is married to Kat Hoyos, an Australian actor, who has starred in a few local films. We are very proud of them both.

Brandon is our baby. He was born at Stepping Hill Hospital, Stockport, when we lived in Bramhall in northern England.

When I told Kieren and Rhys that they had a baby brother, they were so excited and couldn't wait to go and see their mum and little Brandon in the hospital.

Brandon was very clever and always had a great eye for drawing pictures. He followed his brothers into rugby league with the Pennant Hills Stags.

Brandon swapped over to Aussie Rules after watching the success Kieren had enjoyed. He played first grade for Pennant Hills when he was just 17 and made NSW teams.

As a Type 1 diabetic with coeliac disease, Brandon had to overcome a lot of setbacks to reach his dreams. He was drafted by the Swans and made his senior debut against Port Adelaide at Adelaide Oval in 2013, kicking four goals. Brandon played 28 senior games for the Swans, kicking 16 goals. He had a great career that I am very proud of, wearing the number 33 and always giving 100 percent.

He has always had a love of writing and is a published author. His latest book is called *Pissants*, which is about a fictional AFL team. I wish him every success with the book, he deserves it. He has found a love for writing that fulfils him, and he is fantastic at it.

A perfect example of what you work hard at, you will succeed in.

I was very lucky to be in a position to give our kids a good home, with parents that would do anything for them. All three boys had grandparents on both sides that loved them very much: my parents Jan and Keith, and Donna's parents, Wendy and Bill.

We are so proud of the men our three sons have grown into.

Finally, to Donna, such a fantastic mother, wife and now nanny to Alfie, Clara and Hugo.

It takes a very special person to commit to being a nurse, where you put other people's welfare ahead of your own.

That sums her up. Donna always puts her family ahead of herself.

Thank you from the bottom of my heart.

CHAPTER 3

RELUCTANT ROOKIE

DAD turned off the Princes Highway and drove into the car park at Figtree Oval, in suburban Wollongong, just behind the tennis courts.

I sat in the backseat, a nervous six-year-old, peering out the window. Dad opened his door and stepped outside.

"Okay, let's go."

We had arrived at the ground for my first training session with the Western Suburbs Red Devils' rugby league club. I could see my new teammates outside, running around all over the place like you would expect of kids that age.

"Garry, come on."

I'd been looking forward to this moment all week. But suddenly I couldn't move. I was too scared to get out of the car.

Dad gave me a moment to get over it, but things only got worse. I sat there and… started to cry.

Dad climbed back into the car, started the engine, and we left Figtree Oval without anyone knowing we were even there.

It was another 12 months before my father dared take me back. We pulled into the same car park, and he looked back at me with a smile.

"Do you want to get out of the car this time?"

"Yeah, I do, Dad!"

I flung open the door and raced over to meet my new teammates in the Red Devils' under-8s.

It had been a rocky start, but my love affair with rugby league was officially underway.

This would have come as no shock to anyone who knew the Jack family. We had rugby league in our DNA.

My dad, Keith Jack—better known as 'Thunder'—was a tough prop who played more than 80 first-grade games with Wests in the Wollongong competition in the 1950s. He played in the same team as Keith Barnes, who would become a Balmain Tigers' legend and a huge figure in my career.

Dad was an incredibly fit man, running 10 kilometres every day. This was important for his day job as a "bread carter" for Buttercup Bakeries. For more than three decades, he delivered bread around the district, lugging loaves to all sorts of places.

Dad was an old-school guy who wasn't big on delivering compliments.

He would never say to me "that was a good try" or "that was a good tackle". I never held it against him. That's just how he was.

But I know he loved me.

When I was about 16, I made a try-saving tackle at Figtree Oval. Dad wandered over and said: "That was a great tackle. That's something that Graeme Langlands would have done."

"Really Dad?"

"Yep."

I thought, *"Wow, Dad's proud of me."*

The other footy roots in my family came from my grandfather—my mother Jan's dad.

His name was Jim Porter, who played for Mt Keira way back in the 1920s. He was an inspiration to me, and you'll read more about him later.

I never wanted for anything as a kid. I had a great childhood with lots of love.

Mum and Dad were working-class people. They gave me every opportunity to play sport. They always supported me and encouraged me to do my best, even if I *wasn't* the best. While Dad was delivering bread, Mum worked at a newsagent not far away in Dapto.

This worked out nicely for me because I was a massive fan of *Rugby League Week* magazine during my teens. Mum would bring home the latest edition every Thursday after work.

The magazine would include reports on the local Illawarra competition. As I started working my way through the grades, my name would occasionally get a mention, which was pretty cool.

While Dad loved a drink after his shift at the Figtree Hotel, Mum was the opposite. She was a non-drinker and non-smoker.

I was close to my younger sister Mandy, who I used to terrorise. We spent a lot of time together at Figtree Crescent, playing games in our backyard. This was probably difficult for her, as I always had to win… everything. Sorry Mandy!

There weren't too many family holidays, but that didn't bother us. We learned the value of a dollar and didn't waste money (more on that later).

Going back to that under-8's team… we had a fair bit of talent.

There was Craig and Johnny Hobbs—their dad John played for the Manly Sea Eagles in the 1950s. Scotty Moir was another teammate. His dad Ian was a speedy winger who played for Australia.

I don't think I touched the ball much in that first season, although I did score a try.

It was from dummy-half at Scarborough Oval.

A highlight that year was playing in a curtain-raiser game at Wollongong Showground, when the touring Great Britain side played a warm-up match ahead of the World Cup.

In that 'GB' side was a guy called Kevin Ashcroft. Two decades later, he would be my coach when I had a stint with Salford in the UK.

Because we were a bit younger, most of us were still eligible for the under-8s again the following year. With that extra year under our belts, we became the gun side of the competition. Dad was our coach, and we won premierships right through to the under-11s.

Then Dad had to step down because of a horrific accident that nearly claimed his life.

He was doing a bread drop in Dapto when he forgot to check both ways as he crossed the road. He never saw the Volkswagen until it hit him.

Dad went straight over the bonnet, flew over the back of the car, and landed hard on the road.

He dislocated his hip and his shoulder and suffered head injuries. It was a miracle he wasn't killed.

I'll never forget when we got a knock on the door at home. Someone from the bakery came and told us that Dad was in hospital. Mum screamed—she was hysterical.

Thankfully, Dad survived. After six months he was back on his bread run!

Even without Dad calling the shots, we kept on winning.

We won every competition right up to the under-14s, sometimes going through the season undefeated. In that seven-year period, I remember losing maybe two games in total.

I wasn't a fullback in those early days. Not even close. Dad picked me in the forwards at lock.

His advice was to always tackle around the legs; catch the ball on the full; and to run hard. I tried to remember those three things every time I played.

I was never the best player in the team in those early years playing in the forwards. To try and improve, I began modelling my game on the great South Sydney lock forward Ron Coote.

As a result, I became a huge fan of the Rabbitohs, and my form also picked up.

In 1971, I made my first representative team—the Wollongong under-11s. It was a huge thrill for me.

But the following year I suffered a major setback. In fact, it was far more serious than that.

I nearly died.

I contracted peritonitis after my appendix burst. Luckily, I arrived at the hospital just in time and made a full recovery.

Jim Harrod—the grandfather of NRL player Jackson Hastings—took the coaching reins from Dad in the under-12s. Jim was tough on fitness, which I really enjoyed.

We weren't the only Wests Red Devils' team cleaning up the competition. The team one age group below us was bloody good as well. In that team was a boy called Steve Roach.

I was still playing in the forwards at the age of 13 but was thinking I needed a change.

I felt a bit small, as the other guys started shooting up.

I told Dad, who was back helping out the team, that I fancied a switch to fullback. Our regular number 1 had taken off to play soccer, so I knew there was a vacancy.

At the next training session, Jim asked who wanted to take over at fullback. I looked straight at Dad, who was standing next to Jim.

"Garry wants to play fullback," he said.

I nodded my head in agreement.

"Okay—Garry, you're the fullback," Jim responded.

And so, my journey to becoming an Australian fullback of 22 Test matches had begun.

Straight away, I loved the freedom. There was so much room to run. I added my love of tackling too, which I learned from my time impersonating Ron Coote. If someone broke through the defensive line, I would cut them down before the goal-line. I was good at it. I had no fear. I knew I had the right technique. Playing in the forwards had helped me enormously.

Apart from running and tackling, the other important aspect of playing fullback is catching the ball.

I spent hours and hours kicking the ball high into the sky out the front of our house, or down at the park, then running around and catching it.

I would pretend to be Roosters' fullback Russell Fairfax. Or Graham Eadie from Manly.

I wanted to get a bit quicker, so I did some sprint training with Ian Moir. It was all coming together for me.

But the teenage brain tends to wander and suddenly I found a new love. Golf. I was obsessed with it. I was 14 and had a handicap of 10.

Even though Dad had taken over as footy coach for the under-15s, I told him I was out. I wanted to play golf with my mates.

Dad respected my decision and left me at home. He never pressured me to change my mind either. I played golf all year and my handicap came down to five. I was beginning to have dreams of becoming a professional golfer.

At the same time, I was also getting into taekwondo. Bruce Lee was very big in the mid-'70s—everyone was into kung fu fighting.

I stuck at it for about three years, which really improved my flexibility and strength. It added definition to my scrawny body, which was a big aim of mine.

I also loved cricket and surf lifesaving. Those beach sprint relays on Saturday mornings were so important to my rugby league career. You had to get those changeovers exactly right or you would be disqualified from the carnival. I believe this taught me the art of timing my run on the footy field in later life.

I was involved in lots of set-plays at Balmain with Benny Elias. He would dummy one direction, then go the other way and find me in support. I would rarely over-run the pass because of what I learned in nippers at Wollongong South Surf Club.

I left Figtree High School when I was 15. I became a fitter and turner and worked for five years at the BHP Steelworks at Port Kembla.

Even though I didn't really enjoy that line of work, I learned a lot of lessons that helped me later in life.

I returned to rugby league in the under-16s. We went all the way and won the grand final that season. I was physically feeling stronger than ever, and I put that down to taekwondo.

At the age of 17, I played up a year at Wests Red Devils with a teammate who had a huge future ahead of him.

His name was Peter V'landys.

Peter played in the centres and second row and was very fast and elusive. His ability to break tackles was matched by a quick sense of humour.

Even back then, you knew he was going to be a success in whatever he did. He has always had a great work ethic and passion for whatever he sinks his teeth into... apart from woodwork and metalwork. Peter told me he was the only student to fail both in the same year at Keira Boys' High!

I'm not surprised to see him rise all the way to be chairman of the Australian Rugby League Commission. The game is in good hands with PVL as the boss.

He's also run Racing NSW for many years. Even as a young bloke, Peter had an eye for the horses. His best mate, Ian Millward, lived next-door to my nan and pop. Quite often we would all sit at their dining table and Peter would scribble down some tips for the upcoming races at the Harold Park trots.

I inherited that table from Nan and Pop and still have it to this day.

I had one of the best games of my career for the Devils when Peter was in the side. We were playing against Thirroul at Figtree Oval, and I scored three tries.

The next week our first-grade fullback Keith Rugg was called up to play for NSW Country. They wanted me to take his place! I was only 17. The last player that age to play first grade for the club was John Dorahy several years earlier—and he ended up playing for Australia.

Dad ran the idea past Mum, and she was not keen.

"You're not playing first grade, Garry—you're too young."

While I was still raw, I wasn't a babe in the woods. I had left school and was a second-year apprentice fitter and turner.

But Mum was very protective of me, and I loved her for it. She didn't want me to get hurt playing against men.

Even though it was a great honour to be asked, I told Dad that I didn't want to play.

CHAPTER 4

GROWING UP WITH BLOCKER

STEVE Roach and I played 162 first-grade games together at Balmain between 1982–92. That's the most of any partnership in Tigers' history.

We also played together in many State of Origin games for NSW and Test matches for Australia. All up, we were alongside each other for an incredible 211 games at the top level.

Not bad for a couple of boys from Figtree and Mount St Thomas.

We both came through the ranks together from the Western Suburbs Red Devils' club in Wollongong. We were both graduates of Figtree High School.

Even at seven years of age, Steven was the biggest boy in his team. They put him in the front row… where he spent his entire career.

Because of his size, Steve was nicknamed 'Podge' by his teammates. After losing his temper during games and getting into fights, that tag changed to 'Blockhead'… as in, he was always 'doing his block'.

It wasn't long before Blockhead was cut to 'Blocker'. The name has stuck to this very day and is one of the most famous in Australian sport.

I played a year higher than Steve at the Red Devils. Both our teams were virtually unbeatable from the under-8s to the under-14s.

Despite playing in different teams, Blocker and I became friends. We would always argue about which team was better—his or mine.

When I had a year off footy to play golf, I watched Blocker play in the University Shield—a State-wide competition for high schools. Most players are in Year 11 and 12, which means they're aged 17–18.

Blocker played when he was just 14. In one game he more than held his own in the front row against Royce Ayliffe, a guy who went on to play plenty of first grade for Easts and Souths, as well as representing NSW and Australia in his career. Royce was in Year 12, but Blocker didn't care. He was fearless.

Blocker made the move to Sydney a year earlier than I did. When I joined Balmain in 1982, we car-pooled together from Wollongong.

We boarded together at Ashfield, worked together at Balmain Leagues Club, and shared a dream and a desire to play for Australia.

Steve has a great brain for rugby league and that's obvious when you listen to his commentary on Fox League. He genuinely connects with people because he cares. Block is a big softy, beneath that hard, tough exterior.

We were teammates for 11 seasons and developed a great understanding of each other's play. Whether I scored a try for Balmain, NSW or Australia, Steve was always the first one there to congratulate me. I did the same for him—but the big fella didn't score many!

The best thing Steven ever did for me was being involved in introducing me to Donna. He ended up being a groomsman at our wedding.

One of my favourite stories was when we were part of the Australian team that toured New Zealand in 1985.

Blocker and I were having breakfast at the team hotel when I said, "Gee the bacon's great over here."

"Why wouldn't it be?" snapped Blocker. "There's thirty million sheep over here!"

In 1987, Block and I were part of a wild Mad Monday celebration with our Balmain teammates at The Birkenhead Hotel in Drummoyne.

After quite a few drinks, we decided to pinch an idea from the Kangaroo Tour—Big Men versus Little Men, where the smaller guys take on the bigger guys in a (drunken) test of strength.

I ended up on the Little Men's team and, very late in the day, I tried to rip off Blocker's shirt.

This was a very bad mistake.

Block threw a haymaker at me, then followed it up with an almighty uppercut.

By some miracle, they both missed. If they connected, I would have ended up in Drummoyne Bay!

As I counted my blessings, I realised I had ended up on the carpet. When I looked up, there was a very unhappy face looking down at me—and it wasn't Blocker.

Donna had turned up at that very moment to collect me. Her timing was impeccable. I'd been saved from a flogging!

She looked at Blocker and said, "What's going on here Steven?"

"Nothing… nothing."

I jumped off the floor and declared: "We're best mates!"

Then it was time to go home.

CHAPTER 5

HOW I BECAME JIMMY

WHEN I was about 15, I spent a lot of time hanging around the Figtree Pub. It was right next to Parish Park where we used to train. Dad would take me there with our footy coach Jimmy Harrod.

Of course, being underage, I wasn't allowed into the main bar with the grown-ups.

Instead, you could find me and my great mates Craig Berlowitz and Johnny Hobbs inside Dad's Buttercup bread truck, parked out the back of the pub.

These two kids—same age as me—were very daring. Once or twice, they drove the truck around the car park while Dad was inside having a beer!

Even now, I'm mortified thinking about it. But things were a little different back in those days.

'Berlo' and I were huge Rabbitohs' fans. We grew up idolising Ron Coote. We were very sad when he defected to Easts, but we stuck with Souths as our team.

In the late '70s, the Rabbitohs had a fullback called Jimmy Swift. He played a total of 41 first-grade games. Because I was a fullback as well, Berlo decided to call me 'Jimmy'.

My new nickname took off like wildfire.

Berlo was great mates with Steve Roach, so once he told Blocker, soon everyone was calling me Jimmy.

I like the name Garry, but I was comfortable with the new tag. There are worse nicknames than Jimmy.

I must thank Berlo for that!

CHAPTER 6

YOU'LL NEVER PLAY RUGBY LEAGUE AGAIN

WE had a bye during the under-18s' season with the Red Devils, so I made myself available for our under-17s' side as I was still eligible to play in that age group.

It gave me a rare opportunity to play with Blocker.

We were up against Collegians, who were leading the competition. It was nip and tuck the whole way, but I managed to score the match-winning try after a 50-metre run.

One of the Collegians' players, Keith Caldwell, tackled me just short of the goal-line, but I reached out and planted the ball down.

Everyone was very excited, but as I went to join the celebrations, I realised I had a serious problem. I couldn't get up off the ground. My ankle wouldn't take any weight.

Eventually I was helped up by my teammates and left the field to have it strapped and iced.

But things didn't improve. I was hobbling for two weeks. There was a sharp pain on the inside of my leg every time I took a step.

I went and saw a doctor in Wollongong. He put my ankle in plaster and told Mum and Dad everything would be fine.

We went back in six weeks so he could remove the plaster. The doc took it off and said I should be okay to run. That was music to my ears, because it was only July which meant there was still time for me to play in the finals.

But there wasn't much running. I still found it too painful. Five months later, I sought a second opinion from a specialist, Dr Maloney, in January of '79.

He took some x-rays then told me the injury hadn't healed. Dr Maloney said I needed to have surgery. When he saw me thinking about his diagnosis, he added something extra: "If you don't have an operation, you will never play rugby league again."

It was like my whole world was collapsing. My footy days could be over.

It turns out the original doctor didn't set my ankle correctly when he put it in plaster. He was totally negligent.

They had to clean out all the scar tissue, then take bone from my hip to strengthen my ankle. A two-inch woodwork screw kept everything in place. It was quite a serious operation.

A couple of months later when the doctor told me to give it a try, I drove my Holden HT down to South Beach and stepped out onto the sand.

No pain. I knew it had been a success. I was so happy. Now I *could* keep playing rugby league. I had three months to get fit, or the season was done.

I played against Corrimal under-18s at fullback in my first game for 15 months. All the training had paid off; the ankle had healed 100 percent. We beat Port Kembla the following week to qualify for the grand final against Collegians.

Blocker was in our side, as well as future NSWRL first-graders Mitchell Jones (Illawarra Steelers) and John Sparks (Balmain Tigers and Illawarra Steelers).

In the Collies side was Michael Bolt, who would later captain the Steelers. Also lining up opposite me was... Keith Caldwell.

During the game, Keith made a break down the left-hand side of Dapto Showground. I came across in cover defence. All I wanted to do was crash-tackle him over the sideline and put him into the frigging greyhound track that ringed the ground. I wanted to punish him for what he had done to me 18 months earlier. Even though it was just an accident, I blamed him for everything I went through.

However, there would be no 'revenge' on this occasion. Keith stepped past me to score a try. Collegians ran out easy winners, 25–5.

Keith and I kept in contact over the years, and we would always share a laugh—he reckons he made my career! Keith said if he hadn't broken my ankle in that tackle, I wouldn't have come back with such a determination to succeed.

He was right in a way. I learned a lot of lessons out of that injury. I never took footy or my health for granted.

From the moment I walked along South Beach plaster-free, I was totally committed to being the best I could be. If my mates were at the pub drinking beers, I'd be drinking lemon squash.

There are moments in your career that define you as a person. This was mine.

Those words from the doctor, "you will never play rugby league again", scared the hell out of me.

This was a major turning point in my career that I never forgot.

CHAPTER 7

HEADING TO THE BIG SMOKE

BY 1980, I was ready to step up and play first grade at Wests Wollongong.

Our coach was Paul Sait, the former Australian forward. He had retired only a couple of years earlier at the Rabbitohs.

After about six games that season, Paul said to me, "If you want to play in Sydney, I can get you a run at Souths."

I was blown away by the offer. But doubts quickly entered my head.

"No, no. I'm not good enough for that. I just want to play here in Wollongong."

I was confident in my playing ability, but the thought of living in Sydney scared me.

How would I survive? I wouldn't know how to feed myself. I had a pretty good arrangement living at home with Mum and Dad.

We had a great year at Wests and made it through to the grand final against Port Kembla. They were coached by one of rugby league's greatest fullbacks of all-time, Graeme Langlands.

Their captain was Peter Fitzgerald—who ended up becoming my brother-in-law when he married my sister Mandy.

They also had David Boyle, a rugged forward who later became a teammate of mine for NSW in State of Origin.

In a tough game played in howling winds at Wollongong Showground, we came out on top 6–0. I remind Peter about that game whenever I can.

I was named Illawarra Rookie of the Year in my inaugural season of first grade for Wests Wollongong. Other winners in the past included future Test prop Craig Young and NSWRL first-grader Rod Henniker. Suddenly there were write-ups by journalist Charlie Richardson in the local press tipping me to make it in the NSWRL.

My big break came that off-season when I was having a conversation with Dukey Taylor, publican of the Unanderra Hotel. Dukey played for the Western Suburbs Magpies back in the 1950s and we'd talk footy quite a lot.

One day, he mentioned he could get me a trial with the Magpies. Dukey still had contacts there. He wrote them a letter introducing me to them. He spoke about what I had achieved in the Illawarra competition and what my strengths were.

I never thought Wests would offer me a contract. But I figured even if it doesn't work out, at least I'll improve my fitness for another season with the Red Devils.

Dukey followed up his letter with a phone call to Wests' secretary Ray Bernasconi.

By early January, I found myself running laps of Lidcombe Oval — home of the Magpies.

I was one of about 50 players who had turned up outside of the regular Wests' squad, looking to impress coach Roy Masters and earn a contract for the 1981 NSWRL season. Alongside me was my Red Devils' teammate Craig Purcell, who was also given a helping hand by Dukey.

A quick scan of the Magpies' squad was enough to make my knees wobble.

John Ribot de Bresac was there, John 'Dallas' Donnelly, Alan Neil, Bob Cooper, Garry Dowling, Ted Goodwin, Ian Schubert and emerging star, Terry Lamb.

Wests had made the preliminary final in 1980. Masters had again assembled a strong squad for '81.

I tried not to put too much pressure on myself. I had every intention of going back to play in the Wollongong competition. In my mind, I was at Lidcombe Oval just to get fit.

I had been working and training as a lifesaver at North Beach Surf Club for a couple of years and was regularly running about 10 miles to Towradgi and back. I'd also run around Mount Kembla, which was another 10 miles. My endurance base was good, and I was lean, probably only 78 kilos at the time. I could run all day.

So, when the Magpies' trainers ordered us to do 400 and 800-metre runs, that was fine by me. I would win most of those no matter who else was in my group.

I must have made an impact on Roy because he asked me to meet him after training one night. Dad came along too because he would sometimes travel north with me to watch training. Either that or he'd spend the two hours in the nearby Railway Hotel, and I'd collect him on the way home.

We all took a seat in the tiny grandstand at Lidcombe Oval. Roy spoke first.

"I think you should come to Sydney and play for us."

I was genuinely shocked. As the enormity of the moment sank in, Masters continued.

"What are you going to prove having another year in the country? You'd be a better player here."

Most kids my age would jump at the chance, but I was reluctant. My dream was to represent Country in the traditional annual clash with City, which I'd never done before. My dream wasn't necessarily to play in the NSWRL competition for one of the Sydney clubs.

It might sound strange now, but back then playing for Country against City was a huge achievement.

Great fullbacks like Langlands, Les Johns and Keith Barnes all played for Country, so that's what my heart was set on.

Roy said: "I can see you playing five-eighth for us one day. You might start at fullback, but you'll end up at five-eighth."

His idea of moving me to the halves was because of my sturdy defence, which is important when you defend in the front line.

Roy kept talking as night fell across Lidcombe, and I kept going over scenarios in my head. As anyone who played under Roy Masters will attest, he can be very persuasive. Eventually, he talked me into it.

I was paid $5,000 for my first season at Wests. Most established first-graders were on about $15,000–20,000, so it was pretty good coin.

But I made it clear to Roy that I still wanted to live in Wollongong with Mum and Dad. To his credit, he respected that. No one at Wests ever pressured me to move.

That season, I travelled three to four times a week in a little Toyota Corolla station wagon. It was light blue, and I bought it myself, brand new. It was a long return trip to Lidcombe, and I was always relieved to reach the top of Mount Ousley on the way home, seeing the bright lights of Wollongong below, knowing my journey was nearly over.

I also took comfort knowing that other players regularly commuted to play for their clubs in Sydney.

Champion centre Mick Cronin played for Parramatta, NSW and Australia while living in Gerringong, which is even further down the south coast.

Still, I struggled finding my way around. There was no GPS in those days, so locating North Sydney Oval, Kogarah Oval or Brookvale Oval was one of the biggest challenges I faced.

My first appearance for Wests was in a pre-season Craven Mild Cup game against Balmain at Leichhardt Oval. I was one week short of my 20th birthday. I didn't know it at the time, but that ground would later become my second home.

I don't remember much apart from sitting on the bench all game with Craig Purcell. Gary Dowling was the starting fullback. Dowling was the current Australian number 1 and had transferred to Wests from Parramatta.

I started the season proper in reserve grade under coach Laurie Freier. The first game was against arch-rivals Manly at Lidcombe—talk about a powder keg!

This was back in the old 'Fibros versus Silvertails' era, where these teams HATED each other.

Roy would whip the Wests' boys into a frenzy before each game. Face-slapping inside the dressing room was common and became a huge story after *Sixty Minutes* aired a documentary. Everyone was shocked.

I finished my game, then prayed that Roy didn't put me on as a reserve in first grade.

As expected, it was a bloodbath! Dallas Donnelly was sent off after a fight with Les Boyd—a former Magpie who loved the 'biffo'. I just happened to be standing outside the back door to our dressing room when Dallas came storming out.

He was very upset—claiming that Boyd had bitten his finger. I could see the damage too. There was a gaping wound right through to the bone.

Dallas had given me the nickname of 'Cool', after 'Joe Cool', the ex-Wests player John Dorahy.

"Hey Cool, I didn't put it in his mouth! Look what he did to me," he said.

As he showed me his mangled finger, he started puffing on a cigarette!

That was my welcome to the NSWRL. It was a case of just about anything goes back in the early '80s.

I played the first three games in reserve grade before Roy made a big call. He dropped Dowling. The first-grade team was winless, and the current Australian fullback paid the price.

Masters told me I would be taking Dowling's place at fullback against South Sydney on Sunday afternoon at Lidcombe Oval.

Dropping the Test fullback for a rookie was described as a "sensation" in the press. Wests' secretary Ray Bernasconi jumped on the front foot in the papers: "We've got the utmost confidence in Garry Jack. He is loaded with ability."

To try and keep things normal, I went to Wollongong Leagues Club on the Friday night before the game.

I saw Blocker there and told him the news. He was killing it at Balmain in the lower grades but hadn't played first grade yet.

He remarked that I seemed relaxed about it. I agreed. I felt calm and ready.

But all that was about to change.

CHAPTER 8

NIGHTMARE START

THINGS didn't feel right from the moment I stepped into the dingy Lidcombe Oval change rooms on Sunday, April 19, 1981.

You hear players talk of the excitement of making their first-grade debut. Yes, I felt the same way when Roy Masters had named me in the team five days earlier.

But right now, as I looked around our change room, it was a completely different feeling.

I wasn't ready. I was out of my depth. All these thoughts were swirling around my brain.

Here I was, a 20-year-old on debut, watching my teammates slap each other in the face to prepare for a game of footy.

Across in the other change room were players representing the most successful team in the history of the NSWRL, the South Sydney Rabbitohs.

When we eventually took to the field, I stood there thinking, *"Gee, what am I doing out here?"*

Souths kicked-off, I got under the ball… and dropped it. That was the start of my first-grade career.

My only thought at that stage was, *"Ohhh f*&%—I've dropped the ball with my first touch."* I wished I could have dug a hole in the turf and jumped inside.

(That was the only time I ever dropped the kick-off in my 15-year career!)

These days if a rookie makes an error, his teammates will swarm him with encouragement. They'll throw an arm around him or pat him on the backside, telling him everything will be okay.

That didn't happen in 1981. None of my teammates came near me. There were no pats on the back or positive comments.

Things didn't really improve either. It seemed every time I ran the ball back at Souths, I'd drop it. I had put too much pressure on myself replacing a player like Garry Dowling, who was now sitting on the bench as a reserve.

At halftime, Wests' president Bill Carlson shouted at Roy Masters as our coach made his way to the dressing sheds.

"Get him off—get him off now," he demanded.

Roy told me this story 40 years later. He added, "I couldn't take you off, it would have destroyed you."

He was right. It would have.

Roy stuck with me in the second half. But with 10 minutes to go, the home crowd was banging on the fence chanting, "We want Garry Dowling! We want Garry Dowling!"

I felt sick in the guts hearing that. Our own fans were turning against me.

We won the game 20–18, but no thanks to me. I had a shocker.

Afterwards, we went back to the Lidcombe Catholic Club to celebrate our win, even though I wasn't really in the mood. I ended up chatting with our hooker Jack Jeffries.

"Mate, what happened out there?" he asked, sympathetically.

I shrugged my shoulders. I honestly didn't know what to say.

"You know what your problem was? You thought you were playing for Australia. Every time you touched the ball, you thought you had to make a break or set up a try. Mate, you're playing first grade—not a Test match at the SCG (Sydney Cricket Ground). Just do your job."

That conversation with Jack really helped. He was also from Wollongong, and we had spent a lot of time together as we adjusted to life in Sydney. We were good mates.

At training on Tuesday night, Roy grabbed me in front of the grandstand as I was about to take the field.

"I need to talk to you."

I followed him to a more private area, and the coach didn't hold back.

"Mate, we can't have what happened on the weekend—we just can't have it," Masters started.

"You can't be in the side if that's how you're going to play, so I'm dropping you back to reserve grade."

That was it. A short conversation with the coach that left me devastated. I'd blown it after just one game.

There were a million things racing through my head. I kept asking myself, *"Why didn't I just play my normal game?"*

So, the angry Lidcombe mob would get their wish after all. Garry Dowling was in, and Garry Jack was out.

Rugby League Week was *the* publication for all the top footy stories in those days. It contained match reports for every game, along with a rating of each player.

When the magazine came out on Thursday, I grabbed a copy like I always had since I was a kid. I got a 4 out of 10.

It wasn't unexpected, but was still another kick in the guts. It could have broken me, but I'd had enough of feeling sorry for myself. It was time to turn things around.

I tore out the page with the player ratings and stuffed it in my wallet—where it stayed for the rest of the season.

So embarrassed with the way I played that day, the ratings in my wallet would serve as a constant motivator to make sure it would *never* happen again.

I vowed if I was ever given another chance to play first grade, I would take it with both hands.

I still have that crumbled piece of paper to this very day.

CHAPTER 9

MY VOW TO WEAR THE GREEN AND GOLD

THERE was more fallout from my less than spectacular first-grade debut and this was very close to home.

A fallout with my grandfather.

His name was Jim Porter—my mother's father—and his love for rugby league was an inspiration to me. He played plenty of footy in his time and earned the nickname 'Iron Man' because he was so tough.

Pop loved watching me play. He would encourage me when I was a kid by giving me 20 cents if I scored a try. That was like gold back then!

Friday was always payday. We would drop in to see Nan and Pop and I'd collect my cash. Pop would ask me how I went on the weekend. Sometimes I'd score two tries, so he'd give me 40 cents.

One game I really hit the jackpot. It was against Balgownie, and I scored eight tries! So Pop was up for a whopping $1.60! Mum wouldn't let me take it. She thought it was too much money for a kid but eventually relented... after a lot of pressure from me and Pop!

Pop was a dairy farmer his entire life, working seven days a week on the family farm with his brother. On Sundays, he would do a 100-gallon milk run in the morning, leave his horse and cart outside the Harp Hotel in Corrimal Street, then play for Mt Keira at Wollongong Showground. After the game, he'd do the second half of his milk run!

Pop loved telling me stories too. One that stands out was when he was a young front-rower playing against Port Kembla. His opposing front-rower was a guy called Harry Wells Senior. He just happened to be the national heavyweight boxing champion! His son—also Harry Wells—would later play 37 Tests for Australia.

In those days, each scrum was a fiercely contested battle, not like the modern game where it's more of a cuddle between the big men. Getting the loose head gave you a far greater chance of winning the scrum and claiming possession.

In one of the early scrums, Pop was supposed to have the loose head—but Wells was having none of it. The two of them jostled, the young bull versus the old bull, and it was on! The fists were flying!

The referee eventually broke it up and Pop was left with a massive cut above the eye. I guess that's to be expected—he picked a fight with the Australian heavyweight champion. Pop carried that scar for the rest of his life.

Anyway, they both got sent off by the referee. The unofficial rule back then was if two players were sent off for fighting, they would settle things behind the grandstand after the game. This way there would be no referee to break things up.

The alternative venue was down by the creek, which was a short walk from the oval.

Pop decided to head to the creek, mainly so he could wash all the blood off his face.

It wasn't long until he looked up and saw Wells walking towards him. Old Jimmy wasn't stupid. He knew what this meant.

Pop jumped to his feet ready for round 2. Wells approached… then stuck out his giant right hand.

"I just want to tell you that not many blokes would have done what you did today, and I respect you for it."

The pair shook hands and that was it.

That story sums up my pop; a decent hard-working bloke who stuck up for what he believed in. I was very close to him and always wanted to make him proud.

When I got my big break by signing with the Magpies, the local newspaper got in touch. Pop, Dad and I posed for a photo together, and there was also an article.

Pop was quoted saying of me: "I know he's got what it takes, and that's guts."

That's what made this early stage of my career so hurtful, and I take a lot of the blame for that.

When I was named to make my first-grade debut, I told Pop straight away. He was very happy for me.

His mood was a lot different *after* the game though. He wasn't at the game but must have been listening on the radio as I bumbled my way through the 80 minutes against Souths. I dropped into his place after the game, and he got straight to the point.

"What happened?"

"I don't know Pop, I guess I just wasn't ready."

"I'll tell you what happened—you've been carrying on like a big head!"

I sort of laughed, not really knowing whether he was serious or joking.

"You're not as good as you think you are."

I thought I must have misheard him. But it started to make sense when I thought of how I spoke about other fullbacks when Pop and I would watch the footy together.

Once when I was about 16, I was critical of St. George's Brian Johnson after he made a few mistakes. I said things like "he can't catch" and that he was "hopeless".

Now I had my chance in first grade and blew it. This was Pop's way of bringing me down a peg or two.

To really ram it home, he finished with: "Get out of here. I don't want to see you."

So, I left with my tail between my legs. I'd normally see him once a week, but I stopped visiting because I was angry and hurt. This is something I regret, even now.

I didn't return to first grade until round 15 against, of all teams, South Sydney. I played off the bench.

My next start at fullback came in round 19 against Parramatta and we were thrashed 32–5. I kept my place in the team for the upcoming match against Penrith, but I still didn't feel like talking to Pop.

That changed though when Mum spoke to me on the morning of our game against the Panthers. She told me Pop "wasn't well" and I should visit him.

Pop was terminally ill with lung cancer.

He was in bed when I arrived, and we spoke normally. What happened in the past was in the past. It was a huge relief for me to restore my relationship with Pop.

I went out and played a blinder against the Panthers. I scored a try under the posts—my first in first grade—and we won the game 17–15.

I celebrated the win with even more gusto than normal, knowing Pop would have been listening on the radio. It was silly of me to go four months without speaking to him and only reconnect when he was on his deathbed.

On the Tuesday the following week, as I prepared to leave for training, Dad told me that Pop had died. I burst into tears on the spot. Uncontrollable tears.

I cried all the way up the F6 at Mount Ousley and was still crying when I drove into the Lidcombe Oval car park.

After Pop's funeral service, we went to the cemetery with my cousins—Michael and Greg—and my sister Mandy. On the drive home, alone in my thoughts, I made a pledge to myself.

I was going to play for Australia as a tribute to my grandfather and bring him my first Test jersey.

I had only played three first-grade games for Wests, but I was determined to make this happen.

I felt awful that I'd missed all that time with him. He was gone now, but I still wanted to make him proud. I even gave up the drink to give myself the best chance.

Three years later, I made my Test debut against Great Britain at the SCG. The next week, I went to his grave with my first green-and-gold jersey.

"Pop, here it is. I told you I'd bring it to you."

I sat there and talked to him for 15 minutes, in between tears, telling Pop the jersey was a sign of how much he meant to me and how he was my inspiration.

I told him I was sorry for those four months when we didn't talk.

Pop was always in my heart whenever I played. I never wanted to let him down again.

CHAPTER 10

CROC BAIT

AT the end of the 1981 season, I went on a trip with my Magpies' teammates to Darwin. We were going there to play an exhibition game against a local invitational team.

For most of us, it was our first visit to the Top End. We couldn't wait to experience something new.

Adding to the excitement, our opponents featured rugby league royalty—the great Arthur Beetson.

Big Artie had just finished his illustrious playing career. At 36, his best days were obviously behind him, but going up against him for the first time was a real treat for me.

Because there was no way a Darwin invitational side could hope to beat a team from Sydney, a little 'arrangement' was made before the match.

The deal between the two teams was if Darwin scored a try, *we* would be given a keg of beer.

Let's just say that we basically pushed one of their players across our try-line!

Artie showed his class at times during the game, but it was never going to be enough. We won easily.

I caught up with Artie at the bar after the game and was in complete awe. Not just of his physical size, but the aura of the man.

Only a year earlier, he had captained Queensland in the inaugural State of Origin game against NSW. From the moment Artie whacked his Eels teammate Mick Cronin, Origin was on the map.

Yet here he was in a Darwin bar talking to a kid from Wollongong. We had a great chat and it's something I'll always treasure.

Footy out of the way, it was time for us Magpies to relax. For some of the boys, that meant a spot of duck-shooting, which is legal in the Northern Territory.

Even though I had never held a firearm in my life, I tagged along with the 'hunters', including Ted Goodwin and reserve grade coach Laurie Freier. We came across plenty of birds and it wasn't long before we had enough to fill the car boot. We were about to call it a day when Laurie spotted a flock of waterfowl bobbing in the river.

"Go get 'em Gaz," he said.

As I hadn't contributed anything to that point, I picked up a gun and followed Laurie's advice.

I waded quietly towards the birds, careful not to scare them off. With every step, I moved deeper and deeper into the water.

I looked back at my mates, and they were about 100 metres behind me on the riverbank. Another step and I would have been within striking distance of the waterfowl.

At this point, I noticed the water was suddenly up around my chest. For the first time, I felt a bit uneasy.

Suddenly, there was a swish and a splash just 15 metres to my left! I swung my head in that direction and saw a large section of water still churning.

By this stage, the birds had all flown off. Something had spooked them—and it wasn't me.

Paralysed by fear, I stood still, right in the middle of the river.

At the same time, on the riverbank, a local Indigenous man sidled up to Laurie.

"Hey, that white boy is pretty courageous. There are crocodiles out there."

I didn't hear the conversation at the time, but I'd already worked out for myself what I was dealing with here. I was shitting myself.

Any second, I thought, a giant croc would explode out of the river and snap me up in its jaws.

Considering my inexperience with firearms, the rifle was useless. I may as well have been holding an umbrella.

I began inching my way towards the shore, my eyes darting everywhere for the slightest movement in the water. Each step closer to the riverbank drew a sigh of relief.

Thankfully, I made it to shore. For some reason, the crocodile left me alone. Maybe it looked me over and thought I wasn't meaty enough.

I made it back to land and that's when Laurie told me what the man said. My heart started pounding even harder.

I was just 20 years of age. I have no doubt if the croc lunged at me, I wouldn't be here today. Simple as that. I would have been lunch. I still don't think I realised at the time how lucky I was to avoid that fate.

People will read this and think I must have been out of my mind wading into a Northern Territory estuary. But we had been told before we set out that there were no crocodiles.

I'm not sure who gave us that dodgy piece of advice, but it was almost a death sentence for one up-and-coming rugby league fullback.

Thankfully, it's not all bad memories of the Top End.

When we got back to Darwin after our little 'adventure', the other boys were enjoying themselves at an Octoberfest-style barbeque.

It was there I witnessed big John 'Dallas' Donnelly at his best. He had about 100 people gathered around him, singing and dancing, as he belted out some tunes... with a gum leaf.

Yep, that's right—eucalyptus leaves ripped straight off a tree.

Dallas had the place rocking for hours.

CHAPTER 11

MOVING TO TIGER TOWN

THE Parramatta Eels were a team on the rise in 1981. They had some excellent older players, and some of the best young talent in the game.

After three-straight games in reserve grade, Roy Masters brought me back into the starting side at fullback to face the Eels at their home ground, Cumberland Oval.

I was so excited—until I bumped into a good mate of mine, Ian 'Chook' Neil, a director at the Red Devils' footy club.

"Probably not a good game to come back in, this one," he said.

"Maybe wait another week."

Chook was referring to Parramatta's impressive attacking arsenal, who were in white-hot form. They had threats all over the park in Mick Cronin, Steve Ella, Eric Grothe, Brett Kenny, Peter Sterling and Ray Price.

They had yet to win a premiership, but you could see one was coming (in fact there were three in a row!).

I walked into Cumberland Oval for the first time in my life and it was rocking. What an eye-opener! More than 16,000 people were jammed into the place.

Fans in the tiny grandstand stomped their feet in excitement, sending dust and all sorts of crap through the cracks into our dressing room below.

Out on the field, the grass was non-existent. A dustbowl. It felt like a tough afternoon was coming for my return to first grade.

Thankfully, I managed to successfully catch the kick-off, which was a massive relief! But things quickly went pear-shaped.

Grothe, a devastating winger for Parramatta, burst into the clear. With an in-and-away, along with a right-hand fend, he went right past me. He scored two tries as the home side raced to a 23–0 lead at halftime.

After his second try, another long-distance effort, referee Greg Hartley had to leave the field. He'd pulled his hamstring trying to keep up with 'Guru' and had to be replaced by the reserve grade referee!

At one stage, I had a bit of push and shove with Sterling. It was the first time I'd played against him. He came in and whacked me. I said, "Who the $%#& do you think you are?" Later in our careers, we won Origin and Test matches together.

It was a surreal feeling to see Mick Cronin standing opposite me.

A star footballer from Gerringong, just south of Wollongong, I idolised him as a boy. My pop rated him the best player he had seen—and he'd seen plenty of legends like Reg Gasnier and Harry Wells.

Cronin was tough but fair. In an era of biffo, I never saw him punch anyone. Plus, he was a magnificent goalkicker.

Pop would have got a real kick out of his grandson playing against Michael Cronin.

Parra carved us up 32–5. Chook was right after all.

A win over Penrith kept us in the hunt for the top five. We just needed to beat the last-placed Tigers at Lidcombe in the penultimate round to stay alive.

This was my first experience with Balmain's giant Kiwi, Olsen Filipaina. He had beaten two of my teammates and was running full steam ahead, about 10 metres from our goal-line. It was up to me to bring the big fella down. I set myself to tackle him around the waist, but he swivelled and hit me with his hip. BUMP. It was like being knocked over by a bus. I had seen Olsen do it countless times to other poor bastards, but I still couldn't stop him. I hardly even slowed him down as he scored the try.

Another player who beat many fullbacks in his day was Larry 'The Flash' Corowa.

I had been watching Larry beat players with ease with his classic in-and-away since 1978, when he scored 24 tries for the Tigers. Larry just glided over the ground. His modern-day equivalent would be 'The Hammer'; Dolphins and Queensland Origin star Hamiso Tabuia-Fidow.

In this game, I set myself to tackle Larry side-on, but in the twinkling of an eye he was gone! He accelerated like I had never seen before. WHOOSH. Try time for the Tigers.

We lost 17–8, killing off our chances of making the final five.

Our last game was against the Roosters. While first grade was now out of the running for the finals, our reserve grade team had a chance to finish in the top three—and earn two bites at the cherry.

Roy pulled me aside at training and said he wanted me to help the reserve grade team, coached by Laurie Freier.

I'll admit I was disappointed. I was worried how it would look—that I'd been dropped again.

He assured me the Magpies would tell the media the real reason. Roy added I'd still be paid first-grade money.

It would be my final game of the year regardless, because the rules stated you had to play three of the last five games of the year in reserve grade to qualify for the finals. Seeing as I'd already played a total of 17 games in reserve grade that season, it seemed a dumb rule. Anyway, I went out and had the best game of my life!

I scored a hat-trick of tries against 'the Chooks'—the only time I ever scored three tries in a club game.

We won the game and finished in third place, ensuring a second chance in the finals—which turned out to be crucial.

The boys lost their first semi but then bounced back to reach the grand final—and thrashed Parramatta 19–2 to win the premiership!

Even though I didn't play, I joined the team for a lap of honour around the SCG.

With the season over, it was time for me to make a big decision. I was off contract.

Wests had made me an offer to re-sign a couple of months earlier, but I put it on the backburner. They still hadn't followed up on it.

Other clubs were starting to make enquiries.

Balmain had a recruitment guy in Wollongong named Noel Yeomans, a great friend of Tigers' secretary and club legend Keith Barnes. I was best mates with his stepson Mark David.

Noel had helped get Steve Roach, Allan McMahon and Johnny Sparks up to the Tigers. He phoned and said that 'Barnesy' wanted to speak with me about playing for Balmain in '82. I said I would be very happy to speak with Keith.

A day later, there was a knock at my door. It was Keith, along with Noel. I had no idea they were coming over and was completely unprepared.

I was sharing an apartment with a mate, and our only furniture was two beanbags. I offered Noel and Keith a beanbag each, while I sat on the floor.

We talked for a couple of hours about why I should come and play for the Tigers.

Keith was an old fullback himself. He saw me as a good fit to wear the number 1 jersey for Balmain—but there was a catch.

He said I'd have to start the season in reserve grade, because they had Phil Schaefer as their incumbent fullback. It would be up to me to take the spot from him. I appreciated Keith's honesty.

It would have been very easy for me to get swept up in the moment. I was still a rookie, and I didn't have a manager.

I told Keith and Noel that I wanted to speak to Mum and Dad before I committed to anything. They agreed—and we drove straight over to their place, even though it was starting to get late. Keith had played footy with Dad, which no doubt helped make the conversation more comfortable.

We spent an hour chatting with Mum and Dad. It was all so enticing, but there was one thing I wanted to bring up with Keith.

"I want to play in a competitive team—you guys just won the wooden spoon."

Rather than be rocked by this young upstart, Barnesy was straight on the front foot.

He told me about a bloke called Wayne Pearce, who's going to play for Australia. And of exciting young hooker Benny Elias, who was coming through the ranks.

He then spoke of an emerging front-rower I might have heard of—my old mate Steve Roach.

He also threw in the names Olsen Filipaina and Larry Corowa. As if I needed reminding of those two after what they did to me at Leichhardt. If I joined Balmain, at least I wouldn't have to try and tackle them again!

I told Keith I'd come back to him in a couple of weeks. I needed a bit of time. This was a huge decision. I didn't want to rush it.

There were two new teams entering the competition in 1982—the Canberra Raiders and Illawarra Steelers. Both had reached out to me.

I spoke with Raiders' coach Don Furner, but they were never a serious option. I wasn't keen on moving to Canberra.

The Steelers seemed like a logical fit. I was a Wollongong boy still living in the area. Being part of the region's inaugural team in the NSWRL premiership was obviously tempting.

But I was also worried about joining a team that would most likely struggle for a few years.

I met with their club secretary Bob Millward, otherwise known as 'Bobby Steeler'. I had known Bob all my life. He lived next door to Nan and Pop, and I had played with his son Ian in the under-18s at Wests.

When it came time to talk money, Bobby grabbed a beer coaster and scribbled a figure down. He slid the coaster across to me.

$12,000.

I turned over the coaster and said, "Not enough." Balmain had offered me a lot more.

Bob took back his coaster and put a line through the figure, did some more scribbling, then pushed it back to me.

$14,000.

I said, "Still not enough." I told him Balmain was offering me $20,000. Bob shrugged and said $14,000 was their best offer.

I was frustrated by the Steelers' approach. I'd already proven myself in first grade. I knew I could handle it and go to another level.

It felt like the Steelers were taking advantage of the fact I wanted to continue living in Wollongong. They probably assumed I'd jump at the chance to sign.

As I left Illawarra Leagues Club, I bumped into St. George forward John Jansen, who was also heading upstairs to see Bobby Steeler.

He asked me how I went.

"I'm not coming here," I told him. "They can go and get stuffed!"

Another option was Eastern Suburbs.

I spoke to their coach Bob Fulton, but only via a phone call. To be honest, if Bozo went to the lengths that Barnesy did, I may have ended up at the Roosters.

I narrowed my decision down to staying with Wests or joining Balmain. The Magpies had only just missed the finals, while the Tigers ran dead last. It should have been a simple decision if my wish was to play in a competitive team.

I spoke with Laurie Freier, who had accepted an offer to coach the Tigers' reserve grade team in '82. He said he believed in me. He had a lot of confidence that I would thrive at a new club, playing with Wayne Pearce, Benny Elias and Steve Roach, while under the guidance of Frank Stanton, the current Australian coach.

The clincher though was Barnesy. I really appreciated that he drove all the way down to Wollongong to speak with me in person.

I rang and told him that I'd made up my mind—I was joining the Balmain Tigers. Keith told the story for years that I rang him reverse-charge to save 20 cents!

Wests were disappointed when I told them. I think they expected me to stay.

But in my eyes, if someone wants you, they make the extra effort. Balmain really made an effort and that was enough for me.

So began my time in the black and gold.

CHAPTER 12

IN THE WORDS OF GOLDEN BOOTS

A CLOSE footy mate of mine from Wollongong, Noel Yeomans, told me I should take a look at Garry Jack when he joined Western Suburbs in Sydney.

So, I went and saw Garry play one afternoon at Lidcombe Oval. He was obviously impressive.

I got in touch with Garry and made a couple of trips to Wollongong to see him. I knew the family because I used to play with his father, Keith, in the 1950s.

I spoke to his parents, of course, but it was Garry doing most of the negotiating. I had to work hard to get him. He always knew the value of a dollar.

After a few discussions, he agreed to terms for him to come to Balmain.

Whenever it came to contract time, Garry was hard but fair. We would come to terms reasonably quickly.

He was always worth whatever we paid him.

Garry and I would talk a lot. We were both fullbacks and both from Wollongong. We had a lot of mutual friends.

As a player, Garry's greatest qualities were commitment and toughness. He never gave in. He never thought anything was too difficult.

He was a great defensive fullback. He had all the skills and was always involved in the game.

You could rely on Garry playing at 100 percent of his ability every time he took the field. He was so consistent. He was a great player, Garry.

One of my favourite stories relates to his love of a dollar. It was the day Garry agreed to terms with us back in 1981 when he rang from his home in Wollongong to tell me his decision.

Back then, it was an STD phone call, which cost money. The person on the switchboard asked me, "Will you accept reverse charges?" I said, "Yes," straight away.

It was the best reverse-charge call I ever accepted!

Keith "Golden Boots" Barnes

(30 October 1934–7 April 2024)

CHAPTER 13

BALMAIN BOY

MY first day as a Balmain Tiger involved a gym session at the Woolloomooloo PCYC.

I parked nearby in The Domain car park and walked down the hill. On the way, I bumped into this little fella, who was very friendly.

"G'day there mate—great to see you," he said.

I didn't know who he was.

"I'm Benny Elias."

"Oh, nice to meet you—I've heard a lot about you," I replied.

I noticed a confidence about Benny right from our first meeting. It's a big reason why he went so far in the game, becoming one of the best hookers of all time.

My living arrangements for my first year at the Tigers were interesting to say the least.

Blocker Roach and I, being mates from Wollongong, decided to move in together. We ended up at a boarding house in Ashfield, which wasn't too far from our home ground of Leichhardt Oval.

There were 30 bedrooms in this joint and just one bathroom—which was right next to our room on the top level. It was hardly five-star accommodation, and some of our fellow tenants were a little dubious.

The cost was $50 a week each, which included a hot meal every night. After training, there would always be a baked dinner on top of the stove when we arrived home, prepared by the lovely woman who ran the place.

But if we weren't training with the Tigers, Block and I got bored pretty quickly. So, like a lot of young blokes back in the '80s, we would take a drive into Kings Cross to check out the sights.

We never did anything dodgy. We just drove around, then would usually finish off with a trip to McDonald's for a Big Mac.

We stayed at the boarding house for a month, before a couple of incidents convinced us it was time to leave.

I walked into the TV room; it was pitch black with no lights on except for the television. All I could see was 20 sets of eyes looking at me. It was very unnerving.

Then Blocker and I were having breakfast in the common kitchen when a bloke came and sat down opposite me. He put his bowl on the table, then reached in and pulled out a couple of dry Weet-Bix.

As we watched on, this guy crushed the Weet-Bix into smithereens with his bare hands, before repeating the expression, "Mmmm, good. Mmmm, good."

I looked over at Block, who was clearly stunned.

"I think it's time to go, Block."

"Yep, I think you are right Jimmy."

We hightailed it out of there that day.

Thankfully, our Balmain teammate Percy Knight agreed to take us in at his two-bedroom apartment in Abbotsford. Percy was like a father to us—I never forgot how kind he was to me and Block. He'd make us dinner and cups of tea. He taught us how to do our own washing and ironing—all very useful life lessons.

We slept on the floor with just single mattresses. It was very basic, but we were enormously grateful.

Percy was an unsung hero for that Balmain team. He was a classy player, in the Cliffy Lyons mould. Unfortunately, that's the only season we played together because he went and joined the Raiders at the end of '82.

I was seeing Blocker 24/7 because we also worked together at Balmain Leagues Club. Barnesy had lined up a job for me as a gym attendant, while Block worked in the cellar.

I would join Block at the bar on Wednesdays, which was Ladies' Day. We would serve drinks in our smart black trousers, white shirt and fancy bow tie. It was hilarious, serving the regulars, pulling beers and keeping out of trouble.

When people bought a beer, we would give them a ticket. They would tear open the perforation marks to see if they'd won a prize. This could be a free drink, a huge esky, a Balmain Tigers' beer cooler bag or a Tigers' carry bag. A lot of tickets (probably most) had no prizes.

But somehow, the big prizes were disappearing at a rapid rate, which caught the attention of Barnesy. He couldn't work out how they could be going so fast.

The reality was Blocker realised pretty early that if you held a ticket up to the light, you could read what the prize was inside. So, the boys from 'The Gong' were doing 'insider trading' with their mates.

Someone must have tipped off Barnesy, because he suddenly broke us up and put me on the front desk at reception. That was going okay until one morning when I was tucking into a watermelon, bananas and grapes as guests were signing in.

KB (Barnesy) spotted me and said: "What are you doing?"

"Rehydrating."

Next shift I was moved back to the bar.

It ended up being a great decision to work in the gym. While Blocker was lugging kegs around, I took the opportunity to work on my fitness. I was training most days at the gym, which had a big influence on my football.

Our coach was 'Cranky' Frank Stanton, who was also the Australian Test coach. He was well-spoken and very clear with what he wanted.

This was his second year in charge, after picking up the wooden spoon in '81. He was getting tough and clearing out blokes who didn't fit in with his plans.

Frank was a very hard taskmaster. He expected everyone to be fit and to run their arses off at training. His hard-line approach to fitness had seen him enjoy great success with Manly, NSW and Australia.

If you had an injury, Frank would say, "Was that a bit tough for you today? Are you a bit soft?"

He would challenge you like that. He would make you feel like you had to play with an injury. He was always testing you to see if you were mentally strong.

Cranky would try other methods too.

Wayne Pearce once spotted him putting a saucer of milk in front of Paul Sironen's locker after a game. 'Junior' asked what the hell he was doing.

Frank snarled, "Well, the bastard played like a cat today."

Cranky wanted tough players in his team. He especially loved the guys who could churn out 200 and 400-metre runs at training.

This suited Junior, one of the fittest players in the competition. He wasn't the biggest forward, weighing about 90 kilos. But he made up for it with commitment and passion.

Helping Frank with his fitness regime was our conditioner, Les Hobbs.

'Hobbsy' was a quietly spoken man, a true gentleman, but he could fight like a street brawler if needed.

He gave all of us Tigers a harder edge. We would spend weeks of pre-season running around Callan Park in Lilyfield. Centennial Park was another favourite haunt. Hobbsy would always lead the way on every run. If you weren't up to it, Frank would quickly find out.

There was another guy who helped my career enormously.

I first noticed this bloke while I was working at the Leagues Club gym. He would be in there four days a week, from 11 a.m.–1 p.m. If he wasn't running like the clappers, then he was lifting weights like a machine. He was relentless in everything he did.

His name was James Tuite, and he was the conditioner at the Newtown Jets under first-grade coach Warren Ryan.

I was so impressed. We clicked instantly and I took 'Jimmy' on as my personal trainer. It also helped when Jimmy and his new wife Deb moved into a block of units next to Donna and me in Bay Road, Abbotsford.

Jimmy pushed me to my extremes and beyond, increasing my strength, stamina, endurance and flexibility to levels that I didn't know I had.

In addition to my training at the Tigers, I would regularly swim 32 laps at Ryde pool with Jimmy. I spent hours on the punching bag, also doing sit-ups, chin-ups and road runs. It was incredible the amount of work we did, pushing through the pain barrier.

Jimmy was also good for little motivational quotes. Here are a few:

"The only way to succeed is to train hard, while the other guys are sleeping."

"You have to keep the edge all the time, otherwise you're just another knife in the drawer."

"You have to put enough deposits in the bank, so that when it comes time to withdraw, you can cover it."

"Dreams don't come true. You have to make them happen."

"No pain, no gain, if you want to play for Australia."

Jimmy was more than a trainer to me. We became very close, and I was honoured to have him as my best man later in life when I married Donna in November 1985.

I could not have achieved what I did in rugby league without Jimmy's help.

I had the best of both worlds training with Jimmy and Hobbsy. I had put on a lot of muscle since leaving Wests, going from a scrawny 78 kilos to a far more imposing 83 kilos.

The more I trained, the more I loved it. It was like I became addicted to training.

That aspect of my game gave me an advantage over other guys who weren't quite as committed.

I started my first season at the Tigers in reserve grade. Frank was sticking with incumbent fullback, Phil Schaefer.

Barnesy warned that would be the case when he signed me, but I was still a bit miffed.

Phil was a very good player, a good athlete, and I really rated him as a fullback. But I wanted that number 1 jersey. I vowed that when I got my chance, I would take it.

First grade lost the first two games of the season. Coming off a wooden spoon, Frank knew it was time for change.

I had just scored two tries in a win over Parramatta in reserve grade, so my timing couldn't have been any better.

On the following Wednesday, I was called up for our round 3 match against Penrith.

Phil was a Seventh-day Adventist and wouldn't play when it was Easter, so he wasn't available for selection. This gave me my opportunity; I would be making my Tigers' debut on my 21st birthday—not a bad present from Frank!

The guys from reserve grade gave me a birthday card before I ran out to make my Balmain debut. It was a caricature of a bloke pissing on the world. Not sure what it meant, but they signed off with, "All the best Jimmy Jack—go out there and kill it."

But let's just say it wasn't a 'memorable' Tigers' debut.

Panthers' forward Lew Zivanovic made a bust in the first half, and I put my head in the wrong spot as I tried to bring him down. I copped an accidental knee and was knocked-out cold. The trainers loaded me onto a stretcher and took me off.

Then just as we got to the sideline, I suddenly sat bolt upright on the stretcher, like my brain told me to get up or my debut was over.

Johnny Owens was standing a metre away, ready to replace me.

I looked around and said, "What's going on here? I've got a game to play!"

With that, I jumped off the stretcher and ran back to fullback.

I don't remember any of this exchange. Johnny filled me in later. It was a very different time then in terms of how the game dealt with concussed players. These days, there's no way I would be allowed to continue playing. I would have to spend a minimum of 11 days undergoing concussion protocols.

We ended up losing that game to Penrith 15–7. Now the pressure was on everyone.

For me, I vowed to give my best every week as my way of helping the team. I was going to give it everything I had.

Helping motivate me was the iconic *Eye of the Tiger* song by Survivor. It was a tune virtually tailor-made for our team. It was released during the '82 season, and I couldn't get enough of it!

I went out to a nightclub one Friday night (I wasn't playing that weekend due to a leg cork) and when I arrived home at Percy's at 3 o'clock in the morning, *Eye of the Tiger* was playing on the radio. I was living the dream, so off I went for a run.

I was so pumped up I went for a run along Great North Road, across to Lilyfield Road, up past Leichhardt Oval, past Balmain Leagues Club on Victoria Road, over the Iron Cove Bridge, then back to Great North Road. I must have run for three hours—with a leg cork.

I always found *Eye of the Tiger* an inspiring song and love the fact that it still blasts out of the speakers at Tigers' home games to this day.

Fortunately, things turned around quickly after a slow start to the '82 season.

We won five of our next six games. Ironically, the only game we lost, against North Sydney, was when I scored my first try for Balmain. A nice little 20-metre run to the line from a Wayne Wigham pass.

The next game was against Canterbury. This was significant for me, because I was taking on Greg Brentnall, the best fullback in the game and the current Test number 1.

I'd watched Greg as I was coming through the ranks. He was so safe under the high ball. He was the best bomb-taker in the game. I can honestly say that I never saw him drop a ball. I modelled my technique on him, as best I could.

It was a wet day at Leichhardt Oval, but I still managed to catch every bomb that came my way. I wondered if Brentnall was impressed.

At one stage, I caught a line drop-out from Brentnall, about 40 metres from the Bulldogs' goal-line. Throughout my career, I always made sure I ran the first 10 metres the hardest I could, whether I stepped or not.

During this run, I veered to my left, then beat a Bulldogs' defender with a step. I was in open space and could suddenly hear the roar of the crowd.

It was a crucial moment of the game because the score was nil-all and the slippery conditions meant there wouldn't be too many tries. I knew If I could score, we had a big chance of winning.

Out of the corner of my eye, I could see Brentnall coming across in cover defence. Then someone threw themselves at me from behind. It was Steve Folkes—one of rugby league's top defenders.

I managed to pull out of his tackle, just as Brentnall arrived. But he was too late. I scored the try and we won the game 6–0.

I was playing some pretty good footy and began hearing whispers about me being a possible inclusion on the end-of-year Kangaroo Tour. Performing well against Brentnall certainly helped my chances.

A special occasion arrived in round 11 when my good mate Steve Roach was named to make his first-grade debut against Canberra.

Blocker could hardly sleep in the days leading up to the game. One night he said, "Jimbo, I just can't wait to get out there and kill someone!"

Blocker came off the bench as we flogged the Raiders 35–0 at Leichhardt. It was a very proud moment for a couple of old Figtree High School boys.

Next up, we played the Newtown Jets, grand finalists the previous year. A former Tiger, Allan McMahon, was one of their centres.

Allan had a huge boot, and I somehow found myself involved in a kicking duel with him. This was a tactic from the old days where two rival players—usually the opposing fullbacks—would trade kicks to try and gain a territorial advantage.

This wasn't a smart move by me. Allan's superior kicking was gradually pushing me back towards our goal-line. Eventually, I caught one of his bombs and was smashed by their winger Mal Graham.

We lost 27–13 but there were more positives than negatives from this game, because a few days later I found myself having a beer at the Burwood Hotel with Newtown's coach Warren Ryan. Blocker and Percy had organised the catch-up through Allan.

This was my first glimpse into the mind of Warren, who would go on to become one of rugby league's premier coaches.

As we were talking, Allan grabbed hold of some empty schooner glasses and started moving them around the table. He was using them to explain our defensive structures at Balmain, and where we had weaknesses.

It was fascinating. Allan told me that the Jets knew exactly how I ran on a kick return; which arm I carried the ball in; even what foot I stepped off. They knew everything about me.

He looked over at Block and detailed how they knew he could get an offload away like the great Artie Beetson. They knew more about us than we bloody did!

Allan referred all the credit to Warren. He called him a genius.

Warren then spoke to us in very measured terms. He gave us some words of wisdom—football IQ stuff that I had never heard before.

It was a precursor to where the game was headed. Warren was ahead of his time, which we discovered six years later when he joined us at the Tigers.

He had us figured out because when we played them again later in the year, the Jets won again, 30–8.

Another game of note was in round 13 when I played in Wollongong for the first time. It was against the Illawarra Steelers, the team I rejected.

In the opposition were John Sparks and Paul Thompson, my former teammates from the Wests Red Devils. John Dorahy, one of my childhood heroes, played in the centres.

They pipped us 17–16, triggering mass celebrations among the Wollongong Showground crowd of 8,742.

I assume Bobby Millward enjoyed that one!

One of the highlights of the season was knocking off Manly 20–19 in round 24 at Leichhardt Oval.

The Sea Eagles had a great team and made the grand final that year. At one stage, I was in the clear with one man to beat—the legendary Graham Eadie.

I tried to run over the top of 'Wombat', which didn't end well for me. Eadie was about 20 kilos heavier. He hit me head-on and drove me into the ground.

It sounds strange, but it was a good feeling. Graham was one of my idols. He played a heap of Test matches; he won premierships and was one of the greatest fullbacks of all time.

When he tackled me, he never said anything. There was no sledging. That's how Wombat played. A very cool customer.

We finished 1982 knowing we were heading in the right direction. We had worked ourselves off the bottom of the ladder to finish in 11th position.

I had established myself as a regular first-grader. I played 21 games and scored seven tries.

The tide had turned for the Balmain Tigers.

CHAPTER 14

ON THE RISE

TALK of me being a bolter for the 1982 Kangaroo Tour ended up being a fizzer. It didn't happen. The Australian selectors took Greg Brentnall as their only fullback.

But knowing that I had been considered gave me a lot of confidence.

I knew deep down that I had more to give, because I didn't finish the season as well as I would have liked.

Opposition coaches had worked me out a bit. That happens to all new players, and it was a learning curve for me.

Off the field, I'd also lost some focus.

I was a young single guy from Wollongong, away from his parents for the first time in his life, living in Sydney. The party scene was a constant temptation.

I wasn't out *every* night, but I did put in regular appearances at the popular Beattie Street Nightclub in Balmain.

Everyone knew that was a go-to venue for the Tigers' boys. The coach knew it too. He had spies everywhere.

At training one night, Frank called me over for a chat. Someone had told him I'd been at Beattie Street leading up to a game. I told him that yes, I was there but had been drinking lemon squash only.

Cranky Franky was having none of it. He gave me a stern warning to not get carried away with myself.

But the partying continued.

At the end of '82, there was a team trip to Hawaii. It was the first time I had been overseas, so it was very exciting. I roomed with our halfback Steve Martin.

One night, I was on the drink with Greg 'Muscles' Lane and a few of the other boys in Waikiki. We decided to move on to another establishment.

To make the walk more entertaining, we started playing 'leapfrog'. This is a game kids play in the schoolyard. Only this time, it involved grown men on a pub crawl. When it was my turn to leapfrog Muscles, I completely messed it up and came down heavily on the pavement outside the Rose and Crown Hotel, which was a popular haunt for Aussie tourists.

My wrist took the brunt of the impact and straight away it felt sore. Being a young bloke on holidays, I tried to ignore it, but by the time I arrived home in Sydney about 10 days later, my wrist was really painful.

I had an x-ray taken, and sure enough, it showed a fractured scaphoid. I was in plaster for a month.

Barnesy was not happy when he saw me and demanded answers. I told him I slipped over while helping out in the cellar at Balmain Leagues Club.

"I'm not going to cop that Jimmy—don't give me that!" he roared.

I wasn't sure, but maybe he had a tip-off from someone at the Rose and Crown who saw my drunken fall.

Between the two of us, we came up with a cover story just in case a reporter noticed me at training with my arm in a sling.

Our official line was… I slipped over while helping out in the cellar at Balmain Leagues Club!

Luckily, my wrist mended quickly, and I was ready for round 1.

I owed Barnesy after that. So, when he asked me to pose for a photo in a Balmain Tigers' pullover, I could hardly say no.

The woollen pullovers were the latest in rugby league merchandise. All 14 NSWRL clubs at the time were selling them.

My photo appeared in *Rugby League Week* magazine alongside Ray Price from Parramatta and St. George prop Craig Young. It was an honour to be on the same page as those two blokes. Price and Young had won premierships and played plenty of games for NSW and Australia.

The photo shoot did nothing for my back pocket though. I didn't get a cent! Barnesy got me a good one.

My only 'payment' was to keep the pullover, which was worth about $25.

The photo appeared in the magazine every week, so it lifted my profile. I made good use of my new black and gold pullover too—I wore it to every game.

We won our first four games in '83, which had everyone very excited. I could tell we had the nucleus of a really good team.

There was Benny Elias, Steve Roach, Wayne Pearce, David Brooks, Gary Bridge, Olsen Filipaina, Larry Corowa, Steve Martin—so much talent.

Fans and commentators always got Gary Bridge and I mixed up. We were both about the same height, same weight, same Christian name, and had the same, blond-coloured hair.

In one game, I wore a headband to cover up a facial cut from the week before. Our teammates must have also been having trouble picking us apart, because they told me to keep wearing the headband.

I once appeared in a newspaper photo with 'Bridgey' and Steve Martin. We were dubbed, "The Three Blond Bombshells".

A guy I loved playing with was Olsen Filipaina, otherwise known as 'The Big O'.

With his sheer size, he'd always attract defenders, which opened up gaps outside him.

Olsen had a 'hip bump' that was second to none. He was the hardest bloke to tackle in the game.

He did a garbage run every morning and would turn up for training still wearing his garbo gear. This was back in the days when they had to lift the bins onto their shoulders to empty them into the truck. There were no giant mechanical arms to heave the bins up like they have these days. It was bloody hard work. But Olsen never whinged.

Our big test came in round 6 against Manly. The Sea Eagles were beaten grand finalists in '82 and were stacked with internationals.

Junior Pearce had got to know a lot of them on the Kangaroo Tour. He told us not to be intimidated by them, especially their enforcers—Les Boyd and Paul McCabe. Junior wasn't a fighter, but he was talking tough because he knew they would try and bully us.

In the end, it was their flashy backs who killed us. Phil Blake was the 'whiz kid' that year with his chip-and-chase tries. He scored a double as we went down 34–18. The score flattered us, because it was 28–0 at halftime.

Incredibly, after winning our first four games, we had lost our next six! We had plummeted from first to ninth on the ladder.

Our sixth-straight loss came at the hands of St. George. We were belted 45–12 at Kogarah.

Steve Morris scored a hat-trick for the Dragons. I got to know 'Slippery' well later in life—in funny circumstances.

It was at the end of the 1987 season. I was joining Salford, while Slippery was heading to Leeds. We were both travelling to England on the same QANTAS flight.

Morris was seated up near the front with his little twin boys—Josh and Brett. They were yelling, screaming and doing backflips for about 18 hours!

Slippery came back and sat with me for a beer and some peace and quiet. It's remarkable to think those two energetic infants went on to play at the very top level, just like their dad.

We beat Canberra to end our losing streak, but a bigger challenge awaited us: two-time defending premiers Parramatta.

We burst out of the blocks to lead 21–16 at halftime, and a major upset was on the cards.

But the Eels clicked into gear in the second half and ran away to win 42–21. The result showed us we still had plenty of work to do if we were to be genuine premiership contenders.

We played Newtown in round 23, which would prove to be the last ever Tigers-Jets clash, because they got kicked out of the competition at the end of the year.

Their home ground at Henson Park in Marrickville is a fascinating place to play. I found it difficult to get my bearings because the field runs in a different direction to other grounds, which are traditionally north-south. It didn't feel like a footy ground.

There is also a hump in the middle because of a cricket pitch square. Actually, it is more of a hill than a hump. If you are a winger on one sideline, you almost can't see the winger on the other side of the field! That's how big the hump is.

My mate Jimmy Tuite, Newtown's trainer, told me he would regularly get off his sideline chair and stand up… just to see if there was anyone lying down injured on the other side of the field. If he was sitting down, he had no chance of seeing them.

We beat the Jets that day 34–6.

The wins were really starting to flow as we set our sights on a top-5 finish. I had never played in a finals' series, and I was keen for a taste.

By the time we faced Parramatta again in the penultimate round, we had won 10 from 13 games since our last encounter. We were in great form. But the Eels would be our litmus test.

The game took place on a dustbowl at Belmore Sports Ground. Seriously, players these days don't know how good they have it. The grounds of the current era look more like billiard tables.

Despite the dust, Mick Cronin gave me a reminder of his class. He made a break, and I thought I had him covered. 'The Crow' took little steps when he ran, but he was deceptively quick. I left my run a bit late and he scored.

I hit back with a try of my own as we took it right up to the Eels. It was 20–20 near fulltime, then David Brooks gave us a memorable victory with a late goal.

That was Balmain's first win over Parramatta since 1978. It was such a great confidence builder for us young blokes. Parra were on their way to winning a third-straight premiership and we had knocked them off.

We beat Norths in the final round to finish in fourth position, setting up an elimination semi-final with St. George.

The match was scheduled for the SCG. Chatting to Frank, I mentioned I'd never played there before. He told me to go to the ground through the week and get used to it.

So, I went to the SCG on my own and had a walk around. There was no one else in the joint. I took a couple of Steedens with me and kicked some bombs to myself.

I felt better prepared and was grateful for Frank's idea.

The Dragons had beaten us convincingly in our only two meetings that season, but we were clearly the better side in the first half and led 14–6.

Their Wallabies' recruit Michael 'Snoz' O'Connor then put his stamp on the game.

He made a long break, and I was hot on his heels. I got to him and slowed him down, but O'Connor passed to hooker Richard Jones who scored the try.

Slippery Morris then burst into space and kicked ahead. I took him out without the ball and was penalised. Steve Gearin kicked the goal, and it was 14–all when the fulltime siren sounded.

We went to extra-time, but a field goal to O'Connor and another penalty goal to Gearin saw the Dragons home 17–14.

It hurts a lot to lose like that. In the end it came down to brilliance from Slippery and Snoz.

Sadly, our season of promise was over.

CHAPTER 15

THE $3,000 TACKLE

I FIRST fell in love with rugby league when I started collecting Scanlens footy cards in 1969.

We would swap them at school. It was five cents for five cards, plus two sticks of gum. I still have them now, 55 years later.

The thought of ever appearing on a footy card myself was a dream. The ultimate accolade for any aspiring player.

Well, it did happen for me. But my dream became more of a nightmare.

During the 1983 season, footy cards were booming.

In every packet of Scanlens chewing gum there was a pack of cards, containing images of your favourite Winfield Cup players.

They also came as stickers which could go on bedroom doors and schoolbooks to really annoy parents and teachers.

After playing for the Tigers at Leichhardt Oval one day, I went around to meet some of the fans. A group of kids approached me with their cards and pens, asking me to sign.

"No problem boys," I said.

As I scribbled away, I noticed the boys were giggling and nudging one another.

"What's so funny boys?" I asked.

They pointed at the footy card. The photo was of me playing for Balmain against my old club Wests the previous season. I was holding the ball out in front of me, looking to offload. A Magpies defender—I think it's Alan Neil—is doing his best to bring me down. A typical action photo from any game on any given week.

Or so it seemed.

On closer inspection (and I advise against this if you ever happen to find the photo), there is a bit more of me on display than I expected.

As my shorts were pulled at from behind, a different kind of tackle emerged, and it was there for all to see—smack bang in the middle of a footy card!

In those days, I didn't wear the more secure Speedos or Budgie Smugglers, as players do in the modern game. It was whatever undies I happened to pluck out of the drawer as I got dressed.

The pair I had on that day were a little on the flimsy side and it didn't take much for a public showing of the 'crown jewels'.

To say I felt embarrassed is an understatement. These cards were being swapped by kids all over the place!

It had become the most valuable card for traders in every schoolyard. You needed five Wayne Pearce cards to get one Garry Jack!

While others found it amusing, I didn't. I couldn't believe Scanlens failed to notice this X-rated wardrobe malfunction before they published it.

I left the giggling kids and went straight to Balmain secretary Keith Gittoes, who put me in touch with the club solicitor. I left it with the lawyers and mercifully the issue never made the newspapers. It took a while, but Scanlens eventually offered a settlement of $3,000.

At the time it seemed like a decent payout, so I accepted and moved on.

Ten years later, my NSW and Australian teammate Andrew 'ET' Ettingshausen successfully sued Australian Consolidated Press after *HQ* magazine published a nude photo of him in the shower without his consent.

He was awarded $100,000 in damages. In comparison, my settlement seemed a little light.

Even now, I still get reminded about it.

I was working with the SR Flooring company when a guy came up to me with two A3-sized images of the footy card. He wanted me to sign one for himself. He said I could keep the other one if I wanted!

This bloke was in his late 40s. He told me that my lewd footy card was his introduction to pornography as a kid!

You can't be angry forever, and I have learned to laugh about it. Daniel Pain from Dan's NRL Collectables even printed the image onto a coffee mug for my personal use! It sits in my cupboard and comes out only on special occasions.

Certainly not when small children are around.

CHAPTER 16

REJECTING THE ROOSTERS

IN all my years at Balmain, there was only one time I seriously contemplated playing for another club.

At the end of the 1983 season, I received an approach from the Roosters.

Our old reserve grade coach Laurie Freier was coaching the Chooks and making big changes to their roster.

He made it clear he wanted me to be wearing red, white and blue.

Laurie knew my two-year contract with the Tigers had expired. Keith Barnes had made me an offer to re-sign, but it wasn't great. I was holding off.

Easts had a vacancy at fullback. Marty Gurr, the NSW Origin number 1, had left to join the Rabbitohs.

The Roosters were known for splashing the cash in those days before salary caps. They could easily have recruited Test fullback Colin Scott to replace Gurr.

The fact Laurie wanted *me* really made an impact. I told him I would take some time to think about his offer.

I joined the rest of the Balmain squad on a team holiday in the Hunter Valley, which included a stopover at Saxonvale Wines, our major sponsor.

This was the bonding trip to end all bonding trips. We had a few drinks on the bus on the way up from Sydney, then it really kicked-off when we arrived at the winery.

We held a mini-Olympic Games—it was us Balmain boys against the Saxonvale staff.

One of the events involved running around a dam while holding a glass of wine on your head. The winner was whoever finished quickest and spilled the least amount of red.

I have no idea who won, but everywhere you looked, there were Balmain players walking around with a bottle of wine.

It was just young blokes having fun (before smartphones!) and no one got hurt.

Coach Frank 'Biscuits' Stanton was there too. During a break in the festivities, he came and sat next to me.

"Jimmy, what are you doing?"

"What do you mean, Biscuits?"

"Well, I know Laurie has spoken to you."

There are no secrets in rugby league. I didn't even try to deny it.

"Honestly Frank, I don't know what I'm going to do."

I mentioned that Barnesy's offer was a lot lower than what the Roosters were willing to pay.

"OK, I'll chat with Barnesy because we want you to stay."

That was music to my ears. We were all close mates at the Tigers. Our partners got along, and the camaraderie was strong. I didn't want to leave.

A couple of days later, Barnesy increased the offer. I signed on the dotted line.

CHAPTER 17

OFF THE BOOZE AND INTO THE BLUES

THE 1984 season was when my career really went to the next level.

It didn't start well though. I broke my ribs in a trial match against Norths when their big boppers—Don McKinnon and Steve Mayoh—crash-tackled me.

I felt a pop and knew straight away I'd busted a rib. I could hardly breathe—the pain was so intense.

I needed time on the sidelines to recover, and that allowed Steve Humphreys to get the jump on me. He started the season at fullback, while I was picked in reserve grade. Not exactly the start I was looking for, but I knew it was just a minor setback.

We had a bye in round 2, then I was again picked in the 'reggies' (reserve grade) for our game against Manly the following week.

There was a moment in this game that set me on the path to State of Origin honours.

My opposite number for the Sea Eagles was Phil Sigsworth, who had played five Origin games for NSW plus a Test match for Australia.

Manly had a fat chequebook in those days before salary caps, so their roster was chock-full of stars. It wasn't uncommon to find an accomplished player like Sigsworth stuck in their reserve grade team.

'Siggy' made a break from their quarter-line and took off. He had fresh air in front of him. I chased him, coming from the other side of the field, also starting from the quarter-line. He had a decent head-start on me. My only thoughts were, *"I have to get him."* I chased Siggy like no other. He was never going to beat me. I got to him at our quarter-line and tackled him over the sideline.

Keith Barnes said to me after the game that I had made a "critical" tackle. I was surprised to hear him say that. To me, it was just another tackle in a reserve grade game. There were no headlines about it.

But Barnesy said people in high places will now know that I'm quicker than Sigsworth. And even though he was in reserves, there had been talk that Siggy was a contender to play fullback for the Blues in Origin I.

That conversation with Barnesy really grabbed my attention. I was back in first grade the following week.

We attended a club function in Camperdown, put on by our major sponsor Saxonvale Wines. Like we did in the Hunter Valley, we really made the most of the sponsor's products. We then kicked on to Drummoyne Rowing Club.

I came away from that day thinking it was time to get serious. I put myself on a booze ban.

I wasn't a big drinker anyway, but I just thought if my goal is to play for Australia, then I need to give myself every chance.

I was engaged to Donna by this stage and had her full support. She wanted to see me achieve my goals.

Back at Balmain Leagues after a win, the boys would offer me a drink, and I'd turn them down every time. I'd have a lemon squash instead and felt better for it.

I vowed not to have a drink again until I was selected for Australia.

After my chat with Barnesy, I realised there was a really good opportunity for me to break into rep football.

Former Blues' fullbacks Graham Eadie and Greg Brentnall had both retired. Colin Scott was the Queensland and Australian fullback. I knew if I could make the NSW team, I would back myself to get over the top of Scott.

He was a strong runner but was suspect under the high ball and fragile in defence. I was an honest assessor of my fullback rivals and that's how I felt about him.

I watched other fullbacks closely and knew exactly what their strengths and weaknesses were.

In round 8, I was handed a golden opportunity.

We were playing Souths at Leichhardt Oval, and my opposite number was Marty Gurr. He was the incumbent Blues' fullback, having played the final two games of the 1983 series.

I figured I was behind Gurr and Sigsworth in the selection race for the City Firsts' fullback gig. The annual game against Country Firsts was viewed as a selection trial for State of Origin. If I wasn't picked for City Firsts, I had no hope of being selected for the Blues.

I knew I had to play well against Gurr. There was so much riding on it.

In the first half, I broke through the South Sydney defence, just inside their half. The only man in front of me was Gurr, and I had a man outside me in support. I could have drawn Gurr and passed, but I thought *"stuff it"* and took him on myself.

I threw a little dummy to my left, which fooled Gurr, and I ran away for my first try of the season—what a beauty!

In the second half, Souths kicked the ball to our winger Johnny Davidson, who was then tackled on the halfway line. I noticed Gurr was at marker, which meant

Souths had no one defending at fullback.

I called for the ball, then kicked down field and chased hard. It was early in the tackle count, so I knew if it didn't come off, Cranky Franky would probably drag me from the field by my ears.

I got to the ball first but couldn't pick it up cleanly. I kicked it again, then dived on it for a try. We won 16–2. I scored two tries, outplaying Gurr in the process. I was hoping it would prove enough.

The City Firsts' team was announced later that night at Balmain Leagues Club over the public-address system. The first name read out belonged to me as fullback of City Firsts.

I was ecstatic—my first senior rep jersey! All the hard work and sacrificing the booze was paying off.

The mood at the club was buoyant as Wayne Pearce and Steve Roach were also named. David Brooks and Gary Bridge were picked in City Seconds.

It helped that I had a relationship with Frank, who was also the City coach. That was a godsend for me—my club coach was now my representative coach as well. I could talk to him about what he expected from me.

It was before the Origin concept was adopted for the City-Country fixture. Being from the south coast, I found it strange playing *against* Country, which was mainly full of players from the bush.

I was always a country boy at heart. It felt wrong to pull on the City jumper. I didn't consider myself a city slicker.

But I put those emotions aside and helped City to a thumping 38–12 win at the SCG.

When they named the Blues' team for Origin I, we were once again gathered at Balmain Leagues. The place went nuts when they heard Jack, Roach and Pearce read out over the P-A.

To know that Blocker and I would make our State of Origin debut in the same game was just amazing. We had followed the same path from Wollongong and now we would be pulling on the blue jersey together.

It was like a dream.

Queensland had dominated Origin from day one in 1980 when Artie Beetson led them onto Lang Park. They won one-off games in '80 and '81, before taking out a three-match series in '82 and '83.

Wally Lewis was the man pulling the strings. He was well on his way to his status as 'The King'. He was a dominant figure in every game for the Maroons.

We knew we had to take time off Wally if we were to have any chance of winning. I could never understand why previous Blues' teams hung off him when he had the ball. He mesmerised them.

NSW didn't show enough respect for State of Origin in those early years.

The selectors would pick the team on Sunday—then the team would play on Tuesday or Wednesday. Barely enough time for a training run! Just ridiculous.

No wonder Wally was dominating. The Blues hadn't done enough planning on how to stop him.

But with Cranky Franky in charge, things were changing.

This was the first time the Blues went into camp for 10 days before we played. After four years of defeat, the NSWRL had finally decided to get serious.

The long camp was a huge benefit to me, an Origin rookie. It gave me a chance to get to know all the boys.

I was 'roomies' with Manly five-eighth Alan Thompson, who was at the back end of his career. I found Alan good company. I was only 23 and about to make my Origin debut. He looked after me.

It wasn't just Wally we had to worry about. There was also Gene Miles, Mal Meninga, Chris Close… the list goes on.

These were the days before the Brisbane Broncos entered the NSWRL competition. There was a certain mystery about these Queensland legends. We knew who they were. But we didn't *know* them. They played their footy north of the Tweed; we played to the south. Very rarely would we cross paths.

Queensland supporters were also an unknown commodity to me.

That would change though as the NSW bus made its way toward Lang Park on the evening of May 29, 1984.

We were driving past the Caxton Hotel, only a punt kick from the ground, when I started hearing loud bangs on the side of the bus. I looked out the window and saw dozens of yobbos throwing bottles of XXXX at us!

There was no respite once we got to the ground. Before Lang Park was redeveloped, all players had to go through the main bar (yes, true story) to get to the dressing sheds.

As soon as we appeared, I could hear these blokes yelling, "The cockroaches are here!"

We filed past the bar, and they threw the contents of their glasses into the air above us. We had our beautiful Blues' blazers on, but they didn't give a shit. We got drenched in beer!

We had to pull our saturated blazers up to cover our heads, so we didn't get XXXX in our eyes before the game.

It was a diabolical way to prepare for a game. You could feel the hostility. We were the enemy in every sense.

Some guys got off on it. Ray Price loved to feel the hate. It brought out the best in the champion Parramatta warhorse. He got hold of young Blocker in the dressing sheds to help limber up. They started whacking into each other with the shoulders—

they virtually put each other through the walls.

I hung my sky-blue NSW kit bag on a hook. I was so proud of my bag and tracksuit. When they handed it to me at camp in Sydney, I felt like I'd won Lotto!

The touch judges came into our room to check our boots and nails. We were nearly ready for kick-off.

BZZZZZZZZZZZ

A little metal bell in the corner of the ceiling started to buzz like crazy. That was our signal to take the field.

We made our way out the tunnel and then it hit me like a freight train—the jeers of the Lang Park crowd. It was so intense. I couldn't believe that I was out there with Blocker, my Balmain teammate, who I'd played with since the under-17s at Wests Red Devils. I thought to myself, *"How good is this?"*

The hatred of Queenslanders towards anything dressed in blue was real. It felt like I was in another country.

I looked up the other end of the field and saw the Maroons warming up.

Wally was throwing 30-metre passes to Mal. In between, he hoisted bombs to Colin Scott. For someone on debut, I found it a bit intimidating to watch.

Just to give Queensland some extra motivation, their coach Artie Beetson had found out earlier in the day that he'd been sacked as Australian coach.

And guess who was taking over? Frank Stanton—his Origin rival.

When the game kicked-off, the Queenslanders were on another level to us.

Wally was at his magical best. He even booted a field goal just before halftime from about 40 metres out. I watched the ball sail over my head thinking, *"That's not a bad-looking kick."* When it went over, I thought, *"Oh my God."*

The crowd was going crazy.

Their winger Kerry Boustead had a field day, scoring a hat-trick of tries. The Maroons won 29–12, but that scoreline is deceptive. Mal only kicked two goals from eight attempts—mercifully—otherwise the score could have been embarrassing.

I went okay on debut. My aim was to outplay my opposing fullback. I had played against Colin Scott just once before, in the Panasonic Cup. My attitude all game was to get my defence right first, and my attack would look after itself.

Apart from State pride, the other thing that went on the line that night were Test jerseys. The team to play the touring Great Britain side in the first Ashes Test was due to be named after fulltime. We went back to our hotel and were in the function room downstairs when I was called to the phone at the front desk. It was Donna.

"You're in the side—you're in the side!"

"What do you mean?"

"You're in the Australian side!"

I still hadn't heard a thing.

"I just heard on the radio that you're the new Australian fullback!"

I was gobsmacked.

The Australian selectors held their meeting on level 1 of our hotel. We were one floor below—but no one told us a thing!

That's how I found out I would be making my Test debut. I couldn't believe it.

They dumped the incumbent Colin Scott and gave me the number 1 jersey.

After I confirmed my selection, I rang Mum and Dad to share the exciting news. In all the madness, I'd forgotten the time—it was 2.30 a.m.! Mum answered the phone while still half-asleep, but she was very happy to hear from me.

On my way up to my room that night, I shared a very special moment in the lift with Peter Peters and Bob 'Bozo' Fulton—two more Wests Red Devils' juniors. They both congratulated me on my selection and wished me all the best against the Poms.

I reminded Bozo of a conversation he'd had with my cousin Greg 'Scrubber' Brazier six years earlier (see Chapter 55). Scrubber told him I would play for Australia. Bozo remembered, which was nice.

The first Test against Great Britain was played at the SCG. It was always a dream of mine to make my Australian debut at this magnificent venue.

Donna was with my family in the grandstand. She had to attend a wedding on the same day, so I was relieved to see she made it to the game on time.

When I stood in the middle of the ground as they played the national anthem, I was proud as punch. "*This is it. This is what it's all about,*" I thought. *"My first Test match."*

Then they played God Save the Queen. The song struck a chord with me because that's what I sang as a kid at school, before the days of Advance Australia Fair.

I didn't sing it—for obvious reasons—but a part of me felt like it.

CHAPTER 18

WALLY THE BANKER

JUST before kick-off in the first Test, an ugly chant broke out in sections of the SCG.

And, no, it wasn't aimed at the British players. Instead, our own captain was on the wrong end of it.

"WALLY'S A WANKER."

"WALLY'S A WANKER."

Unbelievable. The Australian captain being sledged by his own supporters.

This was where playing a Test series in the middle of a State of Origin series really blurred the lines. The Sydney crowd of more than 30,000 saw Wally as a Queenslander, not an Australian.

They had grown to hate the sight of him because he had become such a dominant force in Origin. Wally had also been handed the captaincy over NSW counterpart Ray Price.

"WALLY'S A WANKER."

"WALLY'S A WANKER."

In later years, Wally laughed it off. He said he always wondered why the crowd thought he worked in the finance industry.

"They kept calling me a banker," he would say.

I found the chant disrespectful. He was captaining Australia for the first time and that's the reception he was given. They hated Wally. It didn't matter what colours he was wearing.

It showed the growing hatred between the States since the introduction of Origin football.

It wasn't just in the grandstand, either. There was also a strange feeling within the team. We didn't know each other.

When the Broncos entered the Winfield Cup in 1988, we played against the Queensland guys all the time. We would share a beer after the game with them.

But in '84, they were still a bit of a mystery to us. We would only see them three times a year—and that's when we were ripping into each other with Test jerseys up for grabs.

This was my first time mingling with the Queenslanders. I was one of only five NSW players in the team.

They had smacked us in the first Origin game, so I found it a bit awkward. They probably thought Colin Scott should have kept his spot. But unfortunately for 'Scotty', Australia had lost their last Test match to New Zealand (in 1983), under coach Arthur Beetson, so a lot of them were on thin ice.

I heard the Australian selectors were split and it came down to the vote of the ARL chairman. Ken Arthurson voted for me, and that was the start of my 22-Test career as Australian fullback. Thank you Arko!

I would have been happy with playing one Test match. I feel very honoured to have been selected for five years.

Some of the Queenslanders were good company, others weren't so friendly. One guy who I really got along with was winger Kerry Boustead. He was my roommate and made me feel very welcome. It would be Kerry's last series for Australia.

I also kept getting a sense from the Queenslanders of, "Why is Ross Conlon here and not Mal Meninga?"

I disapproved of the Wally Lewis chant, but not because we were close mates. I have to say I really didn't enjoy Wally's company in that first series together.

I went into the Test match feeling like I had to prove myself. I knew if I had a bad game against the Poms, I'd be gone.

Early in the game, there was a big punch-up in a scrum, and everyone was into it. It summed up the game. Dirty and very violent. Elbows and knees were dropped in every tackle—mainly from 'the Brits'.

I got hit around the jaw from behind by their second-rower, Chris Burton, as I ran the ball. There were lots of high tackles that they got away with because Test matches between Australia and Great Britain (GB) were always treated differently. 'Refs' were expected to allow a traditional 'softening-up' period. It was wild out there.

My opposite number was a guy named Mick Burke. He was a bit older than me and wasn't the most athletic fullback. But he was a good goalkicker.

GB had Ellery Hanley on the wing, and Garry Schofield in the centres—two future Balmain teammates. They were playing their first Test series against Australia. What an impact they would both have for GB over the next decade.

Wally scored a try under the posts and had four Poms hanging off him. As he went to put the ball down, they were trying to rip him apart. They were raking at his face, anything, just to hurt him. It was terrible. That's when I realised just how tough a player Wally Lewis was—he had a lot more than just talent.

Worse was to come when their bench player David Hobbs came on and elbowed Greg Conescu in the face. Poor old Turtle's teeth went flying into the air, some 10 feet away, that's how hard he was hit.

Hobbs was sent off for his grubby act and later suspended for three games.

Our strength was out wide and that's where we won the game. Once the ball went from Wally to Gene Miles and Brett Kenny in the centres, we had too much skill.

We won 25–8.

CHAPTER 19

THE GRASSHOPPER

THE State of Origin series shifted to the SCG for Game II—and once again it was do-or-die for the Blues.

The selectors reacted savagely to our loss at Lang Park by dropping four players, including Peter Sterling.

We arrived at the ground and realised we were in for a tough slog. Partly because of the Queenslanders—but mainly because of the SCG surface. Torrential rain had turned the field into slop. There was no green grass to be seen, just mud.

The conditions helped propel Noel 'Crusher' Cleal into Origin folklore. He tried to kick a line drop-out from under our goalposts, only to come up with an air swing as the ball got stuck in the mud.

The other 'highlight' was Greg Dowling's try for Queensland. The big prop followed a Wally Lewis chip-kick that bounced off the crossbar. Despite the horrendous conditions, 'GD' somehow plucked the ball up in his fingertips to score a decisive try.

It was also my first experience with referee Barry Gomersall.

Known as 'The Grasshopper', because of his wiry frame and features, Gomersall was always the Queensland Rugby League's preferred choice as referee.

Gomersall came into our dressing room before kick-off to issue the whole NSW team a warning.

"I want you to know if there's any fighting—you'll be sent off. And I'm telling them (Queensland) the same," he said.

Anyway, a fight broke out in the first 15 seconds! I watched Gomersall to see what he would do.

All he did was just watch Queensland pass the ball along their all-star backline like he was mesmerised. He wouldn't have had a clue who started the fight. Well, I can assure you it wasn't NSW, because we'd just been told if we threw a punch we'd be sent off.

I'm not saying he was a cheat, but Queensland seemed to get a lot of calls go their way in games controlled by Gomersall.

I would hear Wally on the field saying, "We need a penalty—come on Barry!"

When we were defending, Gomersall would take us back the required five metres.

Then once we were set, I'd swear there were times he'd take another step backwards and blow his whistle.

"Offside NSW—you're all in front of me!"

But The Grasshopper was actually a very nice bloke when we weren't in the middle of an Origin game. A real character.

Queensland won the game 14–2 to clinch the series yet again.

The Maroons' dominance filtered through to the Test arena. Only three Blues were picked in the starting side for the second Ashes Test: Eric Grothe, Wayne Pearce and me.

Guru and Junior both scored tries in a series-deciding 18–6 win in Brisbane.

I had a better game than I did in Sydney. I liked playing at Lang Park. The pitch was always hard and fast.

I also found that Queensland fans were accepting of us NSW players—probably because we'd never beaten them! We didn't cop the treatment Wally got in Sydney.

The third Test was back at the SCG, and it was a special one for me.

From a kick reception, I put Kerry Boustead away down the wing, then backed up on the inside to score a try under the posts. My first try for Australia—I was so pumped!

Ray Price returned from injury to play his farewell Test match before he retired from international footy. It was an honour to be one of the guys who helped chair Pricey off the field at fulltime.

We won a tough game 20–7 to clean-sweep the series, 3–zip.

Great Britain tried hard and they were skilful, but we were just a lot fitter than them. It reminded me of a quote from Sir Alex Ferguson, the old Manchester United coach: "Hard work will always beat talent, when talent doesn't work hard."

That was so true.

Wearing the green and gold for the first time ranks right at the top in my career.

I consider playing for my country as the ultimate.

CHAPTER 20
TURNING POINT

THERE was a changing of the guard ahead of the dead-rubber third State of Origin match at Lang Park.

After Ray Price's decision to retire from Test football, the selectors agreed to move him on from the NSW team so they could blood new players. Pricey wanted to finish the Origin series and was filthy at being left out. I don't blame him either. He was one of NSW's greatest competitors and deserved to play a final game for his State.

Wayne Pearce was appointed the new captain but had to pull out injured. So, the job fell in the lap of Steve 'Turvey' Mortimer, the champion Canterbury Bulldogs' halfback.

I was becoming aware of an increasing Bulldogs' presence in the NSW team—especially when I opened the door of my hotel room one morning before breakfast.

There in the hallway was Bulldogs' fullback Mick Potter. This was a complete surprise to me, as Potter wasn't in the squad.

"Mick—g'day! What are you doing here mate?"

"Oh, I've been called into the side on the bench."

That was news to me. Potter was having a huge season for Canterbury and went on to win the Dally M award as Player of the Year. Like me, he was a fullback, so naturally I was a little worried. I knew if I didn't play well in Origin III, Potter would replace me.

I had to be on my toes.

Turvey's style of leadership really appealed to me. It was a different vibe in camp before the game—he was a people person.

One day, he called us all into his hotel room. It was strictly players only. Not even coach Frank Stanton was invited. Turvey asked us to "open up" to each other.

He said to me, "Jimmy, I'm really proud of you."

"I know what you will do for us. You are going to go out there and show everyone how good you are."

Turvey believed in all of us. He genuinely believed that we could beat them up there at Lang Park. The problem was we were very raw when it came to Origin football. Eleven of the starting 13 had less than three games experience. Brett Kenny and Turvey were the exceptions. But we were starting to build a team around combinations.

Turvey convinced us this was no dead-rubber game. Maybe it was for Queensland, but not for us. We were going to Lang Park to win.

Turvey's approach worked a treat. We went there and kicked their butts.

Our centres were outstanding. Brian Johnston scored a couple of tries, and Chris Mortimer—on debut—ripped into the big-name Queenslanders. He didn't care if it was Wally or Mal. He was a tough country kid.

We won 22–12 to finish the series 2–1 down. I could see the Maroons were shocked to lose. They didn't see it coming.

Ask any NSW player from that night and they'll tell you the same thing. Winning that game was the start of something big for the Blues.

It was a real line-in-the-sand moment to go up there and win, when all-conquering Queensland was chasing a clean sweep in front of their frothing fans.

It was a turning point in State of Origin.

CHAPTER 21

SOARING WITH THE SWANS

WHILE the 1984 season was a breakout year for me at rep level, things at Balmain weren't quite as rosy.

After starting with so much expectation, we fell short of the finals.

Frank Stanton spoke to all his players after what he deemed a massive failure. He asked me to spend the summer improving my skills in catching and kicking.

I got in touch with the Sydney Swans and started working with their captain, Mark Browning, and teammate, Craig Davis.

Another Swan, Arthur Chilcott, also helped out. I knew Arthur well because as juniors we played golf together at Kembla Grange. He also played rugby league for Dapto before finding his way into Aussie Rules.

I worked with these guys for four months over the off-season, usually at the old Sydney Sports Ground.

Browning spent the most time with me. He would show me how to kick drop-punts and torpedoes. We would also work on my catching, standing 10 metres apart and kicking the ball to each other, honing our reflexes. It's something I still see players do to warm up in the modern game.

The connection to the Swans was a pointer to the future. Two of our sons, Kieren and Brandon, would play for Sydney. I'm a rugby league man, but the Swans hold a special place in my heart.

I went back to the Tigers full of confidence ahead of the new season. Biscuits was so impressed with my new kicking technique that he gave me the job of booting the ball into touch from penalties and doing the line drop-outs. I could now regularly drop-kick the ball for over 50 metres.

Everyone was determined to make amends for the previous season. We even came up with a slogan: "Tigers Alive in '85".

Whether it was our new catchcry or a better attitude, we flew out of the blocks. We won our first four games by big margins: Norths 26–6, Penrith 36–6, Cronulla 32–8 and Wests 50–10.

It was only the might of defending premiers Canterbury that ended our winning run, 20–18, at Leichhardt.

Next up was a mid-week game against Combined Brisbane in the National Panasonic Cup tournament.

These guys were the defending champions and full of big names like Wally Lewis, John Ribot, Colin Scott, Peter Jackson, Bob Lindner, Greg Dowling, Greg Conescu and Bryan Niebling. It was more like a Queensland State of Origin team.

But we smashed them 33–16 at Leichhardt.

We scored a spectacular try in that game that saw me awarded the Panasonic Cup Try of the Year award—even though I didn't score it.

Brisbane kicked-off after Ross Conlon slotted a penalty goal for us. I caught the ball and took off. I'll let Ray Warren call it from there, as he did on Channel 10's coverage:

"Garry Jack making a great run, unloaded to Gary Bridge, who gets it around the corner to Scotty Gale. Gale, making a great run, running like a man inspired, Gale, Gale… he'll score! Look at the jubilation in this Balmain team!"

Dozens of fans jumped the fence to celebrate with Scotty. Watching him run around Colin Scott and leave another three Brisbane players in his wake... it still makes the hairs stand up on the back of my neck. When he put his foot down, he was like The Road Runner.

I was deemed by the judges to have 'set up' the try for Scotty. My reward was a massive entertainment unit worth around $5,000. This thing had a stereo, record player and television all in one. They delivered it to our home in Wollongong.

As a thank you for their roles, I gave Scotty and Bridgey a small bottle of champagne each. Big of me, I know!

Scotty did okay though. He later claimed the player of the series award, which saw him receive $20,000 worth of products from Panasonic.

Scotty was a rare talent. If you look at his highlights reel, it's amazing how much talent he had. He had great speed, a chip-and-chase, and brilliant instincts as a halfback.

He could do things no other player could do.

Scotty could possibly have gotten more out of himself than he did during his career. In later years, they replaced him at Balmain with Gary Freeman, who was more of an organiser.

Scotty was such a lovely fella. I had a lot of time for him. It was incredibly sad when he passed away from motor neurone disease in 2004.

We ended up playing Cronulla in the National Panasonic Cup final. We led 14–12 with 10 minutes to go, when their winger Wayne Smith, a former teammate of mine at Wests, made a break. He was just 15 metres from our line, and I had to somehow stop him, or we were toast.

Smith had a great right-foot step—I rated it as good as 'Changa' Langlands'.

I ran at him to take away his time, then he went BANG off the right foot, just like I knew he would. He beat me, but as I was falling to the ground, I managed to grab him around his bootlaces and bring him down, just short of the goal-line.

It was the best tackle I had made at that stage of my career. It helped us win the game 14–12. It was the first major piece of silverware in my career.

After our win over the Sharks, excitement was building. We were in the middle of a 10-match winning streak across both the Winfield Cup and National Panasonic Cup.

More than 21,000 fans jammed into Leichhardt for our round 22 clash with St. George, which we lost in a thriller, 17–15.

We were still in first place going into our penultimate round clash with bogey team Parramatta. We copped a touch-up, 40–8. It cost us the minor premiership.

We played Canterbury in the major semi-final. It was 8–8 in the second half before our English import Garry Schofield put replacement back Stephen Humphreys over for a try.

As we celebrated what we thought was the match-winning play, referee Mick Stone called it back for a forward pass. He was advised by the touch judge.

There was no way in the world that pass from Schofield was forward. It went backwards out of his hands. The pass was good.

Incredibly, like my only other experience in finals' football, this game went to extra-time.

The scores remained locked until the 100th minute when Andrew Farrar broke clear down the right flank at the SCG. He scored the winning try with me around his bootlaces.

It was very deflating to lose like that. We should have won. We had Canterbury that day.

On a personal note, that was probably the best game I played in my whole career. Sometimes when you touch the ball, everything comes off just the way you want. This was one of those games. I was in career-best form and that was confirmed when I won my first Dally M Fullback of the Year award.

We were flat for the following week's elimination semi-final against Parramatta, who were on a late-season charge.

I scored a try in the first half, but in the end, we were blitzed by the Eels, 32–4.

From sitting in first position a few weeks earlier, we were now out of the finals in straight sets.

It was a bitter pill to swallow. But we knew we had a team that could challenge for a premiership.

Here I am before my final game for Salford in 1994, with Rhys and Kieren

Reflecting at the Isurava memorial on the Kokoda Track in 2015 with Donna and Rhys

Me with the boys after watching Kieren play for the Swans in 2012

Donna with Rhys (left), Kieren (middle), and Brandon (right)

At our home in Cherrybrook, 1995, after returning from England to play with the Tigers

Here we are with Brandon when he received an award as school captain of Oakhill College

Garry and his girls. Here I am with my mum Jan (left), Donna and her mum Wendy (right) celebrating our engagement in 1984

One of the highlights of my sporting career. Receiving my black belt for Brazilian Jiu Jitsu in 2017 from Simon Farnsworth

The love of my life. Donna and I are all smiles during the State of Origin series 1986

Celebrating at home after Kieren was recruited by the Sydney Swans

A sweaty MMA session with Rhys at Universal Combat Academy at Castle Hill

One of my favourite photos. Here I am with a young Kieren, who's holding his beloved football at home

Kieren (left) and Rhys (right) join me in the sheds after a Balmain game. They loved coming to the footy – mainly because they got a Coke!

Feeling deflated during the unsuccessful Alan Jones era.
Rhys and 'Bear' tried to lift my spirits

CHAPTER 22

FEARING FOR MY LIFE

I CHUCKLE when I see players penalised and castigated by the referee for "dangerous throws" in the modern game.

To me, it's like the movie *Crocodile Dundee* when Paul Hogan utters his iconic line to a New York mugger, "That's not a knife ... *that's* a knife."

Dangerous throws these days compared to when I played are not even in the same postcode. They even had a different name: spear tackles.

You were picked up by the defender/s and driven headfirst into the turf like a spear.

It was a terrifying experience for any player, and it happened to me during the 1985 season at Leichhardt Oval.

I was playing for Balmain in a game against Manly. Running the ball up, I was met in defence by Noel Cleal and Paul McCabe. Both were big men weighing around 100–105 kilos. In comparison, I was about 82 kilos.

They grabbed hold of me and instantly I felt myself being lifted off the ground. Crusher Cleal was known for that kind of tackle. He was a strong country boy and picked you up like a bush pig.

Crusher his hand between my legs to lift me, while McCabe had hold of my top half. He used the back of my collar to propel me downwards, while at the same time, Cleal also speared me into the ground, right in front of the Latchem Robinson Stand.

As I saw the turf fast approaching, I put my arm out to break my fall and threw the ball away, so I could fully protect myself.

It all happened in the blink of an eye, but I still had enough time to think of all kinds of terrible scenarios as I was up in the air.

Was I about to end up in a wheelchair—or worse?

Cleal and McCabe finished off the tackle and I thudded into the ground.

Incredibly, I felt no pain. I jumped to my feet, which confirmed no broken bones. I didn't even feel concussed. I couldn't believe my luck. It was a miracle!

The referee blew his whistle and called a scrum, with Manly to feed. He ruled I had lost the ball in the tackle. I don't regret throwing the ball away. That act saved me from serious injury. But I couldn't believe Kevin Roberts took no action against Manly.

Cleal and McCabe weren't even penalised for the tackle.

NSWRL boss John Quayle could have cited both players, but chose not to, which reeked of double standards in favour of Manly players.

Nowadays, they would both be sent off and suspended for a long period of time.

I'm not saying they deliberately tried to hurt me. I consider both of them mates. I played alongside Crusher for NSW and Australia, while 'Macca' was a teammate of mine at Balmain in 1986.

But it was an incredibly dangerous tackle.

A photo of the precise moment I'm being speared into the ground was splashed all over the newspapers. It still sends shudders through me whenever I see it.

The game has now rubbed these kinds of tackles out of the game, making it much safer.

We can all be thankful for that.

CHAPTER 23
HISTORY-MAKERS

STEVE Mortimer was once again named NSW skipper for the opening State of Origin game of 1985.

Turvey had tapped into State pride during the final game of '84, and he was at it again as we headed to Lang Park to open the series. On the team bus, he felt like a few of the boys were a bit quiet.

"STOP THE BUS!"

The driver did as he was told by Turvey, pulling up outside the infamous Caxton Street Hotel. The place was bursting at the seams with Maroons' supporters.

As we sat there wondering what the hell Turvey was on about, he started talking about showing more pride in the blue jersey. He said Queensland cherished their jersey more than us. He reckoned we needed to match that passion.

Just like 12 months earlier, stubbies of beer started raining down on the bus from outside the Caxton.

"Look at them!" Turvey screamed, as he pointed out the bus window.

"They all f*&%ing hate us—have a look at them!"

He was right. This mob in maroon looked like they wanted to storm the bus.

"They have no respect for us. They all hate us," Turvey continued.

"*Everyone* hates us in Queensland."

He then pointed at some random guy in the crowd.

"That bloke over there—he hates us. See that woman—she hates us too.

"Even our bus driver hates us!

"So tonight, we hate them *more*. Let's go out there and hate them more!"

I was so pumped; we could have kicked-off right there and then. Inspired by our captain's passion, we had never been more ready.

That speech by Turvey set the tone for the whole series.

There is *one* thing I should clarify, though.

As we filed off the bus at Lang Park, the driver actually pulled aside one of the boys and whispered, "Just so you know, I actually *don't* hate you guys at all."

On a wet night in Brisbane, we made the home fans even more miserable with a dominating performance.

Thanks to some brilliant tactics from our new coach Terry Fearnley, we were able to shut down Wally Lewis by harassing him and his outside supports.

At five-eighth, Brett Kenny clearly outplayed The King, and not for the first time as it would turn out.

Former Wallaby Michael O'Connor was a welcome addition to our team in the centres. He produced a debut to top them all. Snoz scored all 18 of our points—two tries and five goals.

We won 18–2 to silence the capacity crowd.

It was the first time the Maroons had ever been kept try-less in an Origin game.

Later, the Queenslanders complained that Snoz was one of their own, because he went to university in Brisbane while he was playing rugby union.

Can you believe it? Wasn't it enough that they got two games every year at Lang Park? How's their fair?

Yet still they whinged.

Our victory triggered huge excitement back home. Finally, we were in a position to win an Origin series.

More than 40,000 fans turned out at the SCG for Origin II and once again we got in Wally's face. In his debut series, Benny Elias was leading the charge. He would race out of marker and run straight for Wally at first receiver.

Benny also scored a try as we stormed to a 12–0 lead.

Being the champion he is, Wally wouldn't be kept quiet for long. He made a break around the halfway line, with only me left in front of him. He was about 15 metres from our goal-line when I decided to show him the sideline. The King took the bait and tried to beat me on the outside. I chopped him down one metre short of our line.

I rate that as one of the best tackles of my career, given the pressure and situation of the game.

Despite that, the Maroons snatched a 14–12 lead in the second half. We edged ahead with a penalty goal and a field goal to Snoz.

'Bert' (Kenny) put the game to bed with a late try, throwing a huge dummy to fool The King. It was one of the best dummies I ever saw.

As we celebrated the winning try, Turvey dropped to his knees and kissed the SCG turf in triumph. The passion he had for the Blues' jersey had rubbed off on all of us.

Snoz's conversion gave us a 21–14 win.

We had made history. The first NSW team to win a State of Origin series. The crowd was going bananas!

Turvey was chaired off the field by Peter Wynn, Noel Cleal and Wayne Pearce, with his arms raised aloft. It was to be his final game for NSW. Turvey decided to retire from representative football with immediate effect.

Despite all the celebrations, I was feeling a bit sore and sorry.

I had clashed heads with Queensland's Mark Murray, and the result was my two front teeth were bent back at a 45-degree angle. I didn't even know until our trainer Larry Britton noticed I was bleeding and told me to come off.

The team doctor, Bill Monaghan, did a great job pushing the teeth back into place, and I managed to keep them despite some nerve damage.

This is going to sound crazy, given I played in the world's most physical body contact sport—but it was only after that incident that I started to wear a mouthguard!

The team partied long and loud in the Members Lounge at the SCG with family and friends. I also had the great pleasure of meeting rugby league's first Immortal, Clive Churchill. 'The Little Master', as he was known, was the greatest fullback Australia ever produced.

Defensively, there was no better number one in the game. Clive told me that day, "You have to anticipate what they are going to do and get there before them." I never forgot his advice and always used his philosophy to attack the man with the ball.

Sadly, he passed away from cancer just eight weeks later, aged 58. The conversation I had with him remains one of the highlights of my career.

The beers were still flowing long after the last fan had filed out of the SCG. There were plenty of toasts for Turvey and our coach.

Terry Fearnley's tactics to counter the genius of Wally were a massive reason behind our success. Of all the coaches I worked with at Origin level, Fearnley's strategy was the best.

But despite his success, the coach was about to feel the heat. Serious heat.

CHAPTER 24

BORDER WARS

FOR the second year in a row, a Test series punctuated the State of Origin series.

Australia had named a new coach for the series against New Zealand: Terry Fearnley.

Yes, the same Terry Fearnley who had just engineered the demise of Queensland's Origin dynasty. It was a decision that would have massive ramifications.

The first Test against New Zealand at Lang Park was seven days after we clinched the Origin series in Sydney. Origin III would be played after the Test matches.

The Kiwis were aggressive and thought they could bully us. They had tough forwards in captain Mark Graham, Kurt Sorenson and the Tamati brothers, Kevin and Howie.

We knew the physical assault was coming. Things exploded when Greg Dowling and Kevin Tamati had a punch-up.

The French referee, Julien Rascagnères, sent both to the sin-bin—but made a huge mistake in the process. Instead of holding one of them back for a minute, he stupidly marched both at the same time.

Dowling and Tamati left the field side by side and—surprise, surprise—words were exchanged. GD said something and Tamati responded with a few words of his own—then all hell broke loose!

A jailhouse brawl erupted, right there on the sideline. Headbutts and uppercuts were thrown as both players fought against the Lang Park fence. At one stage GD was on his knees in a gutter.

We won the Test in a really close call, 26–20, but the fight was *the* story.

Rugby league was trying to clean up its image after the wild days of the '70s and early '80s. Les Boyd and Bob Cooper had been given huge suspensions by judiciary chairman Jim Comans for shocking incidents of foul play.

Well, this was just as ugly. Two players brawling against a fence, less than a metre from fans. It was such a bad look for international rugby league.

But Dowling and Tamati only got a slap on the wrist—an eight-day suspension.

It conveniently meant they were both available for the second Test in Auckland.

Dowling and Tamati going head-to-head at Carlaw Park was a promoter's dream. Ding, ding!

My old Balmain teammate Olsen Filipaina was outstanding at Lang Park, and he was again a thorn in our side in Auckland.

The Kiwis deserved to win this game—they were the better team. But we got out of jail to win the series, and I was proud to play a part.

Leading 6–4 with just over 60 seconds left on the clock, Olsen tried to get a kick away for the Kiwis. Paul 'Fatty' Vautin pressured him in defence, forcing Olsen to run instead. He passed the ball to Mark Graham, who lost possession.

We now had the ball, but there was nothing really happening. Then Wally ran from right to left, towards me on the other side of the ruck. I noticed Kiwi forward Hugh McGahan had come up quickly and was out of the line. Wally didn't miss it either. Our eyes met and we both knew where the gap was, just behind McGahan.

Wally passed me a beautiful ball onto my chest, and I went past McGahan and into the clear. I ran for 20 metres with only Gary Kemble to beat. I instinctively dummied on the inside to Wally, then I looked over my shoulder and saw Johnny Ribot unmarked 10 metres away. I passed to 'Reebs' and it hit him right on the chest. It was sheer ecstasy as I watched Ribot run away to score the series-winning try.

I was belly down in the mud at Carlaw Park when Ribot touched down. We had done it. We had pulled off a miracle win, 10–6. Blocker rushed in and gave me a huge bear hug. Wally fell to the ground in disbelief.

It was Fatty's chase that won us the game. If Filipaina got his kick away, then New Zealand would have been camped down our end of the field. It was a huge play from Fatty.

It was an incredible month for Fearnley. He'd masterminded the Blues' first Origin series win, now he was also a winner at Test level.

The easy decision for the coach would have been to keep the same team for the dead-rubber third Test against the Kiwis, also at Carlaw Park.

But Fearnley wasn't satisfied. He knew we were lucky to win both Tests and decided to make changes.

From the starting side, he dropped Mark Murray, Chris Close, Greg Dowling and Greg Conescu—all Queenslanders.

Their replacements were Des Hasler, Steve Ella, Peter Tunks and Benny Elias—all from Fearnley's NSW side.

The whole squad surrounded Terry in a circle as he announced the changes. I could see guys shaking their heads. They couldn't believe what they just heard.

In Terry's defence, I don't think he was favouring his NSW players. Murray wasn't playing well, and neither was Conescu. You could probably say the same about 'Choppy' (Close) and GD.

Terry was within his rights to drop them based on form. But I'll admit it caught me out. I didn't think he'd drop them after winning the series. I walked back to the hotel with Snoz O'Connor. I said to him, "This is going to be huge!"

As a result, things became very icy in camp.

Wally was very close to 'Muppet' Murray. He hardly spoke to Des all week even though they were now Australian halves partners!

In fact, the Queenslanders didn't speak much to *any* of us New South Welshmen. Not even to Benny, who was making his Test debut. Imagine getting called up to play for Australia and half your teammates brush you?

It was a piss-poor reaction.

There was a major split in the team, and it showed the way we played. There was no miracle finish this time.

The Kiwis ran all over us to win 18–0, Australia's worst loss in years. Our team was broken. I wasn't surprised by the result. You can't have players in key positions not talking to each other and expect to win.

Less than two weeks after that tumultuous Test match in Auckland, we headed back to Lang Park with Fearnley to complete the Origin series.

Our goal was to become the first side—from either State—to clean-sweep a series.

The problem was, it had been more than a month since our win in Origin II and momentum was lost. Especially with Steve Mortimer stepping down as captain.

Still angry at Fearnley for being dropped from the Test team, Murray, Dowling and Conescu came out and had blinders for the 'Cane Toads'. Choppy had to go off at halftime with injury.

Queensland hammered us 20–6.

The flashpoint came after a Maroons' try when Dowling made a beeline for the NSW bench.

He found Fearnley and unleashed a tirade. GD flipped him the bird right to his face and screamed, "Get that up ya!"

Even though we won the series, the ugly episode cost Terry his job—for both NSW and Australia.

Wally had taken his grievances to the QRL (Queensland Rugby League) and from there Terry was doomed. The King had a lot of pull.

Years later, I bumped into Terry at a function, and he asked me, "Jimmy, do you think I over-reacted when I dropped those four Queenslanders?"

I told him he made the right decision. I sensed he had some regret.

CHAPTER 25

DOUBLE DELIGHT

WE had finally broken Queensland's dominance in State of Origin—now we were hungry for more.

After the unfortunate demise of Terry Fearnley, our new coach in 1986 was the experienced Ron Willey.

Ron was an old-school style coach who had been around the game for years. His philosophy was that if everyone outplays their opposite number, we'll win the game. Pretty simple.

Going up against Ron was a young coach on the rise. His name was Wayne Bennett.

The first game of the series was at Lang Park. As usual, the hatred for anyone dressed in blue was obvious.

I copped most of the abuse because I'm literally the first NSW player the mad Queenslanders get to lay their eyes on. The fullback always ran onto the field first in those days, because that's how they read out the team.

"For NSW, number 1—Garry Jack!" the ground announcer roared. The boos were deafening.

Personally, I never took offence to being booed during my career. It made me play harder. Booing is designed to put players off their game. I wore it like a badge of honour.

At Lang Park in the '80s, there was always some poor guy in a blue cockroach costume being chased around by a cane toad, carrying an oversized can of Mortein. The cockroach would end up flat on his back, legs twitching, after being covered in spray.

We trailed 16-12 in the second half but finished stronger. I scored my first Origin try, running off a pass from Steve Folkes.

We won 22-16.

Queensland made changes for Origin II at the SCG, including Gary Belcher coming in at fullback for Colin Scott.

One of the first times he touched the ball, Belcher beat about three defenders on a

30-metre run. I knew straight away that was the end of Scott's days as my rival in the Queensland number 1 jersey.

I took a knock to the head in the first half and was concussed. All I remember is running parallel to a Queensland player for 10 metres as he scored a try. I eventually came to my senses and asked Brett Kenny, "Bert, are we winning 4–0 or 6–0?"

He said, "Bloody hell Jimmy, they're up 12–0!"

The game was see-sawing, just like Origin I. But the skills of Sterling and Kenny in the halves was the difference.

We won 24–20 to wrap up our second consecutive series.

Kenny was exceptional. He could sell dummies and take intercepts like no other player. I don't think Bert ever played a bad game for NSW. In my opinion, he should be made an Immortal by the NRL.

It was Wayne Pearce's first series win as skipper. He always led by example. Always gave 100 percent.

Even though Junior was a teetotaller, he would still be front and centre at our 'bonding' nights. He was happy to sip his water or lemon squash. If you didn't know him, you'd swear Junior *was* drunk. That was him being high on life.

We went back to Lang Park chasing a clean sweep.

It was a chance at writing some more history that we didn't want to miss. Crusher Cleal was really revving us up.

Yet again, there was nothing between the two sides. At halftime, the score was 16–16.

After the break, referee Kevin Roberts bravely penalised Wally Lewis for being offside. The Lang Park crowd was furious. One bloke hurled an apple at Snoz as he slotted the penalty goal.

That was the only points of the second half. We hung on to win a nail-biter, 18–16.

The first series clean sweep—and it went to the good guys in blue.

We never expected to win 3-nil, and to be honest it could easily have been Queensland winning 3–nil. Every game ebbed and flowed.

The clash of the champion five-eighths—Kenny and Lewis—was a series highlight. Bert marginally outpointed The King and that was the difference.

They were both in career-best form.

I consider that series as the most enjoyable of all my time wearing the sky-blue jersey.

Five days later, we went straight into a Test series against New Zealand.

We won 22–8 at Carlaw Park, and I was named man of the match which was a huge thrill.

The result was a reality check for the Kiwis. They would have been confident after thrashing us 18–0 at the same venue 12 months earlier.

They made a stack of changes, which included handing a debut to a young halfback named Gary Freeman.

'Whiz' would go on to become one of the most capped Kiwi players of all time, with 46 Tests for his nation. We would become teammates and close friends later in our careers.

One guy who got up our nose was their forward Kurt Sorenson. He used a lot of niggling tactics in back-play that the boys hadn't forgotten. Our front-rowers, 'Tunksy' and Blocker, vowed to sort him out in the second Test at the SCG.

Sure enough, Sorenson started the match with an old-fashioned stiff arm on Wally. Tunksy jumped straight in and let Sorenson know he wouldn't be getting away with that shit today. The Kiwi hardman didn't cause too many problems after that.

Les Kiss—a future Wallabies' coach—made his debut for Australia in that Test match. We called Les 'Lighthouse' because he never stopped blinking! He had a blinder and even set me up for a try.

Les burst down the sideline with me in support on the inside screaming, "Go Lighthouse, go!" The defence got to him, but he threw me a beautiful pass and I scored under the posts to the roar of 34,000 screaming fans.

It was a great feeling to score my second career try in the green and gold. I thought of my Pop straight away. He would have liked that one.

The 'Supercoach' Jack Gibson was calling the game for Channel Nine with Darrell Eastlake and said of me: "That's the difference between a great player and an ordinary one. He had to anticipate and run 50 to 60 yards to score."

Thanks Jack.

That try gave us a 12–6 lead and we ended up running away with it, 29–12.

Blocker was named man of the match. That meant the best players from the first two Tests hailed from the Western Suburbs Red Devils!

We finished the series off at Lang Park with a dominant 32–12 win.

The only lowlight was losing Junior to a knee injury in the first half. That would have major ramifications for our season at Balmain.

But overall, there was so much to celebrate. I had just experienced a series clean sweep over the Kiwis and the Queenslanders.

All I needed now was a premiership.

CHAPTER 26

THE BITE

IN the final round of the 1986 season, there was plenty on the line as we took on the Rabbitohs. We needed a win to keep our finals' hopes alive. For them, victory would hand them the minor premiership and a valuable week off.

Junior Pearce was out injured for the back end of the season after injuring his knee against the Kiwis, so Benny Elias stepped up as skipper. The Rabbitohs were led by Mario Fenech.

Those two played the same position—and hated each other. Their rivalry went right back to their schoolboy battles.

Mario was Maltese, Benny was Lebanese. They came to Australia with their families as kids. Benny was intelligent, good-looking… and had the gift of the gab.

Sometimes that rubbed people up the wrong way. He would get under their skin. But he didn't give a shit. Benny could absorb a lot of punishment. He never got enough credit for his toughness. People just saw the flamboyance.

As a player he changed the role of dummy-half play. He added a different dimension to attack. 'B-E' loved to challenge the defensive line with his running game and clever ball play.

Mario was completely different. He was hard-as-nails and could run over the top of you.

Under Benny's leadership, we flogged Mario's boys that day at Leichhardt, 38–20. But it wouldn't be the last we saw of the Rabbitohs in '86. And next time would be far more controversial.

Three days later, we played the Bears in a play-off for fifth spot at the SCG. We won 14–7 to secure our place in the finals.

The match is best known for some more freakish play from Scotty Gale when he chipped and regathered from halfway, chipped again, and won the race to score.

Up next was an elimination semi-final against Manly on Saturday—our third game in eight days.

That might sound like a lot, but I'd already experienced worse earlier in the season.

How about this for a stretch of games:

Tuesday May 27: NSW v Queensland, State of Origin I, Lang Park.

Wednesday May 28: Balmain v Easts, National Panasonic Cup semi-final, Leichhardt Oval.

Sunday, June 1: Balmain v Souths, Winfield Cup, Redfern Oval.

Wednesday, June 4: Balmain v Parramatta, National Panasonic Cup final, Leichhardt Oval.

By the time we played the Eels, that was my fourth game in just nine days! Not ideal.

They towelled us up 32–16.

It would have been easy to ask for a rest, but I never wanted to let down my teammates. And I've already explained how Cranky Franky felt about his players missing games.

Making matters worse, I injured my ankle during that loss to Parra. This could have been disastrous for me, with Origin, Tests and finals to come.

Enter a guy called 'Shorty'.

His real name was Hilton Hextell, a 68-year-old pensioner who was five-foot tall with magic hands.

Shorty was the long-time strapper/rubber for my home club, the Western Suburbs Red Devils. For over 40 years, he worked as a medical officer in the mines. Eventually he converted his family home in Wollongong to help treat athletes from all sports.

After I injured myself against Parra, I saw Shorty quite a bit. He lived in Coniston, which was just around the corner from our place. I could call Shorty 24/7, and he never complained.

He worked miracles on my ankle. I can confidently say, if it wasn't for Shorty, I wouldn't have enjoyed all the success I had in '86. He was a genius!

The silver-lining from such a hectic playing schedule was that I learned how to play under adversity. I felt like it helped my game.

An older team might have struggled to back up against Manly in that minor semi-final. But most of us were in our early to mid-twenties—still young enough to bounce back from any bumps and bruises.

Plus, we also had the 'Sirro factor' in our favour. Paul Sironen had burst onto the scene that season.

At six-foot-four, and 115 kilograms, Sirro had a high knee-lift when he ran the footy and was a nightmare to stop. He was a Balmain junior who loved rugby league and also played some gridiron in Hawaii.

What a find. He was named Rookie of the Year. Sirro went from kid to Kangaroo in a hurry.

In the knockout match against the Sea Eagles, he was at his rampaging best.

Knowing his raw power, we made Sirro the central figure in a set move from a scrum win. We were on the attack about 10 metres from Manly's goal-line. The ball was passed to Sirro, and he ran straight at poor old Cliffy Lyons, who was about half his size. Cliffy shut his eyes and hoped for the best. Sirro busted the tackle and scored next to the posts.

We won 29–22 to set up another showdown with the Rabbitohs—and this time it was sudden-death for the loser.

It was a tight tussle at the SCG when Benny, as skipper, decided to try something different to break South Sydney's resolve.

Before a scrum was about to pack, he grabbed Blocker and told him to start a fight. An obliging Blocker landed an uppercut on Souths' enforcer Les Davidson—and suddenly there was a wild all-in brawl.

While this was happening, Benny took out his mouthguard… and chomped down hard on his own hand.

As referee Kevin Roberts tried to restore order, Benny came reeling out of the melee screaming at Roberts to look at his hand. Roberts came over and saw a huge bite mark.

"It was Mario! He bit me!"

Roberts replied, "I know Benny, I saw it."

Mario stood there wide-eyed, before protesting his innocence.

"I didn't bite him! I didn't bite him!"

Roberts didn't hesitate. He waved Mario from the field. Souths were down to 12 men for the rest of the game.

Mario was filthy and who could blame him? The referee had been conned by his fiercest rival. He was the skipper. He had to sit in the grandstand when his team desperately needed him.

The game was in the balance until the moment Mario trudged from the field. After that, we romped away to win 36–11.

I don't think Benny needed to do what he did for us to win the game. I would never dream of doing something like that. But that's B-E.

The Rabbitohs had the last laugh when Blocker was cited for a minor headbutt. He went to the judiciary and was suspended for one match—a preliminary final against Canterbury.

Without our two forward leaders—Blocker and Junior—it was going to be a tough assignment against the Dogs.

There was a special moment for me when I scored a try from about 70 metres out. I ran off a pass from Ross Conlon, then beat my opposite number Phil Sigsworth with an in-and-away. Thanks Shorty—couldn't have done that without you!

We gave some cheek, but in the end, they were too strong, 28–16.

I was disappointed to fall a game short of my first grand final. But my mood soon picked up. I won my second-straight Dally M Fullback of the Year award—and even better news was just around the corner.

I was going on a Kangaroo Tour.

CHAPTER 27

KANGAROO TOUR DIARY

KANGAROO Tours were special because they only came around every four years. Unlike these days, you had to be selected for a tour of England and France to be known as a 'Kangaroo'.

It was something I'd dreamed about as a kid.

In 1986, I was the incumbent Australian fullback. I was at home in Wollongong with Donna when the team was announced. It was the highlight of my career, being selected that night.

But the job had only just begun. I had a lot to live up to and felt the pressure as a very capable understudy in Gary Belcher was also selected in the squad.

I was ready to write my own history… so I decided to pen a diary, starting with our pre-tour trip to Papua New Guinea.

Friday, October 3, 1986

The Port Moresby humidity is something else. We trained at 4 p.m. for 30 minutes, trying to acclimatise.

There is good harmony in the team. We realise that we can't take Papua New Guinea easy. This is a sanctioned Test match, so we need to treat it that way.

Saturday, October 4

It's 35 degrees today, but at least I had a good sleep. I sat around the motel and talked for an hour with the boys. Waiting for the game can be hard.

A record crowd of 17,000 people turned up at Lloyd Robson Oval. The place was jam-packed. 'PNG' tried hard and scored a try just on halftime. But we were never in danger, winning 62–12. This was my 10th Test match. It was great to see my Tigers' teammate Paul Sironen make his Test debut.

Australia 62 Papua New Guinea 12

Sunday, October 5

There's nothing to do except sit around the pool. Lost a lot of skin from both my knees, being tackled on the rock-hard ground. The grazes on my knees are stinging and sticking to my tracksuit. We flew back to Sydney. I spent the night at the Camperdown Travelodge with Donna.

Tuesday, October 7

Departed Sydney at 3.15 p.m. for the 26-hour flight to London. Played cards the moment we got on the plane with Benny, 'Simmo' (Royce Simmons) *and 'Sterlo'* (Peter Sterling).

The boys went hard early on the cans of beer during the first leg to Kuala Lumpur but slowed down for the second leg. I think a few of the boys thought it was a holiday, and drank the plane clean out of Foster's in the first six hours! I got about 1–2 hours' sleep.

Wednesday, October 8

Arrived at Heathrow Airport at 8.30 a.m. By 10.30 a.m. we were on a bus to Leeds, a very industrial town. My legs are feeling very stiff after the flight and need a run. We trained in the afternoon.

Thursday, October 9

We are staying at the Dragonara Hotel in Leeds. I'm rooming with Gary Belcher on the sixth floor. There are two single beds in a small room, overlooking the railway station. We are here for seven weeks.

I didn't know Gary before the tour. Instead of matching club teammates together, management has put players competing for the same position together. I don't know if that's a good thing to do. Anyway, when we walked into our room together, and looked at the two single beds, 'Badge' said he will take the one closest to the door. No worries for me.

Training twice a day at 10 a.m. and 4 p.m. I bought some fruit and Mars bars for 20 pence each.

The weather isn't too bad. I'm still getting around in a t-shirt.

We are playing Wigan on Sunday. They have 10 internationals in their top 15 players.

Friday, October 10

Must still have jet lag, woke up at 5.30 a.m. and couldn't get back to sleep. Played soccer at 10 a.m. for training. Getting to know Gary better. But there is still a bit of tension between us.

Played cards with Benny and Royce and won 50 pounds and 68 pounds off them (respectively).

Wally and Sterlo have already bought cars. They were on the 1982 Tour and that's what they did last time.

Saturday October 11

Woke at 7 a.m. to blue skies. Had breakfast by myself. Went to the Yorkshire Cup final at Headingley, Hull versus Castleford. Wow the crowds over here are great. They were singing all game. We were introduced to the crowd at halftime. We got a warm reception.

I made up my mind that I would play over here one day. They love their footy.

Castleford 31 defeated Hull 24. It was all about attack and it was entertaining to watch.

I am in bed writing about tomorrow's first game of the 1986 Kangaroo Tour. I can't wait to play in front of 30,000 fans.

I have always been a huge fan of Kangaroo Tours, getting up at 2–3 a.m. to watch the 1973 and 1978 Tours with my Dad. And now I am on one. Growing up as a boy, you would hear about all the great fullbacks who have represented Australia and written their own history: Churchill, Barnes, Johns, Thornett, Langlands, Eadie.

There certainly was a level of expectation that came with being the Australian Rugby League fullback. I am aware of this and want to continue the tradition. I don't want to let anyone down. It is my time to write my own history, over the next 10 weeks.

Sunday, October 12

Played Wigan at Central Park in front of 30,000.

I set up Mick O'Connor for our first try. I was sin-binned for 10 minutes for a late, high tackle on Wigan captain Graeme West. It was a bullshit decision.

As I was walking up the tunnel, the crowd was sledging me, calling me an 'Aussie bastard'.

We led 20–2 at halftime and won 26–18. What a backline we had in '86—Sterling, Lewis, Kenny, Miles, O'Connor, Kiss, Lamb and Meninga.

This was always going to be our hardest club game on tour. Wigan thought they could ambush us because we only arrived from Australia five days ago. But it backfired.

The Poms think they can win the Ashes, well they haven't seen the best of us yet.

Had a warm bath after the game with Sterlo, Bert, Snoz, Wally and Gene. This is something I have never experienced before. Bert introduced me to his version of the British lion. I couldn't wait to get out!

Australia 26 Wigan 18

Monday, October 13

Two separate training sessions on a foggy day in Leeds. A few players weren't happy with having to do 10 x 200m sprints and 5 x 50m sprints after such a hard game.

But the hard work had to be done now to reach peak fitness and build teamwork.

We watched a replay of the game, with the crew from Channel 10 who were broadcasting the series. There was plenty of stick going on during the game, which I didn't realise at the time. Had a couple of beers. I don't play again until Sunday against Leeds.

Tuesday, October 14

'Baa' (Terry Lamb) *owes me 36 pounds from cards. Said he will pay me off a pound every day—going to be a long wait!*

Did weights at Trafalgar Sports Centre, while the Emus (our Australian 'seconds' team) *go through their moves before playing Hull KR on Wednesday night.*

Channel 10 tell us they have to hire a cherry picker for the lighting. It costs 9,000 pounds each game, which their boss is not happy about.

We played soccer in the afternoon. I think Brett Kenny could have been a great soccer player. He has great feet, just like Mick O'Connor.

Wednesday, October 15

On the way to training, Terry Lamb tells everyone that his wife is pregnant with his second child.

Everyone got weighed and the big units are getting bigger at the all-you-can-eat buffet. My weight is 85 kilos.

Baa celebrated his wife's pregnancy with a 5-try performance tonight against Hull KR. Benny Elias scored 2 tries.

Saw the dirtiest fullback in the world, George Fairbairn. He hits our blokes off the ball but won't take it up himself. He kicks people in tackles. I hope they pick him in the GB team—we'll kill him.

John Dorahy was the captain of HKR. He was my hero growing up, and he was ably supported by Kerry Boustead who was my first roommate for the 1984 Ashes series in Australia.

Australia 46 Hull Kingston Rivers 10

Thursday, October 16

After a two-hour training session, Steve Roach, Paul Sironen, and I went to dinner with Garry Schofield, our old teammate from Balmain. Dinner was at his house with his wife Adele. Had a great English roast—it was the best meal I have had in two weeks.

Sirro tells us HKR (Hull Kingston Rovers) *offered him $110,000 a year.*

Friday, October 17

Had our first run in genuine English fog. Couldn't see further than 20 metres in front of us. Ten of us went to play golf. 'Brandy' (Greg Alexander) *and Baa could have won 16 pounds on the last hole but choked.*

Sunday, October 19

Great crowd at Headingley, around 13,000. The sun was shining. It was a beautiful day.

I scored my first try of the tour. Pretty happy with my game, but as a team we have a lot of improving to do.

Australia 40 Leeds 0

Monday, October 20

Bloody hell, it's getting cold over here!

I am reserve back for the game against Cumbria. Somebody trod on my big toe at training, which is very sore.

Don Furner is lovingly referred to as 'Supercoach'. He said I could get a run on the wing—look out Eric Grothe, here I come!

Came back to the hotel and watched Death Wish II plus a replay of our game against Leeds.

Tuesday, October 21

Three-hour bus ride to Cumbria. Glad I didn't get a run—it was freezing.

After the game we had cold pies, cold sausage rolls, cold Frankfurts, and a hot cup of tea in the Chairman's Lounge.

Sirro was happy getting his first run when GD pulled out injured.

Home at 2.30 a.m. and straight to bed.

Australia 48 Cumbria 12

Wednesday, October 22

Test team picked and Donna called to tell me she was pregnant—boy what a morning! I was selected at fullback for the first Test. Can't wait to see Donna in a few weeks.

Thursday, October 23

After training finished at 10 a.m., I was invited to the Adidas Golden Boot Award, which goes to the best player in the world for that year.

It was an honour to be considered, alongside Brett Kenny, Peter Sterling, Ellery Hanley, and Garry Schofield. Brett won the award—he'd known for a couple of weeks as it turns out.

Saturday, October 25

Steady rain fell on our 90-minute bus ride from Leeds to Old Trafford.

A record crowd of 50,584 turned up for the first Test.

Playing at Old Trafford was a surreal experience for me. It's the home of Manchester United—my favourite English football team.

We led 16–0 at halftime. They tried to take us on out wide but couldn't control the ball inside their own quarter.

Mick O'Connor broke Graeme Langlands' and Mick Cronin's record of most points in a Test match with 22 (three tries, five goals). Gene Miles also scored a hat-trick.

I scored a try courtesy of Sterlo—a perfectly weighted cross kick that I caught above my head. I was onside, even though Rex Mossop in commentary said I was offside.

I became the first Australian fullback to score tries in back-to-back Ashes Test matches (I scored a try in the third Test of 1984 at the SCG)... and the first Australian fullback to score a try in an Ashes series home and away.

I hardly touched the ball in the first half, just couldn't get involved. But I remembered the advice given to me by the great Clive Churchill after State of Origin II at the SCG in 1985.

The Little Master told me: "You are getting too involved, too early in the game.

You need to wait until the last 10 minutes of each half, when they are tired." Great advice from a rugby league Immortal.

We had a couple of beers to celebrate the win.

Australia 38 Great Britain 16

Sunday, October 26

Went to a pub in the countryside, with all 28 players, and played some party tricks with the locals. Played cards on the bus with Badge, 'Rowdy' (Dale Shearer), *and B-E. Rowdy was stacking the deck, which I knew nothing about. Every time I lost, I kept doubling the stakes in a bid to claw back some cash.*

My debt quickly grew to 1,100 pounds. Badge and Rowdy were having a great time. I was the only one not laughing, so I stopped the game.

Monday, October 27

The next morning, I wake up and Badge reminds me that I owe him 1,100 pounds.

I said, "You can't be serious, it was just some fun." But he said, "No, you owe me 1,100 pounds." That was all he said.

I thought, "How am I going to get out of this, he is serious?"

So, I told Badge that my wife was expecting our first child. I had big expenses coming up; getting the baby room ready, buying prams and cribs. I asked if he could let me off.

Badge said, "No, I want my money, and I want it now!"

I told him I didn't have the money. He said I could pay him off in instalments.

Tuesday, October 28

Supercoach has agreed to reduce training to one session a day.

Benny tells me after training that Rowdy and Badge had set up the cards game so they couldn't lose. Yeah, it's funny now but not at the time. I thought my roomie (Badge) *could have let me know a bit earlier.*

The harsh lesson learned by me is don't play cards when you've been drinking!

Went to a town called Knaresborough with Mick O'Connor and Les Kiss. Had coffee in a 400-year-old home, with ceilings just 5 foot 7 inches tall. We also went to the Turkish Baths Harrogate.

Wednesday, October 29

It's game day and Bryan Niebling and I have been appointed 'Duty Boys', which means we have to organise fruit, snacks, sandwiches and drinks for the entire team. Everyone on tour must have a go at some stage. Basically, we are slaves to everyone else on the bus to and from the game. Luckily, Halifax is only 20 minutes away.

Halifax are coached by Chris Anderson from Canterbury, with Manly legend Graham Eadie at fullback.

Graham played well, but we ran over the top of them 36–2. It must have been a surreal experience for Graham playing against the Kangaroos. He is one of Australia's greatest fullbacks, going on two Kangaroo Tours in '73 and '78.

The ground at Thrum Hall drops away about 10 feet from one end to the other, which is quite common in the older English grounds. It feels like you are running uphill or downhill.

Snoz O'Connor copped one of the worst cuts to his chin that I have ever seen. I was talking to him after the game and his chin literally wobbled when he turned his head to speak to me. It was terrible. The poor bloke had it stitched, but it needed a cosmetic surgeon. Poor Mick looked a mess.

On the bus trip back to Leeds, team manager John Fleming warned the boys that anyone getting home late without a key would be fined 100 pounds. There have been a few instances on tour of players banging on doors in the small hours, waking everyone up in the process. 'Flemmo' has had enough.

Australia 36 Halifax 2

Thursday, October 30

Terry Lamb—one of the team's best pranksters—arrived back at our hotel after 2 a.m.

He walked down to Greg Alexander and Dale Shearer's room, which was located directly across the hall from Flemmo's room.

Lamb yelled: "Rowdy let me in—it's Brandy!"

"Please—let me in. I'm not sleeping out here again. Let me in please Rowdy!"

On the bus the next morning, Flemmo got up and demanded everyone's attention.

"I warned everyone yesterday about not having their keys if they got home late, so I am fining Greg Alexander 100 pounds for not having his keys with him last night."

Well didn't Brandy blow up!

"It wasn't me! It wasn't me, Flemmo! It was Terry Lamb! I'm not paying the 100 pounds."

Saturday, November 1

Aussie soccer superstar Craig Johnston organised for the team to go to Anfield and watch his Liverpool team take on Norwich. Craig was out with a knee injury, so we all got to meet him. I found him a very down-to-earth guy. He came to England as a 16-year-old to follow his dreams in soccer.

Back home, Johnston grew up in Newcastle and was a huge rugby league fan.

There were 39,000 fans at the game, and Liverpool won 6–2. They are the best club team in the world. I must say I thought the game was a bit boring, although the crowd loved it with eight goals scored.

Sunday, November 2

It's my first wedding anniversary—and I'm on the other side of the planet to Donna.

Today we played St Helens at Knowsley Road. There is a buzzer in the dressing sheds that gives you a two-minute warning before you have to take the field.

That's when the boys usually take a trip to the bathroom—but there was only one toilet for everyone to use! Can you believe that?

Bryan Niebling ('Horse') *had been in there for a while, so we all started shouting, "Hurry up, Horse!"*

Sterlo, Bert and I were busting, but had to wait our turn.

Horse flushed the toilet just as the three of us raided the cubicle and surrounded the toilet bowl. It was hilarious as Bert and I started peeing into the bowl just like our primary school days. Sterlo was still fumbling around—and dropped his mouthguard into the toilet!

Bert and I just aimed at the mouthguard. We hammered it. Boys will be boys!

Sterlo was the only one who didn't see the funny side. We flushed the toilet and his mouthguard vanished in front of his eyes.

It was time to go, but Sterlo wasn't keen to play without a mouthguard. He used an orange peel instead!

St Helens sent on local forward Paul Round from the bench and within two minutes we had a stink. Both of us were sent to the sin-bin for fighting.

The bloke was a boofhead. He came on and tried to stiff-arm Brett Kenny around the head. What a big tough guy. I pushed him away and then the referee sent both of us off for 10 minutes.

On the way off, this Round character was yelling at me: "Come on you, we'll finish it now you git!"

At first, I had no idea what he was saying, then I realised he was frothing at the mouth and his eyes were about to explode with anger. He wanted to fight here and now, just like the Colosseum days.

I mockingly put my hand out to him, to hold his hand, like he was a big cry-baby. Well, that fired him up even more! By now, the crowd were egging us on.

When we got to the tunnel, he wanted to go again: "You Aussie twat—come on!"

I told him to f&% off.*

We lost Steve Roach with a dislocated elbow during the game, so he was out of the second Test. I felt like we were starting to play our best footy after a month.

Craig Johnston, the Aussie playing for Liverpool, came along to watch the game.

Australia 32 St Helens 8

Monday, November 3

Named on the bench for Oldham game. But with Dale Shearer in doubt, I could be put on the wing. Peter Sterling organised a Melbourne Cup sweep. I'd never heard of the horse I got. It didn't win.

Tuesday, November 4

The Emus took on Oldham, who had my old Wests' teammate Bruce Clark in the front row. Balmain teammate Gary Bridge was also in their team.

I didn't get a run and poor old Bridgey popped his shoulder.

Our boys had to work really hard to get the win.

Australia 22 Oldham16

Wednesday, November 5

I'm named at fullback for the second Test. I discovered the reason why we train at 10 a.m. and not 7 a.m. like the Kangaroos did in 1982 under Frank Stanton.

Turns out Don Furner loves his bed and doesn't want to get up too early.

Donna leaves Sydney today with her mum and will arrive early tomorrow morning. Can't wait to see her.

Thursday, November 6

Donna arrived with her mum, courtesy of a lift with (officials) *John Quayle and Bob Abbott in a taxi. Donna was very emotional when we met in the foyer of the Dragonara hotel. We had lunch together. Donna is looking really good for two months pregnant.*

Friday, November 7

Trained at 10 a.m. Don has a habit of putting up his hands and explaining defensive structures to the team.

"If these three over here come together with the two over there, then we have five defenders," he would say, holding up five fingers.

Bert and Snoz take the mickey out of Don every time he does it. They hold up their hands with seven fingers outstretched, trying to confuse everyone. After five weeks together, you need to have some fun like that.

Watched a video of the first Test with the boys. We played some cricket in the corridor. Rowdy set off the fire alarm when he smashed a ball into the smoke detector!

Dad gave me some timely advice: "Run hard, catch the ball on the full, and tackle around the legs."

Saturday, November 8

No travelling required today because the game was in Leeds at Elland Road.

The build-up for the game was one of the quietest I have been involved in. Perhaps all of us knew what had to be done. We were ready to show GB just how good this team is.

The Lions played very well in the opening 20 minutes, with a crowd of 30,000 getting right behind them.

We led 12–0 at halftime, then I scored a couple of tries off Crusher and Sterlo as we flew out to a 34–0 lead.

Crusher sidestepped the GB defensive line, then drew Joe Lydon to give me a 20-metre run to score under the posts.

Then I ran off Sterlo to score my second try. I became the first Australian fullback to score two tries in an Ashes series.

With five minutes to go, I forced a pass to Mick O'Connor, which I should never have done. Snoz called so I gave him an overhead type of pass, which hit the ground, and Garry Schofield toed it ahead to score for 34–4 at fulltime.

I felt this was my best game of the tour.

Australia 34 Great Britain 4

Sunday, November 9

A day off, so a few of the boys went to Belgium, while Donna and I went north to the Lakes District. We all needed a break from each other and football.

Monday, November 10

We took a 4-hour drive to Scotland, where we saw some beautiful countryside.

Donna and I walked up the historic Royal Mile to Edinburgh Castle. It was about two miles return and it took its toll on Donna.

I bumped my head on one of those big square bridge pylons in front of the castle and nearly knocked myself out cold!

Wednesday, November 12

The boys who went to Belgium with Snoz as the tour guide returned to camp telling us it was a disaster.

According to Wally, Gene and GD—the three greatest critics on tour—it took 16 hours to get there, for one night in Brussels. Gene drank 20 pints. Then it took 14 hours to get back and cost them all 500 pounds.

Not happy. The term 'Snogal Tours' was coined as recognition of Snoz's effort in Belgium.

Of all our tour party, prop Marty Bella is the intellectual among us—just ask him, he'll tell you. So, when we play cards on the bus, if you lose, you have to sit next to Marty for 20 minutes as punishment.

He will bore you silly about the history of each English town we pass through.

The Emus played Widnes tonight. Tony Myler was their five-eighth. He's also the incumbent GB five-eighth. He played with us at the Tigers in '86. He played very well. As usual we were caned 3 to 1 in the penalty count by the referee.

We remain undefeated, but on the downside, Steve Folkes broke his cheekbone, and Les Kiss tore ligaments in his knee and was ruled out for the rest of the tour.

Australia 20 Widnes 4

Saturday, November 15

After training, we went to see Gary Bridge and his wife Tanya, who are living at Oldham. 'Gaz' likes the UK, Tanya hates it. It was a great catch-up, as our time together at Balmain had come to an end. Gaz is joining the Roosters next year. He said the money was too good to refuse.

The bloody fire alarm went off at 11 p.m. in our hotel. But we weren't getting out of bed until we could smell smoke! That's not a very good idea, I know. Anyway, the alarm only went off due to us hitting the sensor when we played cricket in the hallway a week earlier. Thanks Rowdy!

Sunday November 16

This was the dirtiest game on tour. Hull FC used elbows and knees in every tackle.

A fight started in the first 10 minutes. It happened over near the Two Bob Stand at The Boulevard. Suddenly, an old lady leaned over the fence and started hitting me with her umbrella—I couldn't believe it!

She was shouting: "Go home you Aussie bastard—I hate you. Go home!"

I just laughed at her.

I scored a try, which was my fifth for the tour. Some bad injuries though. Noel Cleal broke his arm in the first 10 minutes, putting him out for the rest of the tour. Blocker dislocated his elbow.

Australia 48 Hull 0

Tuesday, November 18

This was the worst weather of the tour. It rained all game at Bradford, and then the fog came in.

Wally Lewis played his best game and was man of the match. GD and Blocker were Duty Boys—without doubt the worst on tour. We had no soap, shampoo, deodorant or towels. The sandwiches they gave us were shit. They would belt you if you asked for anything or throw a can at you if you asked for a beer.

Mario Fenech played for Bradford Northern. This was his first game after being suspended for allegedly biting B-E in the semi-finals. He chased Benny all night.

Australia 38 Bradford 0

Wednesday, November 19

When we win on Saturday, we will equal the 1982 record and become just the second undefeated Kangaroo Tour.

Went looking for a baby bassinet with Donna. She is starting to show. Her clothes are getting tight—must be 10–12 weeks now. Everyone thinks it's a boy, I don't care.

In a big surprise, Don Furner has named Mal Meninga in the second row to replace Noel Cleal. Mal gets the nod over regular second rowers Les Davidson and Paul Sironen. It's just four days before we leave England.

Saturday, November 22

The weather was cold for the third Test, but fine. We ran with the wind in the first half and scored after just two minutes through Geno. Bob Lindner also scored to give us a 12–6 lead at halftime.

Their defence had improved a lot since we last played them. They really stuck it to us and Garry Schofield scored two tries running off his old teammate, Lee Crooks.

In the second half we were looking into the sun and running into the strong wind. GB contained us very well. It was 12–all after 45 minutes.

The French referee awarded a penalty try to Rowdy, when he kicked ahead and was obstructed. Tough call against GB. We led 18–12. The Poms then kicked a penalty goal and a field goal to set up a close finish at 18–15.

Wally put the game to bed with a great try, created from nothing by Royce running out of dummy-half. The image of Wally running around with Sterlo chasing and clapping his hands is something I'll never forget.

Inside the last two minutes, Henderson Gill got clear about 40 metres out. He was a very hard player to tackle. I made sure Gill had no option but to try and score in the corner. The plan worked. He went for the corner, and I tackled him over the sideline five metres short.

We won the game and became just the second team in rugby league history to be undefeated on a Kangaroo Tour. Something we are all very proud of.

Australia 24 Great Britain 15

Next up was the traditional final leg in France, which was a fun way to round off the trip.

During the past month, we had stockpiled bottles of wine that we had received from sponsors. The idea was to enjoy them during a night of celebration before we headed back home.

So, one night somewhere in the south of France, all 28 players ended up in what I can only describe as a forest, ready for a big night.

We had an Aussie-style barbeque and ripped into plenty of 'snags' and steaks. Then it was time to get stuck into the grape juice.

A couple of hours later, our supplies were exhausted. But with almost 30 young men full of grog and high on life, we were never going to end the night quietly.

For a bit of fun, the smallest guys decided they would attack the biggest guy—Mal Meninga. All 110 kilos of him. The bloke has the strength of 10 men.

It was the birth of a Kangaroo Tour tradition: Big Men versus Little Men.

Royce Simmons, Greg Alexander and Des Hasler all set off after Big Mal like a pack of jackals hunting a rhinoceros.

When they finally caught up with him, Des grabbed one of Mal's huge arms, Royce had the other, while Brandy had a leg … and was hanging on for dear life.

Everyone else was in stitches as we watched on.

But Mal wasn't going down without an almighty fight. In trying to shrug them off, he crashed backwards into a tree—with Dessie still hanging onto his arm! The tree was about six inches thick, and Mal snapped it in half when his arm thudded into it.

A lot of us feared the big man had broken his wing. But luckily, we all came through unscathed from our night in the forest.

Our fighting spirit was still strong when the squad enjoyed a night out with our old Tigers' teammate Kerry Hemsley.

'Buckets' was playing club footy in France at the time, so we met him at a nightclub for a drink. He looked pretty banged up after playing a game earlier that day.

Blocker asked him what happened, and Kerry said he copped plenty of 'treatment' from the locals who loved to dish out the dirty stuff—especially when it was three or four on one.

As a foreign player, he didn't get a lot of support from his French teammates.

During the conversation, Kerry mentioned that the same blokes he played against were inside the nightclub. It wasn't hard to figure out what happened next. Blocker wanted to fight every single one of them right there and then!

He marched over to these French guys and demanded the 'matter' be taken outside.

"Let's see how brave you are with 13 on 13!"

While Kerry got virtually zero assistance during the game, he now had the entire Kangaroos team behind him—led by Blocker. The nightclub was like a powder keg.

Suddenly it erupted! About 30 burly footy players came together in a classic bar-room brawl.

Thankfully, it didn't last too long, and no one got hurt. We were all pulled apart before it became too nasty.

But that moment showed the camaraderie of a Kangaroo Tour. Even though Kerry wasn't in the squad, he was still one of us and we look after our own.

France was once a competitive rugby league nation but had fallen away badly in recent years.

We won the first Test 44–2 in Perpignan, and the second Test 52–0 in Carcassonne, where I became the first Australian fullback to score a hat-trick in a Test match.

I was outdone by Dale 'Rowdy' Shearer though, who crossed for four tries.

The big win in Carcassonne completed Australia's second consecutive unbeaten Kangaroo Tour.

That match took place on December 13—two months after we opened our tour against Wigan. That's a long time to be away from home.

The 1986 season was the best of my career. An unbeaten Kangaroo Tour, a State of Origin clean sweep, plus a Winfield Cup preliminary final with Balmain. We also played in the National Panasonic Cup final.

I played 48 games from February to December, at the highest level, for 10 months straight. Even though I wasn't a fulltime player, I certainly felt like one.

I needed a rest.

Donna and I went on a two-week Contiki tour of Europe. By now, the freezing weather was beginning to take its toll.

It was time to go home.

CHAPTER 28

GETTING THE BOOT

FOR the first time since joining Balmain, I had a new coach. Frank Stanton had been replaced by Bill Anderson, best known for his work as a 'sideline eye' on Channel 10's match day broadcast.

I was sad to see Cranky Franky go. He had taken Balmain from wooden-spooners in 1981 to a game short of the grand final five years later.

He had helped develop Steve Roach, Wayne Pearce, Ben Elias, Paul Sironen and me into NSW and Test players.

The Tigers' board felt we needed a change of coach because we couldn't beat the big guns, Parramatta and Canterbury, when the whips were cracking.

The game was becoming more defence-oriented. Anderson, who had coached Souths in the early '80s, was seen as a man who could put the right structures in place to take us to the next level.

He was a schoolteacher by trade and a very smart man. He hadn't played the game at the top level but had learned a lot about coaching while working under the great Jack Gibson at Easts in the mid-70s.

Keith Barnes, who signed Bill, looked like a genius when we won eight of our first nine games.

We opened the season with wins over 1986 grand finalists, the Eels (30–6) and Bulldogs (11–8), in consecutive weeks. The board must have been doing cartwheels to see us beat these guys.

We did it without Blocker, who suffered a serious knee injury in the pre-season. He didn't return until the final rounds.

Our form extended to the mid-week National Panasonic Cup. We fought hard to beat Souths (11–10) and Easts (14–12) to qualify for our third consecutive final.

It was another tough grind in the decider against Penrith. We led 12–2 at halftime and hung on to win 14–12. Benny was named man of the match.

After this, we went winless for four matches, slipping from first to third on the ladder. Our hectic schedule, especially for us representative players, was starting to take a toll.

Apart from City-Country and State of Origin commitments, we also played a one-off Test for Australia against New Zealand at Lang Park on July 21.

The Kiwis were at their bruising best as they caused a massive boilover, 13–6. It was our first Test match since the unbeaten Kangaroo Tour. The Kiwis, led by Hugh McGahan and Dean Bell, gave us a real wake-up call.

Back at Balmain, we fell away over the closing rounds and limped into the finals in fourth place.

The Rabbitohs eliminated us 15–12 in the minor semi-final—sweet revenge for Mario Fenech after what happened 12 months earlier.

A highlight of 1987 came in June when I was awarded the prestigious Golden Boot Award.

This recognises the best player at international level over the preceding 12 months.

During '86, I played nine Tests against New Zealand, Papua New Guinea, Great Britain and France. I scored nine tries.

I played with some great players who helped me win this award. Peter Sterling, Wally Lewis, Brett Kenny, Gene Miles and Michael O'Connor—what a backline to have in front of you as a fullback. So much natural talent, speed and footy IQ. It was a dream come true to have played with them.

I joined Wally (1984) and Brett (1985) as winners of the award.

I was told by one of the judges after the ceremony that I had actually finished equal with Brett for the '85 award. But they gave him the nod due to his man-of-the-match performance for Wigan against Hull at Wembley in the Challenge Cup final.

In 1987, Peter Sterling and Kiwi Hugh McGahan shared the Golden Boot after finishing on the same number of points. It made me think about the '85 judging—I could have had two Golden Boots if they let me share with Bert!

I was blown away to join such elite company and in later years the Golden Boot would be won by legends like Johnathan Thurston and Andrew Johns.

It was an incredibly proud moment for me.

CHAPTER 29

QUEENSLAND HIT BACK

FOR the opening game of the 1987 State of Origin series, my roommate was glamour boy Andrew Ettingshausen. He was making his NSW debut. I figured the selectors wanted to pair up the two best-looking blokes in the team!

ET was the fresh-faced pin-up boy who was doing great things for the Sharks. He was an excitement machine with blistering speed.

I told him to take a photo of himself and then have another look after playing at this level for 15 years. I warned him he won't look the same. But he actually did! Lucky bastard.

Origin I was at Lang Park (yet another home game for Queensland to start a series) and we broke Maroons' hearts right on the bell.

Mark McGaw chased through a kick and beat a few Queenslanders to touch down just millimetres inside the dead ball line. Referee Mick Stone ruled a try and Wayne Bennett threw his head back in anguish up in the grandstand. The budding master coach had lost his fourth Origin game from four attempts.

Replays showed Stone made the right call.

We won 20–16 and were now the dominant team in State of Origin. Of the last eight games, we had won seven. The tide had turned. It was now Queensland who were under pressure—especially their coach.

The big positive for them was the debut of a little halfback called Allan Langer. He was a controversial selection ahead of the more experienced Laurie Spina.

Langer was only five-foot tall, and we were told in the lead-up to the game that we would literally run over the top of him. How wrong they were.

Alfie's a tough bugger and he tackled anything that moved that night. He made a mockery of the critics who reckoned he wasn't up to it. I could see he was something special. His short kicking game and footwork gave us plenty of headaches.

A packed house of 42,000 fans turned out in torrential rain at the SCG for Game II to see if we could make it three-straight series victories.

We knew Queensland would be desperate—and gee they had some help.

The refereeing of Barry Gomersall was shambolic. He caned us 6–1 in the penalty count in the first half.

The most farcical moment came when Gomersall penalised Peter Sterling for an incorrect scrum feed. The only problem was Sterlo didn't even feed the scrum—it was Langer for Queensland! Sterlo pleaded with The Grasshopper, but it fell on deaf ears.

The Maroons won a tough game, 12–6, to square the series.

There wasn't a struck match between the two teams, which is why I was stunned when I heard our line-up for the decider. NSW selectors had made 10 changes!

The biggest mistake of the lot was they moved our champion five-eighth Brett Kenny out to the centres. What a dumb move. Brett was 26 and at the peak of his powers. Wally Lewis must have breathed a sigh of relief when he heard the news.

The selectors brought in Cliff Lyons to play with Sterlo in the halves. Cliffy was going great in a Manly side on its way to winning a premiership.

But splitting up a Parramatta Eels combination that had won four premierships together? Before an Origin decider? Crazy stuff.

Cliffy didn't go badly, but it takes you at least a couple of games to find your feet in State of Origin. He and Sterlo had never played together before.

Queensland led 10–8 at halftime and we just couldn't find a match-winner in the second half. The Maroons defended really well, but our combinations didn't click under pressure because of all the changes made by the selectors.

It was a scoreless second half, giving Queensland its first series win since 1984.

Langer was named man of the match. Bennett had his first Origin series win.

I chatted with Wayne years later when he was coaching the Great Britain team. We spoke about that '87 series and the relief he must have felt.

Wayne told me that a Queensland official let him know that he was "gone" if they lost the second game at the SCG.

We could have finished the master coach's career!

State of Origin had become a massive product. The Australian Rugby League decided to use the series to try and gain traction in the untapped market of the USA.

For the first (and only) time, a fourth game was scheduled in 1987. It was to be played in Los Angeles on August 6.

I didn't want to go. Donna had only just given birth to Kieren, our first child, so I made it known to the NSWRL that I wasn't available for selection. It was already tough enough on Donna, who was suffering from postnatal depression. I'd been away from home enough with my footy commitments. It was time for me to put family first.

The NSWRL didn't see it the same way. I was the reigning Golden Boot winner as the best player in international rugby league and they argued I should be involved in promoting the game to a new market. They threatened me with heavy fines and suspension if I didn't go.

John Quayle was running the game and was behind it all. He was acting like a dictator.

No one could see it from my point of view.

It wasn't a real Origin game anyway—more of an exhibition game.

Quayle and the NSWRL board wouldn't have a bar of it. They feared I could spark a surge of players pulling out of Origin games to play for their clubs instead. Their official argument was that I hadn't made myself unavailable for representative football at the start of the season, which is when those decisions were made.

I was ordered to attend a judiciary hearing to justify why I shouldn't have to go to LA.

I thought it was pretty obvious—I wanted to be with my wife and newborn son!

It was none of their business. Personal reasons are personal reasons. But in the end, I had to explain what Donna was going through at home.

One of the officials asked me, "Does she tell you that she loves you?" I nearly fell off my chair.

They suspended me for two Tigers' games and threatened to fine me $1,000. This was the first time I had been suspended in my career, going back to the Under 7s.

Life was very difficult with all the media attention. A photo of Donna and Kieren appeared on the front page of one newspaper with the headline, *Why We Cost Garry Jack $1,000.*

These days players are applauded—and rightly so—for putting their family first.

I had given four years to the sky-blue jersey. I'd given it everything I had—and this is how they treated me?

It left a foul taste in my mouth for years.

CHAPTER 30

GET HOME JIMMY!

PLAYING in the English competition was something that appealed to me.

I'd seen my mates from Test and Origin level—Brett Kenny and Peter Sterling—go over and play starring roles. Those two even went head-to-head in a final at Wembley.

So, when the Salford City Reds gave me a call in 1987, I jumped at the chance.

Their offer was a bloody good one. For just four months of footy, I would make more money than I was earning for a full season at Balmain!

I saw it as a chance for our family to get away and spend more time together. Kieren was just three months old.

I'd been working 40-hour weeks with Wade's Action Office Equipment in Wollongong, selling photocopiers and fax machines. I'd been doing this for around three years—on top of all my commitments with the Tigers.

I was hardly at home. You can imagine how tough that was on Donna. Going to England was an exciting adventure for us.

Salford's home ground was a place called The Willows, where the freezing winds of mid-winter would cut you in half. It was a relic of a venue, built in the 1890s, and it was always bloody cold.

It was my first taste of being a full-time professional player. It was common in soccer but not in rugby league. In the 1980s, everyone held down a part-time job to help make ends meet.

I loved where we stayed in Monton. We had a lacrosse field out the back, and I would be over there running or kicking a ball just about every day.

Our coach was Kevin Ashcroft, a former hooker for Great Britain. He had an attacking mindset. Defence was not the main priority like it was back home.

Another couple of Aussies were in the team: Greg Austin from Manly, and Queenslander Steve Gibson. I really enjoyed playing with the Salford lads: Ian Blease, Peter Williams, Keiron O'Loughlin and Martin Birkett were all great guys.

We had some good wins and by mid-January we were on track to avoid relegation from the top league, which was the main reason they brought me over.

Then out of the blue, I received a phone call from Australia. It was Keith Barnes. And he sounded stressed.

"Jimmy, Jimmy, you've got to come back now—the (Balmain) board is not very happy."

"What do you mean Barnesy?"

"They want you back in Sydney this week."

"I can't come back this week. We've got a Challenge Cup game. I'll be back at the end of the month."

"Oh no Jimmy, you don't understand. They're not happy. They want you back now. They don't want you over there for any longer."

I was stunned. I spoke to Ashcroft and Salford management, and thankfully, they were very understanding. I returned home two weeks earlier than normal.

The reason behind Balmain's haste to get me home?

There was a new top dog in town.

CHAPTER 31
THE WOK

I RETURNED from the UK to meet my third Balmain Tigers' coach in the space of just three seasons.

Warren Ryan came across from the Bulldogs where he had enjoyed enormous success during his four years as coach.

The Dogs won back-to-back titles under Ryan in 1984–85 and were regarded as one of the best defensive units that the competition had ever seen. They lost the grand final to Parramatta in '86 by the barest of margins, 4–2, then fell away to miss the finals in '87.

'The Wok', as he was known, had fallen out of favour with Bulldogs' supremo Peter 'Bullfrog' Moore and his time at Belmore was over. Keith Barnes never missed an opportunity, and he quickly snapped Ryan up.

It signalled the end of Bill Anderson's one-year reign as Balmain coach. I liked Billy but he was probably too nice to make it as a first-grade coach. He never yelled or got upset. I think some players took advantage of his gentle nature.

Warren Ryan was a completely different beast.

We had all heard stories about his time at Canterbury. He was clearly a great coach but had a difficult personality and could rub people up the wrong way.

He gave it to me quite a few times.

One Saturday morning, I turned up for training at Leichhardt with Kieren, who was still in nappies. I handed him over to our trusted staff member, 'Wimpy', who always looked after the kids while we trained.

Warren didn't like this arrangement at all. He was very cranky that I'd brought my toddler to training and called me out in front of the whole team.

"C'mon Jimmy, what are you doing? It's not bloody Romper Room!"

I never brought Kieren to training again.

At least it gave a few of the boys a laugh. Steve O'Brien still sings out "it's not Romper Room" whenever he sees me!

But overall, Warren really made an effort to get along with us senior Balmain players. Junior, Blocker, Benny, Sirro and I were all part of the Australian team. The Wok knew we were the key to making this work.

Overall, I got on well with Warren. Maybe he had fond memories of our drink together after a Tigers-Jets' game back in '82!

I always found him very honest and straightforward. He said what he thought—he never left you guessing.

Warren's philosophy was good defence will always beat good attack. It was his defensive tactics and aggression during his time at Canterbury that stopped Parramatta's winning streak at three premierships. If it wasn't for Warren, the Eels would have won six-straight premierships from 1981–86.

The Wok had his fingerprints over everything we did. He would look at videos of our opposition and within five minutes he had developed a game plan on how to beat them.

Warren changed our defensive structures and wanted us to play a whole different game. There was no room for natural ability. It was all about getting to certain parts of the field and then putting on a set-play.

We were playing chess. Everyone else was playing checkers.

Blocker and I had a move called "Strain". This was essentially an inside ball from Block to me. I would float up behind him in attack and if I spotted a lazy defender, I'd shout 'Strain' and make sure I was in the right position to take the pass.

Why did we call it 'Strain'? It was derived from a Warren Ryan saying. He told Block to "strain" the defence. In other words, stretch it to the maximum by ball-playing *before* the line, not at the line. This worked a treat against Brisbane at Lang Park in round seven, when Block put me through for a try from 40 metres out.

Another call we had was "Ten".

Benny would be involved in this as well. He would make space with his skills out of dummy-half, before passing to a rampaging Roach. If we called 'Ten', that would be me taking a pass off Blocker's outside shoulder.

It might surprise some people, because he had a prickly reputation, but Warren did have a sense of humour… albeit a very dry one.

One of his favourite gags was an IQ test. The question to catch out the dummies was, "Captain Cook made three journeys to Australia. On which journey was he killed—the first, second or third?"

Blocker would say to Sirro, "Watch out mate—it's a trick question."

Warren always said the secret to coaching was to keep the three blokes who hate you away from the 10 that aren't sure. I was to learn this first-hand later in my career.

There was always a bit of truth in Warren's humour.

We made a slow start to the 1988 season, winning just one of our first three games. After falling to competition new boys Newcastle 20–16 in round 3, there may have been a few doubts creeping in.

The turning point was beating the Brisbane Broncos.

It was the Broncos' first season in the NSWRL, after being added along with the Newcastle Knights and Gold Coast Giants.

With Wally Lewis and Allan Langer pulling the strings, the Broncos started like a house on fire. They won their first six matches—including a 44–10 thrashing of premiers Manly in their debut game.

But we went up to Lang Park and rolled them in front of their home fans, 26–18.

That game gave us enormous confidence.

We were right behind The Wok.

CHAPTER 32

WALLY DOESN'T GIVE A XXXX

AFTER the controversy surrounding my no-show for the game in Los Angeles, I was keen to bounce back in the 1988 State of Origin series.

Unfortunately, I had to sit on the sidelines for the opening game because of a farcical suspension.

Balmain played a National Panasonic Cup semi-final against Souths at Scully Park in Tamworth.

There was a flashpoint during the game when Blocker and I combined to stop Mario Fenech from scoring a try with a burrowing surge out of dummy-half. As we turned him onto his back, Block gave him a 'squirrel grip'. Mario's palm then flew out and hit me flush on the nose. In a purely reflex action, my boot flicked forward, just missing Mario's head. The referee, Greg McCallum, put me on report.

"But I didn't kick him," I pleaded with McCallum.

If I wanted to kick him, I wouldn't have missed from 12 inches away. My foot never went back in a traditional kicking style, it just flicked forward. Thankfully, there was no contact.

We won the game 19–4, but I was later cited for allegedly kicking Mario. I'll admit it didn't look good. But my boot made no contact with Mario whatsoever.

At the judiciary, the touch judge testified that he had a clear view of the incident. "I saw Mr Jack lash out with his foot and kick Mr Fenech, who was lying on the ground, in the head."

He went on to say, "In my view, there are three types of kicks: there's the vicious one, a medium range one, or a tap. This one was medium range, but getting towards vicious."

My solicitor quickly interrupted. "You're not colouring your evidence to make it sound worse are you?"

Earlier, Fenech reluctantly gave evidence, saying he wasn't even aware that I had allegedly tried to kick him.

The NSWRL suspended me for two matches.

That's the only time I was ever suspended for an on-field incident. It was hard to accept, because I knew I was innocent.

I was rubbed out of the City-Country game and also the first Origin match.

Replacing me for the Blues was Jonathan Docking, the diminutive Sharks' fullback.

Under a new coach in John Peard, the Blues were soundly beaten 26–18 in Origin I at the newly opened Sydney Football Stadium (SFS).

I was recalled for the next game at Lang Park—a match that is forever etched in Origin folklore.

We had done extremely well to lead 6–4 with 18 minutes left on the clock. Then it all went pear-shaped when our prop Phil Daley and Queensland hooker Greg Conescu were sin-binned for fighting.

Wally Lewis fronted referee Mick Stone and gave him a gobful—so Stone sent him to the sin-bin as well!

This was uncharted waters for Wally at his home ground. He kept questioning Stone as he reluctantly left the field.

The capacity crowd were livid at seeing The King being marched from the field.

Suddenly a can of XXXX came flying out of the grandstand, cartwheeling across the turf right in front of us. Then came the rest. Hundreds of cans flew onto the ground like an angry plague of locusts.

These weren't empty either. Most of them were full. I know, because I made the mistake of picking one up and underarming it back towards the fence.

Then another 200 came straight back at me!

Wally's antics had incited the crowd, and it was getting ugly. Play was paused as police entered the field to protect all the players and match officials (I don't think Queensland players were in any danger!).

At this point, I had fears for our safety. A full can of beer to the head could cause serious damage.

Thankfully, none of us were hit and order was eventually restored after about five minutes.

When play resumed it was a different game. With a rabid crowd behind them, the Maroons lifted two or three gears.

They scored two tries to win 16–6 and take the series.

It was another example of the influence of Wally Lewis. He used the crowd to lift his side. He was the master manipulator of his generation.

We returned to Sydney for the dead-rubber Origin III. I was given Bears' rookie Greg Florimo as my roommate.

Greg was just 21 and on debut. He turned up at the team hotel on a skateboard with his cap on backwards. At 27, I suddenly felt old!

Our preparation was awful after Phil Daley was dropped from the squad for breaking team camp.

Phil hadn't gone out to a nightclub or anything like that. He was going to see his wife who was about to have a baby. Something had happened and he needed to be there as a matter of urgency.

Back then there were no mobile phones, so it was difficult to let people know. The NSWRL didn't care. Rules are rules and it was their way or the highway. It brought back a lot of bitter memories for me.

The world was changing. Players were becoming professional, and the administrators expected more and more from the game's elite.

After the highs of Origin the previous few years, it was a different story at the SFS. A crowd of just 16,000 turned up.

Despite the flat atmosphere and rows of empty seats, we flew out to an 18–6 lead at halftime.

But that was as good as it got.

Big Sam Backko steamrolled us for a couple of tries and Queensland won 38–22, notching their first series clean sweep.

I felt sorry for John Peard. He lost the series and lost his job.

CHAPTER 33

MYSTERY SIGNING

KEITH Barnes did some amazing things during his time running the Balmain Tigers. One of his best moments came midway through the 1988 season.

Ellery Hanley had just led Great Britain to a stunning upset win over Australia in the third Test at the SFS, 26–12. I was on the wrong side of his brilliance that day.

Keith had been communicating with Ellery for weeks, looking to bring him over for a cameo. His performance just made Barnesy even more determined to close the deal.

He hopped in his car and drove over to Manly where the GB team was staying. Barnesy was in a hurry because the Brits were flying home the next morning—plus the NSWRL's deadline for mid-season signings was just days away.

He met Ellery in a hotel car park. After a very brief discussion, Ellery signed a Balmain Tigers' contract on the boot of Barnesy's car!

I played against Ellery again a few weeks later when Australia took on a Rest of the World team at the SFS. We won 22–10.

The next day, I turned up at Leichhardt Oval for Balmain training. I saw Ellery Hanley, putting his boots on.

I said hello and asked why he was here. When he told me, I was stunned.

None of us players had a clue that the Great Britain captain was playing for us until he showed up at training that day!

Barnesy had pulled off one of the great signing coups—and—kept it a secret. That's no easy task in rugby league.

The deal was later made public, literally five minutes before the signing deadline.

At that stage of the season, we were drifting along just outside the top five in the Winfield Cup.

Yes, we had made a fourth-straight mid-week final, losing to St. George 16–8. We were a team with plenty of potential. But something was missing.

Barnesy reckoned the team needed more 'X-factor' to win a premiership.

I knew Ellery was an elite player from our battles at Test level. But I didn't realise what a great attacking weapon he was until he started playing for us.

Ellery played mainly lock for Great Britain, but we brought him as a centre.

He debuted against the Sea Eagles in round 20, which we lost 8–4 in front of a huge crowd at Brookvale.

Ellery didn't score a try that day, but over the next eight weeks he would transform our team, instilling self-belief that we could win a premiership.

And it was all thanks to the smarts of Keith Barnes.

CHAPTER 34

BLOCKER BLOCKED

THE loss to Manly really stung us into action. We felt everything went against us, but we still nearly beat the defending premiers on their home turf.

Referee Greg McCallum sent Mick Pobjie, Sirro, Blocker and me to the bin at different stages of the game.

The Blocker sin-binning was a joke because it also cost us a try.

Gary Freeman had dived over to give us a 6–2 lead. But McCallum listened to a report from his touch judges and sent Blocker to the sin-bin. They said he punched Manly's Phil Daley in the lead-up. Replays showed it was Daley who threw the first punch and Block retaliated.

He took the try off us and gave Manly a penalty. I'd never seen anything like it.

It was a crucial call considering we were still fighting to secure a place in the finals.

We came away from 'Brookie' knowing we were a genuine premiership chance. We just needed to make the final five.

Next up, we faced the Panthers at Leichhardt Oval. This game is probably best remembered for Benny Elias being absolutely flattened by Brad Izzard. It was a legitimate hit, technically perfect. Look it up on YouTube—it's had plenty of views!

I was right next to poor old Benny at the time and was thinking, *"Holy shit!"* Most players would leave the field on a stretcher after a hit like that.

But Benny eventually got to his feet, dusted himself off, and kept playing!

We finished in a tie for fifth place with the Panthers, so we faced them again in a mid-week play-off at Parramatta Stadium.

The Panthers had been in the top three all season but now had the wobbles. We finished them off 28–8 to book a knockout semi-final appointment with Manly.

During the game, Blocker and Panthers' rival Matt Goodwin were sent off for headbutting. Two front-rowers headbutting each other was the second oldest profession in rugby league, just behind two front-rowers throwing punches at each other. Both were later exonerated.

However, it wasn't all good news. There was another problem—a much bigger problem.

Blocker was cited for a late and high tackle that took Chris 'Louie' Mortimer out of the game in the 11th minute. The incident happened in back-play and no one really knew anything about it at the time.

Block was mates with Louie from our time playing together for NSW. Louie wasn't too bothered by Blocker's tackle. He told Block there was nothing in it and that he would help get him off at the judiciary. But the NSWRL refused to let Mortimer come and give evidence. Blocker reckons Louie had been told by Peter 'Bullfrog' Moore (his old boss at the Bulldogs) not to appear.

Steven went in front of the panel and was suspended for four matches.

It was a disgrace that he got four matches for that. An absolute disgrace. Blocker had been rubbed out of the entire finals' series.

Our premiership hopes had just taken an almighty hammering. Blocker was so important to everything we did.

But then Keith Barnes had another moment of genius.

He hatched a plan for Steven to go over to England and work off some of the suspension in their competition. He would then come back and play in the grand final—if we qualified.

The club came to an arrangement with Warrington and put Blocker on the next flight to the UK. The English season had just started. Barnesy did the maths and worked out Blocker would sit out two games for Warrington, by which time he would already have missed two games for Balmain.

There are your four games. Blocker would then be eligible for the Winfield Cup grand final.

But Barnesy came under an enormous amount of pressure from higher powers in the game to 'pull the pin' on his idea. Eventually the plan was aborted while Blocker was still over in England.

It left a bitter taste in our mouths because South Sydney's Mario Fenech was allowed to serve a suspension in 1986 while playing for Bradford Northern. But for some reason, it was different for Blocker. It was a clear case of double standards.

This whole episode just fuelled my suspicion that certain people running the game felt threatened by Balmain. In those days, the Sea Eagles and Bulldogs wielded a lot of influence.

Steve Roach was the best front-rower in the game. Him being suspended from the finals would boost their chances of winning a premiership.

CHAPTER 35
ELECTRIC ELLERY

JUST four days after beating Penrith in the play-off for fifth spot, we had to face Manly at the SFS in a knockout minor semi-final.

It was a ridiculous schedule which would never be allowed in the modern game due to player welfare regulations.

I was also faced with another dilemma.

Donna and I had bought a new home in the north-western Sydney suburb of Cherrybrook, which was very exciting for our young family. After completing the sale, we agreed to move into our new abode on the Friday of that week.

I packed up all our belongings in Wollongong and drove them to Cherrybrook—a two-hour drive—the day before we were due to play our biggest game of the year.

Kieren was only little at the time, so Blocker and his wife Cathy kindly looked after him while we moved everything. They brought him up to us later that night.

On reflection, it was such a stupid thing to do before a big game. I don't know what I was thinking.

This was the stage of the season when our English import Ellery Hanley grabbed everyone's attention.

He scored two tries against the Sea Eagles as we ran out 19–6 winners, knocking the defending premiers out of the competition.

Ellery scored again the following week as we put the Raiders out of business, 14–6. Hanley fended off Peter Jackson, Sam Backo and Gary Belcher—not exactly three mugs. They all played for Australia.

A crucial part of our win was a booming 43-metre penalty goal from Ross 'Rosco' Conlon just before halftime. We had been trailing the Raiders 6–0, so Rosco's goal really put a spring in our step going into the sheds.

Conlon was the best goalkicker I ever played with. He struck them high and long.

He did a little skip and a stutter, then would kick the cover off it. It was all timing.

Rosco changed the momentum in plenty of games for us with his goalkicking.

Our next opponents were minor premiers Cronulla in the preliminary final.

This was a real dogfight. The Sharks led 2–0 at halftime, but a penalty goal from Rosco and a field goal to Benny edged us ahead 3–2.

There was a moment in the second half when the game was in the balance, and where all my hundreds of hours of catching practice came into play.

Cronulla five-eighth Michael Speechley launched a bomb on the last tackle, about 40 metres from our line, and my God it went high! The wind was blowing, the ball was floating all over the place, but I never took my eye off the Steeden as I tracked it towards our goalposts, with Andrew Ettingshausen breathing down my neck for the Sharks. I had to take a left-hand turn so I didn't crash into one of the uprights, but I grabbed the ball with my outstretched arms just ahead of ET.

It was one of the best takes of my career.

The game hung in the balance until another moment of Ellery magic inside the final 10 minutes.

Paul Sironen and David Brooks combined in our own half with some clever ball play, sending Mick Neil racing away up field. 'Meggsy' started to stumble, but luckily Ellery loomed up on his outside. Meggsy gave him the pass and he did the rest, giving us a 9–2 win—and a ticket to our first grand final!

Ellery could read the game so well. He always knew where to be. He had incredible strength through his hips, a powerful fend, and was one of the best support players to ever play the game.

Hanley scored in four-straight games—which just happened to be our four biggest matches of the season. He had become our weapon and was getting plenty of headlines.

Watching on were the Bulldogs who had already qualified for the decider. They would have seen what a threat Hanley was to their premiership chances.

I'd never felt better after a game than I did when we beat the Sharks. Knowing we were in a grand final…it was the best feeling ever. I had won State of Origin games and Test matches. But this topped them all.

This would be my first grand final and the excitement was already hitting home.

I'd be playing against my old mate Steve Mortimer, who was in his final year at Canterbury before retirement.

A quote of his popped into my head as I thought about the week ahead. When Mortimer led NSW to our first State of Origin series win in 1985, I remember Turvey saying, "Well done boys—this is almost as good as winning a grand final."

That comment really made an impression on me. I thought, *"Shit, if winning a premiership is better than winning Origin—then I want to win a comp!"*

Balmain had won 11 of our past 12 games to reach the big one. We had a good chance of becoming the first team in history to win a premiership from outside the top three. Winning form is good form, and our confidence was sky high. We had huge momentum.

Even though Canterbury was installed as favourites, we felt we could win. We were on a massive roll, even without Blocker leading the charge.

Also, we knew how to beat the Dogs. We knocked them over in our only encounter for the year, 19–8 in round 10.

The local Balmain community was absolutely buzzing. The Tigers hadn't made a grand final for almost two decades, not since upsetting Souths 11–2 in 1969.

While this was new territory for most of us, Warren Ryan had plenty of runs on the board. He had already been part of four grand finals as a coach, with Newtown (1981) and Canterbury (1984–86).

The Wok said we had to try and keep things as normal as possible, despite all the craziness going on around us.

There was a bit of a hiccup through the week. 'Brooksy' put a nail through his foot on a construction site. He was a builder by trade, and these were the days when players juggled work with footy.

He was in hospital on a drip right up until game day. We weren't even sure if he'd play, but Brooksy's a tough kid from the bush and was never going to miss a grand final.

However, he wasn't the only Tiger facing a fight to prove his fitness.

CHAPTER 36

BAD DOGS

WARREN Ryan was a very paranoid coach who trusted no outsiders.

Before every training session during the season, he would scan Leichhardt Oval like a hawk, searching for any uninvited guests.

He would insist that staff members check the bathrooms to make sure no one was in there secretly filming our session.

The fact that our home ground was a public facility didn't help. Any old Joe Blow could walk through the joint.

The Wok was particularly suspicious of anyone sitting behind the goalposts. That is the best part of the field to assess our set-plays. You can also see how we number up in defence. He figured anyone sitting there must be a spy.

Warren would confront people, demanding to know what they were doing. In his mind, they could have been sent over by a rival coach like Tim Sheens or Phil Gould.

The Wok knew this was a possibility—because he regularly did the same thing. He often sent his staff to watch other teams train in the week before we played them.

In grand final week, Warren's paranoia reached new heights.

One day we were having a closed training session at Leichhardt when he spotted a television crew filming us from an adjoining property. There is a heap of terrace houses with clear views into the ground.

One homeowner probably made some easy cash by allowing a TV news crew to film from their veranda.

But Warren was having none of it.

He stopped our session and said we weren't restarting until the camera crew had gone. He even sent someone to the house to tell them to take off.

Not wanting to cop a media ban from the fairytale team of the grand final, the crew obliged, and we were able to carry on.

I had played in plenty of big games in my career. But a Winfield Cup grand final was a whole new experience.

On the morning of the game, I pulled open the curtains and my excitement levels shot through the roof. Our neighbour's kids had put a sign on our front lawn overnight, covered in black and gold streamers, with a simple message.

"Good luck Garry!"

It was a beautiful gesture.

Leading up to the grand final, I had been dealing with something I kept quiet from just about everyone except Donna and my coach.

A broken rib.

In the game against the Sharks, we ran a set-play that didn't end well for me.

We had tried the same move a week earlier in our win over Canberra, and apparently Sharks' coach Allan Fitzgibbon reviewed the game and saw exactly what we were up to.

Fitzgibbon told his tough prop Dan Stains where to wait for me as our set-play unfolded. Stains did as he was told, lined me up and—WHACK!

X-rays confirmed a crack in the rib. It was bloody painful—every breath hurt like hell.

But there was no way I was missing a grand final. The Wok asked if I would be okay to play and I said, "Absolutely."

I had a pain-killing injection before kick-off, and it felt better immediately. I also wore some padding around the area for extra protection. I was confident the Bulldogs didn't know about the injury.

Because of my experience in big games, I knew how to conserve energy in the lead-up to kick-off. Some players complain of feeling flat by the time the game starts, because of all the nerves and excitement.

Even though it was my first grand final and I had a busted rib, I felt ready.

We didn't fear Canterbury.

We knew we could beat them. Parramatta was always our bogey side in the 1980s, but for some reason we always troubled the Bulldogs.

The only downside for us was that Steve Roach was in England listening to the game on radio, instead of being in the middle of the SFS with us.

The Bulldogs came after us right from the start, like we knew they would. In one tackle, Paul Dunn tried to take Paul Sironen's head off.

A bit later, Paul Langmack flew in and grabbed hold of Benny, after a fumble from their fullback Jason Alchin. Langmack flung Benny to the turf for no reason. During the melee, Steve Folkes unloaded a series of uppercuts at B-E.

"There's Folkes on the right—his arms are going like windmills!" roared Rex Mossop in commentary.

Once order was restored, referee Mick Stone awarded the Bulldogs a penalty—figure that one out!

Their prop Peter Tunks also trampled over Benny—*after* Stone had blown his whistle for an infringement. For good measure, Tunks aimed a kick at Benny while he was still on the ground. Stone sent him to the sin-bin for 10 minutes. I reckon Tunks was extremely lucky not to be sent off for attempting to kick a player in the head.

We would soon see that Benny Elias wasn't the only Tiger on the Bulldogs' hit-list.

The Dogs grabbed a 4–0 lead from two penalty goals to Terry Lamb, but I felt we were right in the game.

Benny then launched a bomb into the Bulldogs' in-goal, which Mick Neil contested and deflected backwards. Waiting for the crumbs, Benny pounced to score the first try of the grand final. Conlon converted and we led 6–4.

Then came one of the most infamous moments in grand final history.

Ellery Hanley had just passed the ball when he was hit low by Andrew Farrar. The broadcast follows the ball, but in the corner of the screen you can see Terry Lamb come in and hit Ellery high.

Our English ace was knocked-out cold.

I didn't see much from where I was positioned on the field. All I knew was that the guy who played a huge role in us being in a grand final was lying flat on the ground and not moving.

No one saw what happened. The referee, touch judge, no one.

Ellery was eventually taken from the field, rubber-legged. His eyes were rolling around in his head. There's no way he could have made it off the field without assistance.

I thought, *"Shit, he might not be coming back on."*

While Hanley was off the field trying to work out where the hell he was, the Bulldogs attacked his side of the field and scored a long-range try through Mick Hagan.

We hit back with a penalty goal to Rosco which cut the margin to two points.

At halftime, we trailed 10–8.

The grand final was up for grabs, but the big concern was Ellery.

In today's game, there is no way he would be allowed to come back on the field in his condition. Player welfare is everything.

But back then, before we knew everything we now know about the effects of concussion, you dusted yourself off and played on.

Warren Ryan went up to Ellery in the sheds during the halftime break and asked if he was okay to go back on. Ellery peered up, still with a dazed look in his eyes.

"Yes mate, I'm okay," he said in his broad northern English accent.

Warren could see things weren't right.

"Nup," said The Wok. "You're not okay. You're not going back out."

Our biggest attacking weapon had just been ruled out of the grand final.

When you combined that with Blocker's suspension, it was going to take a mighty effort to knock over the Dogs from here.

We repelled wave after wave of Canterbury's attacks early in the second half, until we eventually cracked. Some quick hands saw David Gillespie touch down just inside the corner post. Benny and I came flying across in cover defence but couldn't quite stop 'Cement' from scoring.

Lamb and Glen Nissen scored further tries for the Dogs, and suddenly the game was gone.

Bruce McGuire scored a consolation try for us in the dying stages. But my first grand final had ended in extreme disappointment.

We lost 24–12.

While disappointed, I felt it was a great effort just to be there on the biggest day of the year. I'm not saying that we didn't want to win. But when you consider where we came from—ninth place halfway through the season—we were proud of our achievement.

The one thing that disappointments me to this day was the leniency shown towards foul play from the Bulldogs.

They tried to bash us out of the game.

I heard they put up pictures in their dressing shed of the two Tigers' players they wanted to take out: Benny Elias and Ellery Hanley.

Everything came off Benny around the ruck. He was so clever. And everyone had seen what Ellery had been doing.

The next day, Lamb was cited for the tackle on Ellery. It was big news that he'd taken out our star player without any sanctions.

But NSWRL boss John Quayle took a look at the incident and said Lamb didn't have a case to answer, even though he clearly struck him in the head with his forearm.

Compare that to Blocker copping four matches for a high shot on Chris Mortimer.

Years later, Baa apologised to Hanley in person for what happened. Hanley accepted it as part of the game. He still has no memory of the incident.

I know Baa well from playing with and against him my whole career. We toured together with the Kangaroos and shared some great memories.

Terry Lamb is a winner, and when he played, he would do whatever was required to win.

The Dogs knew that taking out our gun player would destabilise us. They had loads of grand final experience, while we didn't. It was a terrible oversight by Stone and his touch judges. We lost our best player, while the Bulldogs lost no one.

I have no doubt the Hanley knockout and suspension of Steve Roach cost Balmain the 1988 premiership.

But nothing could take away how special it was to be part of that Tigers' team.

On a personal note, '88 was one of my best years.

I won a third Dally M Fullback of the Year award. The *Rugby League Annual* by

David Middleton named me in the top five players of the year, along with Benny Elias, Wally Lewis, Allan Langer and Dally M Player of the Year-winner Gavin Miller.

I had learned so much from Warren Ryan in just one season. I had become a better player.

CHAPTER 37

BRITS BITE BACK

A STRANGE thing happened during Australia's Bicentenary celebrations of 1988.

For the first time in a decade, we lost a Test match to Great Britain!

We won the first two Tests comfortably 17–6 (Sydney) and 34–14 (Brisbane).

In the Lang Park Test match, their halfback Andy Gregory eye-gouged me with some Dencorub. There was no action taken by the referee, but he definitely got me. I had blurred vision for a while.

I shouldn't have allowed it to distract me, though. It's exactly what Gregory would have wanted.

We returned to the SFS for the dead-rubber third Test.

Interest was sadly low in Sydney—a mere 15,944 fans turned up to see if we could win another clean sweep against the Old Enemy.

An unnamed official blamed the poor crowd on the tourists' lack of appeal, saying that trying to promote a Test against Great Britain was like "flogging a dead horse".

The Poms were the better side right from the start at the SFS. They led 10–0 at halftime and went on to win 26–12.

It was their first Test match win in Australia since 1974 and snapped a 15-match losing streak to the green and golds.

I played all three Tests in the series. My fullback rival at State of Origin level—Gary Belcher—was selected on the bench for all three matches. Badge was a specialist fullback like me, so I found it a strange selection.

Before the first Test, chairman of selectors Ernie Hammerton told Peter Peters from *Big League* magazine: "Australia has always had great fullbacks; from Clive Churchill, Graeme Langlands, Les Johns, Ken Thornett, through to Graham Eadie in the modern era.

"Jack or Belcher will carry on the tradition in 1988."

Hardly a glowing endorsement from the chairman of selectors considering I'd played 18 successive Tests as Australian fullback from 1984–88. I was also the current holder of the Golden Boot.

Gary Belcher hadn't even started a Test at fullback yet. I found that to be an amazing statement from the chairman of selectors.

Australian coach Don Furner was also on the Belcher bandwagon—because he coached him at club level with the Raiders. During a training session, Furner told me he wanted me to pass the ball like Badge.

"Well, I'm not Badge," I told him.

It was clear to me they were grooming Belcher, and had been since the 1986 Kangaroo Tour, when they put us together as roomies for 10 weeks.

The selection backfired in the third Test when our halfback Peter Sterling was forced off at halftime with a dislocated shoulder. Badge was our only back, so Furner put him on the wing and shifted Tony Currie to halfback.

Currie had never played halfback in his career. What a calamity.

During the second half, I called "mine" to take a bomb from Gregory. Badge also called for the ball out of habit. We collided and the Poms picked up the crumbs to score.

I told Badge afterwards, "If I call 'mine', just leave it."

But I don't blame him for what happened. 'Gaz' was just trying to make an impression, but it was difficult playing out of position on the wing. Instead, I blame the selectors and coach Furner for ratifying the selection in the first place, ahead of Terry Lamb or Des Hasler. They offered more utility value as bench players.

In those days, you were only allowed two reserves, unlike today where you can name four. Naming a specialist fullback on the bench was costly.

We lost a Test match we should never have lost.

But of course, it was the players who got the blame—not the administrators who approved the team.

Our next Test match was against Papua New Guinea a couple of weeks later. I held my position, while Belcher was dropped and replaced by Hasler—surprise, surprise.

It was a one-off Test at a sold-out Eric Weissel Oval in Wagga Wagga—the first time Australia had played a home Test match outside of Sydney or Brisbane.

We overpowered PNG by a record score of 70–8. Michael O'Connor smashed the world record for most points in a Test, scoring four tries and kicking seven goals for a personal haul of 30 points.

Blocker Roach didn't play, but he was kept very busy at a civil reception for both teams. All the PNG boys queued up in front of Block, patiently waiting for his autograph. They loved the big fella!

A couple of weeks later, we took on a Rest of the World team at the SFS.

They had a quality side featuring the likes of Kevin Iro, Mark Graham and Kevin Ward.

I don't think I ever played a tougher Test match. Both sides ripped into each other.

We won 22–10, but unfortunately all the talk was about Mal Meninga after he broke his arm for a third time, just a month after his latest comeback.

After the disappointment of losing a grand final with Balmain, I had a chance to finish the year on a high with the World Cup final against New Zealand.

Under the old format, the finalists were decided from results in the final Test match of each series over the preceding four years. This was so teams would take dead rubbers seriously—because World Cup points were up for grabs. Wally and I were the only two players in the squad to play in all eight qualifying games in that period.

This was the most hyped rugby league Test match to be played across 'The Ditch' in history.

There was no way the Kiwis' traditional base of Carlaw Park in Auckland could handle such a massive occasion, so the fixture was transferred to the much larger Eden Park—home of rugby union powerhouse, the All Blacks.

The match was declared a 46,000-seat sell-out well before kick-off.

The Kiwis were doing cartwheels at how rugby league was suddenly the hottest ticket in town. So were we—but for completely different reasons.

We feared the Kiwis at Carlaw Park. They were always tough to beat there. It was like a mini version of Lang Park.

Yes, Eden Park was new to us—but it was also unknown territory for the Kiwis. Without realising it, they had given away their biggest advantage. Eden Park was a rugby union field. It was hard and fast, which suited us perfectly compared to Carlaw Park, the mud-heap.

Our team was full of Bulldogs and Tigers' players who had played in a grand final just a couple of weeks earlier. We were battle-hardened.

I lined up with my Balmain mates—Junior, Blocker, Benny and Sirro. It was the only time all five of us played together in a Test match… and Gary Freeman was in the Kiwi team. A very special moment for all of us and the Balmain club.

The big crowd was baying for an ambush, but they got the opposite. By halftime you could hear a pin drop. We led 21–0.

Wally Lewis didn't return for the second half after breaking his arm. Thankfully, we had another five-eighth on the bench in Terry Lamb, so we didn't miss a beat. The selectors had learned their lesson after that farce against Great Britain.

We scored again straight after halftime, before finishing 25–12 winners. Allan Langer had a blinder, scoring two tries.

That would prove to be the 22nd and final Test match of my career.

The Kiwis did score a small victory over us—thanks to the quick wit of Whiz Freeman.

The little halfback tried to inspire his side by taking a run up the middle of the ruck into the teeth of the Australian forwards.

Blocker was waiting for him and gave Whiz a big stiff arm, followed by a spray.

"If you run here again Freeman, I'm going to bite your head off!"

"Well, if you did Block, it would be the first time you ever had any brains in your head!"

Freeman 1, Roach 0.

CHAPTER 38

BAD BREAK

OUR bid to go one step further in 1989 began with a pre-season game called the Alpha Romeo Challenge.

It was a new addition to the rugby league calendar, a clash between the grand finalists from the previous season.

We lined up against our old mates the Bulldogs at Parramatta Stadium.

Our defence was soft to start the match, with Canterbury's forwards making plenty of inroads. When their second-rower Brandon Lee broke free, I had the shits. I came flying in from fullback determined to pull off a big hit and show the boys how it's done.

It couldn't have gone much worse.

My right arm collected Lee across the top of his head, which felt a bit like hitting concrete. It bloody hurt, but I played on… until I heard a sickening 'click' come from my arm when I was tackled a few minutes later.

I came off and scans later showed a clean break. The doctors said I probably suffered a hairline fracture in the initial incident with Lee, then snapped it completely when I was tackled.

I had surgery with a six-inch plate inserted as well as 10 screws. I was out of footy for three months.

We ended up winning the game against the Bulldogs 28–16. We held up the trophy to a half-full Parramatta Stadium, but it gave us no sense of revenge. It sure didn't make up for losing a grand final.

The Alpha Romeo Challenge ceased to exist after just one season. You will learn the fate of the trophy later in the book.

With me sidelined, my arm in a sling, the Tigers won the $90,000 Nissan Sevens tournament. It was great to see the boys have some success, but I hated not being part of it.

Of all the injuries I suffered during my career, this was the most challenging from a psychological sense. When I came back in round 8 against the Gold Coast, I wore a big, bulky arm guard.

We weren't really setting the world alight for the first half of the season. And we knew there would be no Ellery Hanley cameo to boost us like last year. He had signed to play out the season with Wests instead.

We did find another British import though—centre Andy Currier.

He didn't have Hanley's profile, but he was very elusive and could kick goals. He formed a potent combination with our schoolboy star Tim Brasher. Andy finished the season as our top point-scorer and equal top try-scorer.

We used to call him 'Milk Bottle'. Andy was tall, skinny and white. There was no real shape to his body. He was like a milk bottle from Widnes.

A game that stands out for me that season was in round 18 against the Broncos at Leichhardt Oval.

Brisbane prop Greg Dowling collapsed a scrum and, on the way down, kneed our halfback Gary Freeman in the face. Whiz lost a couple of teeth and Dowling was rightly sent off by referee Greg McCallum. 'Dish-head' later copped an eight-match suspension.

I saw Whiz at halftime and his mouth looked in terrible shape. But he went back out for the second half, and we won the game 24–6.

That spoke volumes as to how tough Gary Freeman was as a footballer. It also showed what we were prepared to do to win a premiership.

In the final round of the regular season, we hosted the Panthers in front of a ground-record crowd of 22,750 at Leichhardt.

Penrith would finish in second place no matter what the result. But we needed to win to join them in the all-important top three.

Benny made sure we hit the scoreboard first... in unusual fashion.

We'd been given an early penalty deep in Penrith's territory, so he decided to take a quick tap then bang over a field goal. Yes, we led by the soccer-type scoreline of 1–0! I still have no idea why Benny did it.

The Panthers lost forward John Cartwright when he was sent off for a late hit on Benny in the 21st minute, which made our job easier. We ran away to win 33–6.

We went in very confident the following weekend when we played the Panthers again in the major semi-final. We won 24–12 to set up a blockbuster with minor premiers Souths.

The SFS was packed to capacity, and we eventually overpowered them. When Currier scored a try in the second half, we knew we were heading to our second-straight grand final.

We won 20–10, but there were no celebrations. We had learned from 1988 that the job was not done yet.

With the weekend off, Warren decided to take us to the preliminary final between Souths and Canberra. Channel 10's broadcast would occasionally show us sitting in the grandstand, watching to see who we would play in the grand final.

The Raiders were on a big roll and the Rabbitohs couldn't hold them. Canberra won 32–16.

I don't think it was the smartest idea from Warren. Watching our eventual grand final opponents win in such emphatic style could have potentially psyched us out.

The Raiders had experience in Mal Meninga, Gary Belcher, John Ferguson and Dean Lance, plus rising stars Ricky Stuart, Brad Clyde, Laurie Daley and Glenn Lazarus.

We knew it would be a challenge. But we were confident we could beat them.

CHAPTER 39

MY BLUE WITH THE SUPERCOACH

I WAS excited to hear that the NSWRL had appointed Jack Gibson as our coach for the 1989 State of Origin series.

We were looking to bounce back from consecutive series defeats and who better to help us than the man famously dubbed 'Supercoach'?

Gibson had never coached at Origin level before but had won a combined five premierships with Parramatta and Eastern Suburbs.

Here was my chance to experience the magic of Jack Gibson, which I'd heard all about from my good friends at the Eels, Peter Sterling and Brett Kenny.

But by the end of the series, I didn't see what all the fuss was about.

Right from the start, Gibson wanted to do things his way. He tossed out the team camp, which had become a tradition. He reckoned camps were for boy scouts. Instead, players checked into the team hotel on the Monday morning before the game. We played Origin I on a Tuesday night, the next two games were on Wednesday nights. As you can see, we didn't spend much time together.

Gibson gave the impression he didn't rate Balmain too highly. He overlooked Steve Roach because of Blocker's alleged ill-discipline. And he wasn't keen on Benny Elias either, despite his outstanding form. He preferred Benny's arch-rival, Mario Fenech.

He picked Paul Sironen for Origin I, then dropped him for the rest of the series. Blocker, Benny and Sirro were all part of Australia's World Cup win in 1988, but now they weren't considered good enough for NSW.

Gibson picked Gavin Miller as captain. Gav was playing well for the Sharks, but he hadn't played an Origin game in six years—now he was captain! To me, it was a baffling choice.

We went into the cauldron of Lang Park with a rookie captain and just 39 games of Origin experience. In comparison, Queensland had 124 games!

What followed was 80 minutes of carnage. Jack had a simple game plan of taking two runs infield, then switch back to the blindside for Gavin. Somsone told Jack it wasn't working. He said, 'We will wear them down'. We were blown away 36–6, a record loss at the time. We were lucky the margin wasn't worse.

I was incredibly frustrated. It all came spewing out when I was having a chat with my old Balmain teammate John Davidson a few days later. Davo was now at the Sharks, and he asked me what I thought of Gavin Miller. I told him that I didn't rate him highly as Blues' captain.

During that shellacking in Brisbane, as we kept gathering behind the goal-line after Queensland tries, Miller constantly trotted out the line, "Let's just do it for each other."

If you closed your eyes, you'd swear it was Jack Gibson. That was one of his big sayings. Miller had become a clone of the coach.

My comments to 'Davo' were nothing personal against Gav. It's just that I'd played under Steve Mortimer, Wayne Pearce and Peter Sterling during the previous five years for NSW, and Gav simply wasn't in their class as a skipper.

I felt Benny Elias should have been captain, but he couldn't even get a start in the team. He was creative, tough and a proven performer at this level, unlike Mario. It was a poor decision by the coach.

My chat with Davo was a private conversation that would come back to bite me on the backside.

Game II was at the SFS, but I was under an injury cloud in the lead-up. I had taken a tumble down the stairs at home. There were fears I'd broken my right arm again, but thankfully, the scans cleared me.

More than 40,000 fans turned up to see if we could square the series. But this game really highlighted how ordinary we were as a team.

Queensland suffered a heap of injuries—Allan Langer, Mal Meninga, Paul Vautin, Michael Hancock and Bob Lindner were all busted and forced from the field.

The battered Maroons finished the match with just 12 men, but somehow won 16–12 to seal their third-straight series.

I was left shaking my head. We had no idea how to play as a team. We lacked combinations—that's what you need to have success in Origin. Gibson and the selectors could have picked Blocker, Benny, Sirro and me to utilise our chemistry at the Tigers. But they didn't for some strange reason.

In the end, it was a try for the ages from Wally that set up Queensland's win.

From a standing start 30 metres from our goal-line, The King beat the tackle of a young Laurie Daley, then he beat Chris Mortimer, which is no mean feat. I was the last line of defence. Wally came at me, and I went too high and was palmed off. He carried a couple of us over the line with him to score.

I wish I had a dollar for every time that bloody try is replayed. When I see it on TV at State of Origin time, I think, *"Here we go again."*

Wally was a hard bloke to bring down if you went high. He had a good fend. And he was quicker than he looked over 20 metres.

The moment Wally scored was when I realised that I still didn't have full confidence in my arm. I had only been back for five games since I broke it. My instinct was to dive at Wally and hit him low—which I'd done many times before—but I didn't do it. I just stuck my hands out to grab him.

Subconsciously, I was protecting my arm. I knew it still wasn't 100 percent.

But that's the thing about playing fullback. You can make a tackle that wins the game. Or you can miss a tackle that's going to make the other bloke look great.

It's those moments that define you as a player. Being able to back yourself, and having the courage, without fear of consequences.

For the first time in my career, I felt fear.

We had a team dinner before the final dead-rubber game in Brisbane. I ended up sitting across from Gibson and his right-hand man Ron Massey. I wasn't expecting much conversation. Jack was famous for not saying much. He preferred a dry one-liner.

As we started on the entrees, Jack looked up at me and said in his legendary slow delivery, "I hear you have something to say about Gavin as captain."

I stopped eating my entree.

"I don't know what you're talking about, Jack."

"You know... 'Let's just do it for each other.'"

I knew exactly what he was talking about. Jack slowly cocked his head and eyed me from across the table.

"Jack, I don't know what you're talking about."

Gav was there at the dinner too, of course. He was sitting just two places down from me.

Gibson kept up the pressure.

"Is there something you want to say to Gav?"

"No, there isn't, Jack. I really don't know what you're on about."

I should have spoken up.

I should have said, "Yep, I don't believe Gavin should be captain based on what I've seen so far; I don't believe in your tactics; I don't like your defensive structure; and I don't have a lot of faith in your selections".

But I didn't. Jack Gibson was a very intimidating coach, and I didn't want to argue with him the night before we were due to play.

I eventually found out that Davo had mentioned our conversation to a few of the Sharks boys and word got back to Jack and Gavin, who weren't too thrilled about it.

Team morale wasn't great going into the final match at Lang Park. But we put together a strong first 40 minutes to hold a surprise 12–10 lead.

After the break though, we imploded again. Queensland piled on the points to win 36–16.

It was a second-straight clean sweep for the Maroons. They had won eight games in a row. NSW was in disarray.

My relationship with Jack Gibson deteriorated further when he hooked me midway through the second half. It came not long after I had fumbled a Wally grubber-kick in our in-goal, allowing Kerrod Walters to score. It was my one and only error of the game.

I was dealing with that disappointment when I noticed one of our reserves, Phil Blake, had come onto the field.

"Jimmy, you're off," he said.

"What?"

I thought, *"Get f*&%ed."* I hadn't been replaced during my entire career. And it was about to get worse.

I was substituted on the far side of Lang Park, literally the furthest point from the NSW bench. My long walk back gave Queensland fans time to have a good crack—and they didn't miss their chance.

"You're a f$#%en wanker, Jack!"

"You're a cat, Jack!"

"You're f&^%en hopeless, Jack!"

"You're shit, Jack!"

That happened all the way around the perimeter of Lang Park. When I finally made it back to our dugout, I saw Jack and asked him why he took me off.

He mumbled something back. I asked him twice. I still couldn't gather anything meaningful from what he said.

Gibson was obviously a brilliant coach at club level. But in my view, he had underestimated Origin and was trying to blame me for the loss.

We had no defensive structure at all. Jack's plan was to "kick it to the seagulls" (a part of the field where there were no opposition players) and then go and defend it.

But Queensland coach Artie Beetson was too smart. They would find numbers everywhere. We had no plan for how to keep them out.

It was a shame the series finished on that note because I had already decided it would be my final State of Origin game. The only person I'd told was Donna.

I was coming off a big six years of playing club football both here and in England, plus Origins, Tests and mid-week competitions.

Between 1984 and 1989, I'd played a total of 214 games—averaging 35 games per season!

I was exhausted. I needed a break.

There's not always going to be a fairytale finish. I understood that. But that was a disappointing way to go out. Being replaced uninjured and being abused by 35,000 Queenslanders.

Gibson had effectively ended my representative career. I still wanted to play for

Australia in the upcoming Test series against New Zealand but couldn't see them picking me after I was hooked by Jack.

I kept thinking, *"Would Artie Beetson drag Gary Belcher off the field for one mistake?"*

Badge dropped a bomb in Origin II that allowed Laurie Daley to score a try under the posts. Beetson didn't replace him.

He gave him the chance to make up for his mistake. That's all I wanted, and I think I deserved the chance to do so.

Before I was replaced, I'd made 12 runs for 112 metres. I'd made four tackle busts. During my 17 Origin appearances, I averaged 176 metres and 5 tackle busts per game.

To rub it in, Gibson moved Des Hasler to fullback. Des was a halfback—he'd never even played fullback before.

It was a bullshit decision.

I think Jack wanted to make an example of me for what was said earlier in the camp about Gavin Miller. I was a scapegoat. It took the focus off his flawed selections and lack of tactics.

The selectors named the Australian team at the Travelodge Hotel in Brisbane. I found out I'd lost my place in the Test team in the same room where I was named to make my Australian debut in 1984. A cruel twist of fate.

In that Australian side there was only one player who had played more Tests than me—Wally Lewis.

Belcher was named fullback. Badge had taken his game to another level, so I certainly felt no ill-will towards him. He was always on the attack in a team that had just won three State of Origin series in a row. He had earned his shot in the green and gold.

I did attempt to make a comeback the following season, at the end of 1990. I put my hand up for the Kangaroo Tour and was picked in the train-on squad.

Australia coach Bob Fulton phoned me on the day the official team was named and told me that he wanted me on the tour. Bozo said to me I deserved to know that I had his support. I thanked Bob for his loyalty and honesty.

Later that night, I was left out of the 1990 Kangaroos' team. So much for our chat!

The selectors stuck with Belcher after he'd won a second-straight premiership with Canberra. Greg Alexander was named as his understudy.

In 1991, they gave Broncos' fullback Paul Hauff the nod, but he failed and never played for Australia again. Then in '92 they selected Tim Brasher, who was playing in the centres at Balmain.

I felt like I deserved to get picked. My form was strong. In the 1980s, no one had played more games for NSW—I was level with Brett Kenny on 17 appearances.

Lots of players have been given a second chance in 'rep' footy, but sadly not me.

I don't want to sound ungrateful though. I'd had a great career at the top level and have so many cherished memories.

On the fly with Balmain as a 21-year-old in my first season since switching from Wests

You beauty! The boys are all over me after scoring the match-winning try against Canterbury in 1982 at Leichhardt

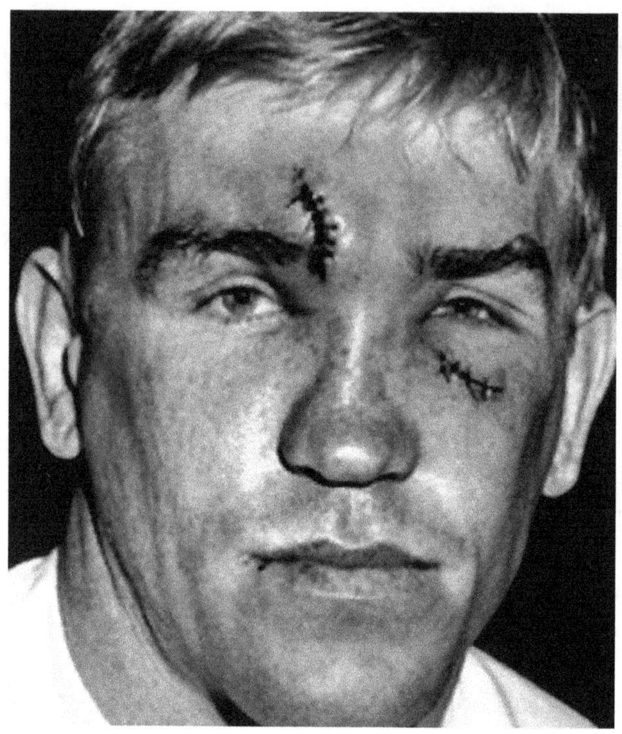

24 hours after the Ian Roberts assault. My face blew up even more after this. A low point of my career

Cooked chooks! Here I am splitting the Roosters defence in 1984 on my way to scoring a crucial try

I'm mobbed by Steve Martin and Benny Elias, while the Roosters look on in anguish

Time to party! Peter Sterling and I after winning the 1986 State of Origin series 3-zip

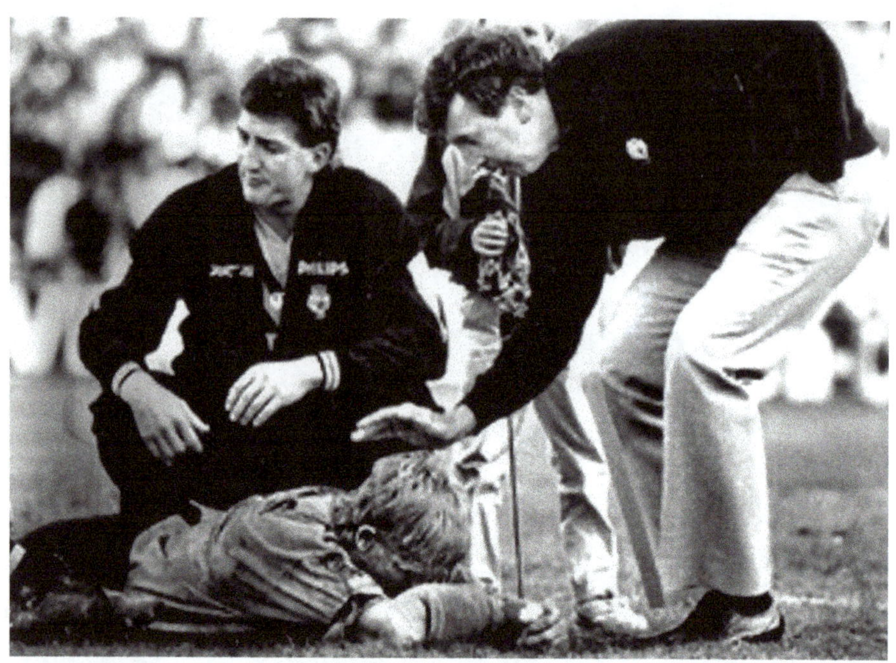

Utter devastation. Warren Ryan tries to console me after the 1989 grand final. The only time I ever shed a tear on the footy field

The greatest hooker I ever played with. Here I am with Benny Elias after becoming the first team to beat the Broncos at Lang Park in 1988

Steaming onto a pass from Noel 'Crusher' Cleal. I was named man of the match in a Carlaw Park mudbath. Second Test versus Kiwis, 1986

I learned how to tackle by watching the great Ron Coote as a kid. He'd be proud of this effort against Manly

Playing with some serious padding after breaking my arm at the beginning of the 1989 season

Mick 'Meggsy' Neil looks pretty impressed by my clearing kick at Leichhardt Oval in 1991

I was 19 when I signed for Western Suburbs Magpies

Controversy in the 1989 decider. Raiders players including Ricky Stuart clearly offside, but no penalty, despite Benny's field goal attempt being charged down

On the burst for Balmain at Leichhardt Oval. I wish I still had those quads!

CHAPTER 40

TOOTHLESS TIGER

I BECAME a headline writer's dream in a game against the Bears at North Sydney Oval, late in the 1988 season.

Their captain Mark Graham had burst through our defensive line. There was only me left standing in his way.

Let me paint you a picture of Mark Graham. This bloke was as tough as they come and arguably the greatest player to represent New Zealand. He was a six-foot-four lock forward and a maniac once he crossed that white line.

As Graham steamed towards me, legs pumping, I knew I had my hands full. I decided the best way of stopping him was to try and wrap him up with a ball-and-all tackle.

Graham crashed into me and used his ball-carrying arm to try and bump me off. As he did this, his elbow rose and smashed flush into my mouth.

Three of my teeth came flying out, roots and all. A fourth one was whacked so far out of place it went through my lip.

I looked down at the turf. My teeth were just sitting there in the grass.

By this stage, I was feeling the pain of the tooth embedded in my lip. There was blood everywhere.

I started picking up my teeth, one by one. The thought of going off for treatment never entered my head. The game was in the balance. There was no way I was going off. I didn't care how much it hurt.

I looked at my teeth in the palm of my hand, wondering what to do with them. Then I stuffed them in the top of my socks and played on!

The adrenalin must have really been flowing because I ended up having one of my best games of the season.

Not long after Graham's dental work, I leapt high to take a dangerous bomb that was launched by my rival fullback (and childhood hero) John Dorahy. That gave me a lot of confidence.

At the 70th-minute mark, I received a line drop-out from Greg Florimo and took off downfield. I busted the Bears' defence and had only Dorahy in front of me. I slowed and pretended I was going to pass to winger Daryl Powell, then accelerated to score the match-winning try.

My three teeth were still in my sock as I scored.

When our trainer Paul Hockam came out to check on me, I handed him my dislodged pegs and told him to hang onto them.

"I'll put them back in later," I said.

Paul's wife was a dental nurse, which I thought was ironic.

I did a few interviews after the game and was questioned about wearing a mouthguard. During my career I wore a guard for the top teeth, but never the bottom ones.

I arrived at a dental clinic in Glebe just after 6 p.m. The dentist asked me roughly what time my teeth were dislodged.

"About 20 past 3 this afternoon."

The dentist shrugged and said there was nothing he could do. He told me that teeth must be reinserted within 20 minutes of coming out, otherwise they die.

I was about three hours too late!

They saved the one that went through my lip, but that was pretty badly damaged and had to come out later in life.

I still wear dentures to this day, courtesy of my run-in with Mark Graham.

He nearly got me again later that year during the World Cup final at Eden Park.

Graham broke through our line and once again it was just me left standing in his way.

I attempted a ball-and-all tackle, and sure enough, he put the elbow up again—but this time I backed off at the last moment and he missed me.

Graham wasn't even cited over the incident at North Sydney Oval, which was hard to believe. My teeth didn't fall out on their own.

The headlines after the match all read the same: *Toothless Tiger.*

CHAPTER 41

WARDROBE MALFUNCTION

I FELT we were ready to break Balmain's 20-year premiership drought when we arrived at the SFS for the 1989 grand final against Canberra.

We had taken a lot of learnings from the experience of playing in the decider 12 months earlier against the Bulldogs.

Once inside the change rooms, I looked around at my teammates. Everyone was calm, there was a quiet confidence. We had enjoyed a week off and felt fresh.

This was our time.

Sure, the Raiders had won nine games in a row. But I felt like we had them covered, especially in the forwards. We had a great pack led by Junior, Blocker, Benny, Sirro and Bruce McGuire. They had been our strength all season.

Also, we had beaten the Raiders in our only meeting of the season, 18–12, on their home turf at Seiffert Oval in round 15.

Our gear steward appeared in the change room and began handing out our grand final edition jerseys. Back then, a red badge sporting a picture of the Winfield Cup trophy was sewn onto one of the sleeves on every jersey.

When I held my jersey up to get a good look at the exciting red badge, there was something wrong.

It was about five times too big for me!

I flipped it around to make sure I didn't have Sirro's or Blocker's jersey by mistake. When I saw the number 1 on the back, I was horrified. Then I heard a roar from the other side of the room.

"5XL—WHAT'S THIS SHIT!"

Blocker was blowing up deluxe. Every single player had been given a 5XL jersey—the absolute maximum size. They were big enough to host a wedding.

I always wore an L for large. Sirro and Blocker, our biggest players, would wear a 2XL. Mick Neil and Gary Freeman both weighed about 70 kilos wringing wet. They looked at their jerseys in disbelief. I watched as Meggsy measured his against his whippet-like frame. The jersey came down past his knees! It looked more like a nightdress than a footy jersey.

I pulled mine on and it ended up halfway between my hips and knees.

Clearly no one from the club had checked them when they were collected from the warehouse or wherever they came from.

Maybe everyone was too busy looking at the special red grand final badge to notice the jerseys were five times bigger than they should have been.

If there wasn't less than an hour until kick-off, it might have been funny. But no one was laughing—least of all Blocker. He was still going off and rightly so.

There was obviously no time to scramble a new set of jerseys. With the clock ticking, we had to think on our feet.

A pair of scissors were produced, and we all became instant tailors. My sleeves came down past my hands, so I hacked both off (the sleeves, not my hands!). I then scrunched up the acres of material from the lower half of the jersey and jammed it into my shorts as best I could. I pulled the drawstring and hoped this nightmare was over. When I looked down, my jersey had poked through the legs of my shorts, but there was nothing I could do about it. All the boys had the same problem.

This was the biggest game of our lives. Instead of passing around a copy of The Wok's game plan, we were handing around a pair of scissors.

It's the last thing we needed.

Eventually, we said, "Enough is enough." It was time to put the wardrobe malfunction behind us.

Destiny awaits.

CHAPTER 42

LOSING THE GREATEST GRAND FINAL

IT was close to the perfect start. Winger Jimmy Grant swooped on a stray pass from Raiders' prop Brent Todd and scooted over to score the opening try.

Todd wasn't known for his passing game. Maybe the Raiders thought they would catch us off guard. I really didn't care. We were up 6–nil.

Mal Meninga kicked a penalty goal to put Canberra on the board, before Sirro sent Tigers' fans into a frenzy just before halftime.

Blocker started the play when he spotted a chance down the short side in our own half. The big fella put Andy Currier into space with a great pass. As the Raiders' cover defence converged, the Englishman kicked in-field. Gary Belcher surprisingly let it bounce and Jimmy Grant was on the scene again to grab it. Just as he was about to go into touch, he flung the ball back inside to Currier, who found Sirro on the burst.

In commentary, Graeme Hughes roared, "Sironen charging, charging—they won't stop him!"

He wasn't wrong. Once Sirro had the legs pumping, no one was bringing him down. Brad Clyde tried valiantly but he had no hope. With Currier's conversion, we were up 12–2.

The Raiders were down but they were still a threat.

Their winger Matthew Wood broke away down the touchline, about 40 metres from our goal-line, and pinned his ears back.

As a fullback, this was my bread and butter. As I came across in cover defence, I knew as long as he didn't step inside me, I could catch him before he got to our line.

I made it my job to know about our opposition. Everything I had seen on Wood made me confident he would go for the corner. I positioned myself to take the option away for Wood to step inside, just in case he thought of trying something different.

As I expected, he set sail for the corner. I hit him low just as he was preparing to put his arm out and plant the ball down for a try. The momentum of the tackle spun him, and his legs went over the sideline before he put the ball down.

I'll admit I cut it pretty fine though!

We took a 12–2 lead into halftime, which was a bit deceptive because we had been on the back foot a lot during the first half. Thanks to referee Bill Harrigan caning us 6–1 in the penalty count, we seemed to always be coming out of trouble.

The reality was we had two chances to score, and we took them both. Things were looking good.

The second half of the grand final is littered with moments that people still talk about to this day. Here are the main ones:

THE MCGUIRE PENALTY

The Raiders kept throwing plenty at us after the break, but the boys were hanging tough. We were tackling our arses off. Whenever they threatened, someone in black and gold would turn up to shut it down.

Matthew Wood again went close, but this time it was Junior who smashed him into touch.

A bizarre penalty from Harrigan soon swung momentum.

Bruce McGuire had got up to play the ball after being tackled inside our own half early in the tackle count. He looked up and saw there was no marker. In those days, if there was no marker, you could tap the ball forward, pick it up, and run.

Bruce did this just before Steve Walters arrived at marker. The Raiders' hooker got in Bruce's way, appealing for a penalty. Bruce ducked behind Walters as he ran the ball forward.

We heard Harrigan's whistle and expected to see Walters penalised for being offside. Instead, his arm was pointing towards the Raiders. Harrigan had chosen to penalise McGuire—and no one knew why.

Bruce asked Harrigan why he was penalised. Harrigan said, "For using the Canberra player as a shepherd."

Junior, as our captain, then went over and asked, "What was that for Bill?"

Harrigan replied, "For not playing in the spirit of the game." Why did Harrigan change his answer? What does that even mean?

This was the first time I had ever heard of that type of penalty. And Harrigan decided to drag it out of nowhere. In a grand final.

Bruce had done similar things in the past and never been penalised. The fact is that Walters shouldn't have been there. He hadn't got to marker in time, which means he was offside.

If the NRL Bunker had been operating in 1989, it would have been a penalty to us every day of the week.

I know Warren Ryan was fuming about that call. He said he'd swear until the day he dies that the penalty should have gone to us.

We weren't having much luck with Harrigan.

We didn't receive a single penalty in general play, which would have allowed us to kick the ball out and set something up. That was a specialty of the Wok.

In our only other game against the Raiders that season, back in round 15, he caned us 11–4 in the penalties.

From the very next set after the McGuire penalty, their veteran winger John Ferguson compounded Harrigan's bizarre penalty with a moment of magic.

Long passes from Ricky Stuart and Gary Belcher found Laurie Daley steaming onto the ball inside our quarter. He turned the footy back inside for Ferguson, who zig-zagged past a few of our blokes as they hurtled across in cover defence.

As we struggled to get our hands on 'Chicka', Belcher ran another change of direction. He took the pass on the inside from Ferguson, again catching us on the wrong foot.

Badge broke free from Currier and darted over to score. Mal's conversion made it 12–8.

THE ANKLE TAP

Warren Ryan was a great coach for set-plays in attack. In the lead-up to the grand final, he had identified Meninga—a colossus of the game—as a potential weak link.

Big Mal was almost 30 years old and wasn't too quick on his feet. The Wok reckoned we could isolate him and come up with a result by getting on his outside.

The play he devised, in consultation with us senior players, would be called "Crash".

Benny was to pass from dummy-half to Blocker, who would hit it up like he did 50 times a game. The trick was, this time, he'd turn and pass the ball to Gary Freeman who would sweep around the back. All going well, Whiz would then have a few options to hit out wide and hopefully catch Mal out.

The plan was for Crash to come from a penalty tap. But guess what? Harrigan hardly gave us a penalty and when he did, we were never in the right position to have a crack at Mal.

The call finally went out after a Raiders turnover deep in their half. Whiz yelled out, "Two up for Crash!"

Everything unfolded exactly how we wanted. Mal came out of the defensive line just as we had planned, and went straight for McGuire, who was supposed to get the pass from Whiz. At the last second, Whiz hit Meggsy with a perfect flat pass instead of McGuire.

Meggsy hit the hole left by Mal exactly as The Wok had mapped out. He had 10 metres to run to wrap up Balmain's first premiership since 1969.

Mal realised straight away that he'd gone for the wrong bloke (McGuire) and that Meggsy was past him on his outside. In sheer desperation he turned and flung out his left arm—still heavily padded to protect a previous fracture.

It was enough to contact Meggy's right leg, which clipped his left and down he went. By the time he tried to get up and go again, the Raiders were all over him.

He was less than a metre from scoring.

Rex 'The Moose' Mossop in commentary roared: "Certain try—Neil was in for a certain try if not for the ankle tap, no question!"

JUNIOR'S DROP

Even though Meggsy was brought down, we were still on the attack.

I was at dummy-half and popped a pass to Sirro who crashed into the Canberra defence, before flinging the Steeden out the back when he realised there was no way through.

The ball found its way to Benny, who could see we had a three-on-one overlap to the right. He lobbed a long pass to Junior, who had an unmarked Tim Brasher outside him.

Unfortunately, Junior couldn't take the pass cleanly above his head and knocked on.

It was a difficult pass for Junior to take. He had suffered a detached retina in a game eight years earlier, so his vision wasn't the best.

I look back at that passage of play with regret. When I picked up the ball at dummy-half, I should have gone with my first instinct.

Run.

Canberra's defence was stretched, they were scrambling to get back in position. The Raiders knew Laurie Daley was stuck defending that overlap and they had to shift left to help him out.

There was a chance for me to barge my way over from dummy-half and score. I was only a metre from the line.

Instead, I gave it to Sirro and the play broke down not long after that.

BENNY—SO CLOSE

A rare penalty from Bill Harrigan gave us some breathing space with about 10 minutes left. He picked up an offside play from Stuart, allowing Currier to boot us to a 14–8 lead.

When the clock showed less than seven minutes remaining, our young prop Steve Edmed made a charge deep into Canberra's quarter. We were 15 metres from the goal-line, right in front of the posts.

It was the last tackle and Stuart spotted Benny getting ready for a crack at field goal. Stuart ran in late in a desperate bid to get to marker, so he could try and charge-down Benny's field goal attempt.

Replays clearly show Stuart never got there in time. Yet he was able to join Mal Meninga in chasing out from marker—and Mal ended up smothering Benny's field goal attempt.

This happened right in front of Harrigan. But he did nothing. We should have had an offside penalty in front of the posts. Currier would have kicked the goal for 16–8, game over.

Despite that, we still had the ball after Mal's charge-down. A couple of plays later, Benny again had the ball in front of the Raiders sticks.

A field goal here would have given us a 15–8 lead with just over five minutes to play.

Benny took the pass cleanly and struck the ball with his right boot. It was a wobbly old effort but—most importantly—it was heading in the right direction.

The ball seemed to travel in slow motion. Probably every player out there was thinking the same thing: *If this goes over, it's game over.*

DING!

I can still hear it now. The footy slammed into the middle of the crossbar and came back into the field of play, where Gary Freeman knocked-on.

I looked at the posts and could see the mark of the Steeden on the black dot painted on the middle of the crossbar. That's how hard it hit.

If Benny's kick had just been a couple of millimetres higher, it would have been a match-winner.

Benny Elias kicked 33 field goals in his career for Balmain, NSW and Australia. That's the only time I can remember him hitting the crossbar.

This moment was to become even more painful a decade or so later, when our chairman John Chalk approached me with a look of disbelief on his face. He told me he had some news to share.

'Chalky' had been talking to his Raiders' counterpart John McIntyre, who let slip a stunning revelation.

McIntyre apparently told Chalky that when the Raiders shifted home base from Seiffert Oval to the more modern Bruce Stadium for the 1990 season, the ground staff had no idea about the specifications needed for the goalposts.

They asked McIntyre, who told them to copy whatever the measurements were at the SFS, presumably because that was the most recently built stadium in the competition.

So, the Raiders had someone visit the SFS to measure the height of the posts and crossbar. They then used that for their own posts.

A couple more years down the track, they had to change the posts at Bruce Stadium, and this time someone checked the *official* specifications with the NSWRL. That was when a gobsmacking discovery was made.

The crossbar at the SFS for the 1989 grand final was two inches *above* the required height.

Two inches too high! Five centimetres.

When Chalky told me, it was like he'd punched me in the guts. I could hardly breathe.

If the crossbar had been two inches *lower* like it was supposed to be—Benny's kick would have gone over.

At that time during the game, it was disappointing—another missed opportunity. But we still led 14–8 in the shadows of fulltime.

In commentary, Graeme Hughes exclaimed: "Balmain are so close—they can smell it!"

CHICKA'S HEART-BREAKER

A huge moment—among many huge moments—came when Stuart chip-kicked for Daley, just inside our half. A roll of the dice from Ricky with under two minutes to go.

Meggsy, Currier and I converged to try and shut down the movement.

Daley ended up lying flat on the turf and raked at the bouncing ball, desperately trying to regain possession.

He knocked it on. I was right there. I have no doubt about it.

Not only did Harrigan disagree—he ruled six more tackles! That was the game right there and then.

Our old teammate, Kerry Hemsley, missed it. He'd already left his seat in the grandstand to go and grab the magnum of champagne, which had been chilling all game.

'Buckets' thought we were home and he was ready to celebrate. Most of the 40,500 fans at the SFS were probably thinking the same thing.

About the same time Buckets had his hands on that giant bottle of bubbles, Raiders five-eighth Chris O'Sullivan was hoisting a cross-field bomb towards our goalposts.

I launched myself at the footy in conventional fashion, like I had a million times in my career.

On this occasion, however, a guy called Steve Jackson came flying through for the Raiders and tapped the ball backwards. I never even touched it.

If I had tried to take it above my head AFL-style, it could have been a different outcome.

But I don't regret going conventional. No one knew who Jackson was, let alone that he could contest the high ball.

His tap-back found Daley, who threw a basketball pass to Ferguson, like he was playing for the LA Lakers.

Coming back against the grain, Chicka stepped off his left foot three times, beating our guys along the way. I was still on the ground after being knocked over in the contest to catch O'Sullivan's bomb. I was watching this like a train wreck unfolding before my very eyes.

Chicka kept coming, he ducked down low and carried a couple of us over the line with him as he scored. The Raiders and their fans went nuts.

When Chicka took that pass from Daley, the safest option for him would have been to set sail for the corner. He would have scored comfortably. But it would have been a difficult conversion attempt for Meninga.

By cutting back inside, Ferguson scored close to the posts. It gave Mal a much easier kick and he slotted it. Scores were level, 14–all.

We kicked-off and the siren sounded about 10 seconds later. That's how close we came.

No grand final had ever gone to extra-time until then. There had been drawn grand finals in 1977 and 1978, but they were replayed the following Tuesday.

At this point, I wasn't thinking about being part of history.

We had a grand final to win.

THE SUBSTITUTIONS

As we all caught our breath at the end of regulation time, our old coach Bill Anderson in Channel 10 commentary detected trouble straight away.

"A worry for Warren Ryan is his strike players are off the field—Roach and Sironen."

Blocker had been substituted by The Wok inside the final 10 minutes. If you watch the replay, it's obvious the big fella didn't want to come off.

Sirro was replaced after Ferguson had scored in the dying seconds. He was one of our defenders who tried desperately to stop Chicka from scoring.

This was the pre-interchange era. Once you were replaced in those days, you couldn't come back on.

The sight of Steve Roach and Paul Sironen on the bench and out of the game—as we prepared to enter extra-time in a grand final—was a head-scratching moment.

With the score 14–8 heading into the final stages, there was a big chance the game would go to extra-time and that's when you want your best players out there.

Roach was the current Australian front-rower, he was our leader. His ball-playing ability set up Sirro's first try. He had missed the '88 grand final because of suspension. Why would you replace him in his first grand final?

Warren pushed Bruce McGuire to the front row to replace Block. Bruce was also an Australian player in '89, but he was a backrower and didn't have the dominance and aura that Steve had up front.

Canberra's forwards started to run without fear of being belted in the ruck and it changed the whole momentum of the game.

In his autobiography, Doing My Block, Roach says: "I was filthy on everyone when I was replaced. I just couldn't believe it. I was too angry to think straight. The only thing going through my head was, 'Why did he do it?'. I'm still asking myself the same question years later."

Mick Pobjie was told to replace Sirro with about five minutes to go in regulation time. He didn't get on until Ferguson's try.

I still can't work out what they were thinking up in the grandstand. They had a chance to change their minds about taking Sirro off, but didn't.

Pobjie told me years later that there was a problem with the radios, and he should never have gone on. He apparently didn't receive a message from the bench telling him to stay off.

So, Mick went on and replaced Sirro in the second row—a position he had NEVER played in his 10-year career. He was primarily a centre. Yet in the biggest game of his life, he's thrown into a completely new position.

With all this going on, I couldn't help but think... *"Holy f&^%. What else could go wrong?"*

EXTRA-TIME

Mal Meninga kicked-off the first stanza of extra-time and the ball came straight to me. I took the catch no problem, and ran back towards the Raiders' defence.

I tried to palm Laurie Daley ... and that's when it happened.

The force of the impact dislocated the middle finger on my right hand. I played the ball and then repeatedly tried to put the finger back in place, but it was no use.

At this crucial stage of the game, my right hand was causing me extreme pain and—worse—couldn't function properly.

Next thing I know, Ricky Stuart is launching a clearing kick in my direction. Ricky had kicked the leather off the ball all day. He had it on a string.

Trying to protect my dislocated finger, I went to catch Ricky's kick left-handed. It wasn't natural for me and the ball ricocheted off my chest and bounced out of my grasp.

Knock-on. In front of our goalposts.

From Canberra's ensuing scrum win, Chris O'Sullivan kicked a field goal to give them a 15–14 lead.

It was the first time we had trailed all afternoon.

With our two best forwards out of the game, you could feel the Raiders lift. Suddenly their pack was making easy yards up the middle, where Block and Sirro would normally be patrolling.

The knockout blow came late in the second period of extra-time.

Andy Currier decided to grubber kick just outside our own quarter-line. It was an aimless kick and Big Mal bent over and scooped it up with ease.

He held off Tim Brasher before passing to Steve Jackson. I got to him first and speared in low in defence, but Jackson's legs were pumping and he bumped me off.

Shaun Edwards and Mick Neil were also unsuccessful in stopping the little-known Raiders' bench forward in jersey number 20. Kevin Hardwick and Gary Freeman got to him near our goal-line, but Jackson somehow reached out and scored with them hanging off his back.

It was a remarkable try.

Meninga missed the conversion, but our fate was sealed.

The fulltime siren that followed was like a dagger to the heart.

We had lost the grand final.

THE AFTERMATH

It was a feeling of utter devastation.

We lost to Canterbury 12 months earlier, but this was far more painful.

We led 12–2 at halftime and 14–8 with 90 seconds left.

The only thing I could think of doing was to lay on the turf. I looked around and all my teammates were doing the same thing. Russell Gartner, who didn't play that day, came over and consoled me with a pat on the back.

I was completely exhausted. I had never been this spent in my career.

Raiders' players were jumping up and down in celebration. Brad Clyde was awarded the Clive Churchill Medal as the best and fairest player. They were all screaming their heads off.

When they went on stage to collect their medals and hold up the Winfield Cup, I couldn't bring myself to watch.

There's a famous photo of Bill Harrigan signalling full-time, as all the Canberra players were celebrating. I'm not sure why, but I kept a copy of that photo.

At the press conference, Warren Ryan was grilled about his decision to replace Steve Roach and Paul Sironen.

He explained it was because bigger forwards naturally tired towards the end of a game. Warren felt it was a chance to get more mobile defenders out there.

Back in the dressing room no one said a word. Nothing. Complete silence. It felt like a morgue.

It was the same on the bus ride back to Balmain Leagues Club. It must have been an hour before anyone felt like talking.

That night we ended up at Kings Cross, getting stuck into a few drinks to help wash away the bitter memories of what happened.

Feeling hungry, a few of us dropped into McDonald's for a feed. I was ripping into some French fries starting to feel better about myself, when I was stopped in my tracks.

A television monitor was playing the late news and there it was: footage of Canberra players and fans going berserk over their maiden premiership.

That sobered me up in a hurry. Time to go home.

Years later, I was fascinated to read a story by journalist Tony Durkin about the awarding of the Clive Churchill Medal for that grand final.

It was revealed that *I* was judged the winner of the Medal, as voted by the three Australian Test selectors who were given the duties.

They were required to lodge their votes 5–10 minutes before fulltime. With us leading 14–8 at the time, I was declared the winner.

But after the Raiders fought back to win in extra-time, John Quayle apparently didn't like the nomination. Up on stage, he even spoke with Prime Minister Bob Hawke about what to do. Hawke reassured Quayle that he could disregard the vote, as he was the boss.

So, that's what Quayle did. He made an on-the-spot executive decision and gave the award to Clyde instead.

I never watched a replay of the game until 2009.

Fox Sports was celebrating the 20th anniversary of the grand final with a special documentary. They invited a handful of players from both teams to watch the game and provide a few insights.

It wasn't something I jumped at. I was thinking, "Do I really want to put myself through that all over again?"

Eventually, I agreed and I've got to say...it was a bloody good game of football. I didn't realise how good it was until I watched that replay.

But hearing people—to this day—calling it the *greatest* grand final ever played, still gives me no comfort.

I'd rather have won and had everyone call it the *shittiest* grand final ever played.

It gutted all of us—and not just the players.

When he got back to his office at Balmain Leagues Club after the game, Keith Barnes was still filthy with the result.

He spotted on the mantlepiece our trophy that we won for taking out the pre-season Alpha Romeo Challenge.

Barnesy picked this thing up and hurled it across the room, smashing it into smithereens. The poor old trophy was spread all over the carpet.

John Chalk watched it happen. He says it's the only time he ever heard Keith Barnes swear.

CHAPTER 43

THE RED FOLDER

NOT talking about the 1989 grand final seemed like a good idea at the time.

The result hurt like hell. Most of us just wanted to try and forget it ever happened.

But that approach backfired. The wounds festered for months.

Then we gathered for pre-season training at Leichhardt Oval. The mood felt volcanic. Like all this tension just below the surface was about to bubble over.

Warren gave a speech about how we must pick ourselves up and "go again". It was a new season.

We just stood around listening, not knowing quite what to say.

Then Blocker broke the ice with, "Why did you take me and Sirro off?"

Blocker and Sirro being replaced was one of the main talking points after the grand final.

Warren tried his best to explain. He told Block he was tired, and we needed to make changes for the good of the team.

Looking around, I could see he wasn't winning over the players with his argument.

It was clear to me that Warren got it wrong. He shouldn't have taken them off.

Blocker was our forward leader. He was the one keeping the middle of the ruck tight, so Glenn Lazarus and Brent Todd couldn't march through.

To take him off with the game in the balance at 14–8 ... he shouldn't have done it. Same thing for Sirro.

I was to learn years later that it wasn't completely The Wok's call to replace our two best forwards.

During his time with us, Warren employed a coaching co-ordinator named Brian Satterley. Warren would always listen to Brian. They had known each other a long time and Warren trusted him like no other.

A comparison would be the relationship between legendary Parramatta Eels' coach Jack Gibson and his offsider Ron Massey in the early 1980s, when they won three-straight premierships.

Satterley was famous among the players for his red folder. Everywhere he went, the red folder went with him. It was full of notes and stats about the team that he would share with the coach.

When the score was 14–8 after Gary Belcher scored Canberra's first try, the game went to another level. It was frenetic, end to end, with high completion rates and kicks staying in play. All of this in temperatures around 30 degrees. For around six minutes, the ball never went out of play—the most exhausting passage of play I can remember ever being involved in.

High up in the grandstand, Satterley pulled out his red folder, scribbled a few notes, and leaned over toward Warren.

"Block's walking."

In other words, Steve Roach needs replacing.

Keith Barnes and John Chalk were sitting nearby. They saw the red folder emerge and heard Blocker's name mentioned.

Barnesy made a firm point to Satterley in his thick Welsh accent: "You can't take him off."

Then he turned to Chalky and said, "Tell him to put the red folder away."

I loved Chalky. He always had a very distinct way of getting his message across.

"Ahhh, you won't be needing that—put it away."

Satterley took the tip, but then brought it out again. Quick as a flash, Barnesy elbowed Chalky in the ribs.

"He's got the red folder out again—tell him to put it away!"

It was too late.

Warren had sent word for Blocker to be replaced.

The only reason Block was 'walking' was because of that crazy six-minute period. He was just catching his breath when there was finally a break in play as a scrum was packed.

The decision to replace him, followed by Sirro, changed the whole momentum of the game.

Warren should never have done it. But I know why he did.

The red folder.

CHAPTER 44

SQUEEZED DRY

THERE seemed to be no escaping the Raiders.

Our second game of the 1990 pre-season competition, The Channel Ten Challenge, was against the 'Green Machine'. It was a quarter-final in Goulburn and both teams were virtually full strength.

I took a run and was grabbed by Glenn Lazarus, who went to the ground and pulled me down with him. I fell in an awkward, backwards motion and knew straight away I was in trouble. My knee had buckled under the weight of Lazzo's tackle.

My opinion of the Raiders at that point was not great. They had seriously wounded me twice in about five months.

Just to rub it in, they thrashed us 26–8 and went on to win the tournament.

I saw Dr Sam Sorrenti the next day, and he informed me the medial ligament in my left knee was completely ruptured. He told me it was one of the worst he'd ever seen.

I was about to turn 29, so that news shook me up. Suddenly, I was a bit worried about my ability to come back. But the doc assured me I could recover and play footy again.

For the second-straight year, I'd been struck down by an injury in the pre-season. All the hard work from November to February had been tossed out the window.

I was in the grandstand at Leichhardt for our opening Winfield Cup game against Manly.

A beautiful March day suddenly gave way to menacing skies. The rain came sweeping in before halftime, but that was just the start.

During the second half, hailstones started hammering down on the players! There was lightning, thunder and torrential rain like I'd never seen before.

Referee Eddie Ward called out the two captains, Benny Elias and Michael O'Connor, and asked if they wanted to go off.

Snoz O'Connor said, "No, let's keep playing, Sir."

So, they stayed on as the hail kept falling. Manly won 14–12.

My injury gave Tim Brasher a chance to show his wares at fullback. Since coming into first grade as a schoolboy, he had played in the centres, but I always felt he played his best footy with the number 1 on his back.

I made my return via the bench in round 5, with The Wok keeping 'Brash' at fullback. Two weeks later, I was back in my old jersey.

Next up, we played the Raiders in a grand final rematch in front of more than 23,000 at Bruce Stadium.

They got us again. This time 14–0.

We scored a couple of wins after that to move into third place on the ladder. Things were looking good.

Or so I thought.

We were out in the middle of Leichhardt Oval getting ready for training, when Keith Barnes headed over in my direction. Just behind him were Warren Ryan and Brian Satterley.

"Hey Jimmy, you got a sec?"

I went over to Barnesy, who looked nervous.

"Jimmy, this is the hardest decision I've ever had to make."

"Oh yeah? What decision."

Before he could answer, Warren stepped in.

"We'd like you to play reserve grade this week," said the coach.

"You're not as good as what you were, and we'd like to move Brasher back to fullback for this game against Cronulla. He's got a bit more spark than you."

I had never been dropped in all my time at the Tigers.

I'll admit I wasn't quite back to full speed after my injury, but I didn't think I was going too bad.

The fact Barnesy was part of the discussion showed what a huge decision this was from The Wok.

As CEO, Keith oversaw everything that went on at Balmain. That's why he was involved. Warren couldn't have dropped me without running it past the boss.

Warren went on to say that the ball was in my court.

"You can play reserve grade, or you can take a week off to fully get over your injury."

I didn't have to think about it. I took the week off.

That weekend we got rolled by the Sharks, 18–10.

The following week I was back in the side at fullback. I was also captain, because Benny and Junior were out injured.

We thrashed Easts 22–2 and went on a four-match winning streak.

The fourth win of that sequence was against Illawarra at my old stomping ground, the Wollongong Showground. Heading back home to the South Coast brought out the best in me—I scored two tries and kicked the only goal of my career in Australia!

After I scored a try under the posts, we realised our regular goalkicker Ian McCann had left the field. Someone said, "You may as well take it Jimmy."

I agreed. All those years of practice at training and I'd still never taken a shot at goal in almost a decade of first grade.

When the ballboy emptied his bucket of sand on the ground in front of me, the nerves took over. I was right in front of the posts, but it felt like I was kicking from the sideline, 40 metres out.

My hands were visibly shaking as I tried to steady the ball on the mound. I was thinking just one thing: *"For f*&%'s sake—don't miss it."*

I went back three steps back from the ball, took a deep breath, then came in and toe-poked it over.

It meant a lot to me, not that too many at Wollongong Showground seemed to care. I ran back to halfway with a spring in my step. I had my first and—as it turned out—only goal in Australia. I kicked the only other goal in my career when I was playing in England.

The next weekend saw the creation of an iconic moment in rugby league.

We were playing Manly at a jam-packed Brookvale Oval and the home team was on top. The match exploded when referee Eddie Ward sin-binned Blocker for five minutes over a minor incident (there was a five-minute sin-bin option in those days).

As Ward waved Blocker from the field, my old mate did something that has gone down in folklore.

He patted Ward on the head.

As soon as I saw the big fella do it, I knew he was in strife. It was only a pat, not even enough to ruffle Eddie's hair.

But you can't touch a referee.

Blocker wasn't finished. He sprayed the touch judge for his role in having him sin-binned. Block called him a "wombat", with some colourful language also involved.

He was suspended for four matches and fined $5,000.

Round 21 was a special occasion as Wayne Pearce played his final home game at Leichhardt Oval. There was a big crowd and black and gold everywhere you looked.

Unfortunately, Parramatta didn't get the memo, and our old mates Peter Sterling and Brett Kenny spoiled Junior's party with a 14–10 win.

To the strains of *Up Where We Belong*, Junior set off on a final lap of his beloved home ground.

Just to show what a machine he was, Pearce ran his farewell lap. You're supposed to walk around and soak it up. But Junior never walked when wearing the black and gold, and he wasn't about to start now.

Bruce McGuire and I eventually caught up to him. We hoisted Junior onto our shoulders and let him enjoy the rest of his lap. He deserved it. What an incredible career for club, State and country.

In the final round, we played the Knights in front of a record crowd of 32,217 at Marathon Stadium. The home team was fired up as they chased a maiden finals' appearance.

Even with Blocker back from suspension, we couldn't get the job done, going down 16–14.

We had lost three of our last five games to crash from second to equal fifth on the ladder with the Knights. We now had to beat them in a play-off to make the finals.

The match was scheduled for a Tuesday night at Parramatta Stadium. Tries to Junior and Steve O'Brien got us home in a tight one, 12–4.

This booked us a date with Manly in a knockout semi-final. The Sea Eagles had beaten us in both games that season, so it was a tough assignment—especially being our third game in six days.

Not surprisingly, we were very flat and failed to score a point, losing 16–0. That was Junior's final game of footy.

The season just never got going for us.

I don't think we ever recovered from our grand final defeat in '89. It was always in the back of our minds.

We might also have lost a bit of belief in Warren Ryan. Maybe he sensed it too, because straight after we were eliminated by Manly, The Wok announced he was moving on.

After three seasons Ryan said he had "squeezed the lemon dry" at Balmain.

Some saw that as an insult, but I could see where he was coming from. If you look at his record at other clubs, a three-year stint is about the maximum for Warren. By then, his abrasive style starts rubbing people up the wrong way.

He went and joined Wests.

Then came the real bombshell.

CHAPTER 45

THE ALAN JONES ERA

WHEN Keith Barnes told me who was taking over from Warren Ryan as coach, I was completely caught off-guard. I couldn't work out why they would appoint someone with *zero* rugby league coaching experience.

But Alan Jones had other assets.

He had proven highly successful in rugby union, guiding the Wallabies to a Grand Slam in 1984—beating the "home nations" (England, Wales, Scotland and Ireland). More than 40 years later, their achievement still hasn't been matched.

Jones was known as a master motivator and was making a name for himself on Sydney's airwaves as the big-money breakfast host on radio station 2UE.

He was doing so well financially; he didn't even ask Balmain for a cent—he was coaching for free! Jones told Barnesy he just wanted an opportunity to coach a team in the Winfield Cup.

Although Jones hadn't coached in rugby league before, we still had a core of senior players to help him through that early adjustment period.

Junior and Kevin Hardwick had retired at the end of 1990, while Bruce McGuire had joined the Bulldogs. But we still had Blocker, Benny, Sirro, Brash and me. We'd bring the footy nous, Jones the motivation.

That's what I thought would happen. It didn't turn out that way.

The first sign that things might be veering off track came before a ball was even kicked, when Jones announced his big new signing—sprint star Darren Clark.

At the peak of his powers, Clark ran fourth at the 1984 and 1988 Olympic Games in the 400 metres. He won gold in the same event at the Commonwealth Games in Auckland in 1990. He was one of Australia's biggest names in track and field. He was even dubbed "the fastest white man in the world".

The first thing I noticed about Clark when he turned up for training were his ridiculously large hamstrings. Enormous. They were the biggest I'd ever seen.

There was a bit of a buzz about his arrival and Alan was loving it.

Clark was picked on the wing for our first trial match. After winning a scrum in our own half early in the game, we kicked the ball downfield and Clark hared past everyone to get to the ball first and score a try. With his first touch! The guy had blinding speed.

If you kicked ahead for him, Clark was great. But if you threw him the ball, he didn't know what to do. He didn't know how to hit a gap or beat a man one-on-one.

These are skills often taken for granted in rugby league. He had little idea in defence either.

Clark played in the pre-season Nissan Sevens tournament, but he never played a premiership game. He returned to athletics after seeing out the year in reserve grade.

Jones had to undergo neck surgery as we were preparing to kick-off the '91 season. He checked out of hospital and made it to training, even though he was still in a lot of pain. I could see his clothes were loose and that he'd lost a lot of weight.

Jones spoke for about 45 minutes of how proud he was of our performances in the trials. I could see he was physically hurting as he addressed us. I was impressed by his dedication.

But hopes of an exciting new era under the former Wallabies' mentor were quickly dashed.

Whiz Freeman was sent off in the opening round against Canterbury for a high tackle on Darren Brown off the ball. We led at the time but were over-run 26–16.

Freeman was suspended for two matches, and Mick Neil was also missing with a broken ankle.

In the opening seven rounds, we didn't win a game. A 12–all draw with Newcastle was the only thing keeping us above last-placed Parramatta.

We took on the Eels in a battle of the cellar-dwellers—and lost 16–15. We were now last on the ladder.

Just 18 months after missing out on a premiership by the barest of margins, we were the worst team in the competition.

Everything we learned from Warren Ryan was out the window. All the success we enjoyed was a thing of the past. Morale was at rock-bottom.

While Freeman was serving his suspension, Jones signed a rugby union halfback named Brian Smith. He told us our new number 7 would be the next Ricky Stuart, able to kick the bladder out of the ball and throw 20-metre cut-out passes.

I was on the end of a Smith pass against the Gold Coast. It was straight from 'Ward Nine', allowing Wally Lewis to bury his shoulder into my ribs. As I picked myself up off the ground, Wally said he felt sorry for me!

But Smith was always a Jones favourite. After an 18–9 loss to Easts in round 4, Jones publicly scolded us for not providing Smith with better service.

"We have got one of the best tactical kickers in the world in Brian Smith, yet they couldn't have found him with a radar set."

Smith was straight into the Jones inner sanctum... which spelled the end for Whiz.

Freeman had been with us for four years, playing in both our grand final appearances. I thought it was disgraceful that Jones dropped him after a few games to bring in the new kid. Whiz was left stranded in reserve grade.

I was angry at his treatment because Whiz was as much a part of Balmain as myself, Blocker, Sirro and Benny.

But Balmain had paid big money for Smith, so Jones had to justify the expense.

He underestimated the fight in Freeman though. He eventually got out of his contract, went to Easts in 1992, and won the Dally M Medal as Player of the Year. Whiz proved him wrong. Class is permanent, form is temporary.

Jones introduced several 'initiatives' in his first season at the helm. One of those was the 'Team of the Week'.

After each game, he would announce a special team comprising the best players from all three grades. Jones would make a big speech at training, explaining why he picked each player. It was a chance for him to talk up some players… and tear down others. One night, he tore shreds off one of our young up-and-coming forwards.

"There's one player I won't be picking in this team—that's you, Shane O'Grady," Jones declared.

In front of the entire playing squad, he ripped apart O'Grady's performance from the weekend. When he finished his spray, I walked up to Shane and asked if he was okay. I told him he didn't deserve that. Shane was upset. He was only 21.

Jones had brought him through the grades, then he cut him down in humiliating fashion.

Any confidence the kid had was gone.

Pressure was building on Jones, just a few months into the gig.

Barnesy tried to end the speculation by reminding everyone that Jones had a two-year contract, and the Tigers were not looking to make any changes.

We upset the Broncos, but then backed it up with a disappointing 22–12 loss to Norths.

The game against the Bears was special for me—my 200th in first grade. I had also gone past Barnesy as the most capped Balmain player of all time (195 first-grade games), which was a huge honour.

To mark the occasion, I scored a try and later had photos taken with Kieren and Rhys sitting on my lap in the change rooms. The photos appeared in the newspaper the next day.

We found some form mid-season to climb off the bottom of the ladder. But we still finished well short of playing finals' football, ending up in 12th place with just eight wins.

It was the first time Balmain had missed the finals since 1984.

When we returned from our off-season break, I organised a meeting with Jones and us senior players to work out how to improve on what was a diabolical year. The meeting was held at Jones' apartment, and I had Blocker, Benny and Sirro with me. I also had a copy of Warren Ryan's playbook from his three years at the Tigers.

I wanted to share this with Jones, because I thought it could help. What a waste of time that proved to be. Jones wasn't interested. In fact, I didn't even get a chance to open the book.

That meeting was three hours of my life I'll never get back. I left Jones' apartment and straight away said to Blocker, "We've forgotten more about rugby league than he'll ever know."

CHAPTER 46

IMPOSSIBLE TO WORK WITH

MY relationship with Alan Jones is probably best summed up by the events of 1992.

It was my 11th season at Balmain and the club decided to honour me with a testimonial dinner, for which I was very grateful.

The event was held in April at the Hilton Sydney and Jones was the keynote speaker. Jones has a way with words, and I was truly blown away with what he said about me up on stage.

He described me as a "warrior" and if you were going into battle, "you'd want Jimmy Jack alongside you".

Jones added that my form was so good, I should be considered for a recall to the Australian side.

Donning the green and gold again was a huge goal of mine. For him to push my cause like that, in such public fashion, made me think I had been a bit harsh on Alan Jones.

That's why I was left so angry and confused just two days later.

We were playing St. George at Kogarah Oval, when a clearing kick from the Dragons headed towards the sideline. I tried to get to it, but the ball beat me into touch.

It's a scenario that plays out every weekend. The ball goes out, we feed the scrum and get the ball back.

As the forwards from both sides slowly congregated to form a scrum, I noticed our reserve back James Grant standing on the sideline anxious to get on the field. We were only 30 minutes into the game, and no one was injured, so I was surprised to see him.

"What are you doing out here mate?"

"Jimmy, you're off."

"What?"

"You're off. Jonesy said I'm coming on for you."

I couldn't believe what I was hearing. What had I done wrong? To replace a fullback was a waste of an interchange by Jones.

The substitution took place on the opposite side of the field to where the Tigers' bench was, so it was a long walk back... it showed me very little respect.

By the time I got back to the Tigers' bench, I could see Jones sitting there. I asked him straight away why I was replaced.

He didn't respond as he continued to watch the match. I started thinking of how Whiz was treated. I asked Jones again, and again I was ignored. I blew my stack.

"You've f*&%ed this joint!"

With that I stormed towards the change rooms. I could feel my Balmain teammates on the bench watching me, and also the St. George boys who were sitting not far away.

I kicked open the door and Donny the strapper was there, preparing for the halftime break. I repeated what I said about Jones. I was mad.

A few seconds later, Keith Barnes and John Chalk appeared. They had seen the commotion and were attempting to calm me down. It didn't work.

"You know what this bloke is doing?" I snapped. "He's f&^%ing this joint up! It's disgraceful."

Let's get one thing straight. I never considered myself irreplaceable as a player. I could accept being demoted if it was warranted. But that was the problem. I still had no clue *why* Jones dragged me from the field.

To make matters worse, the Dragons were toying with us. By halftime, we were down 16–2. We rallied in the second half to level the scores at 16–all. Then future dual international Andrew Walker came off the bench—his first-grade debut—and booted a freakish 40-metre field goal with his first touch to give the Dragons a one-point lead.

After another slow start to the season under Jones (two wins and four losses), defeat here would be disastrous. There were under 20 minutes left on the clock. Keith Barnes approached Jones.

"I think it would be a good time to put Jimmy Jack back on."

I watched this interaction take place. Jones listened to Barnesy then wiggled his finger at me.

"Come here."

I went over but could hardly bring myself to look at him.

"I'm going to put you back on. Get to the ball early."

Get to the ball early? What the hell was he talking about? Whatever he said was just bullshit. I was hardly listening.

I went back on, and James Grant scored to give us the lead. With just seconds left on the clock, Walker launched an almighty torpedo bomb from about 40 metres out from our goal-line.

Walker was the pioneer of this kick, which is now a deadly weapon in the modern game.

These swirling, spiralling bombs are the stuff of nightmares for fullbacks and wingers. One second, you're standing under it ready for the catch. Then it can suddenly curl away from you, making you look like a fool.

When Walker sent the ball into orbit, my first thought was, *"Hooooly shiiiiit!"* I turned and tracked the flight of the ball toward our goalposts. I could hear the footsteps thudding behind me as the desperate Dragons' chasers poured through in search of a miracle match-winning try.

I knew Walker's kick would curl away from me at the last second, but I couldn't afford to let it bounce. I covered more than 20 metres, keeping one eye on the ball and another on the goalposts which were looming very quickly. At one stage, I thought I was going to crash into them.

I eventually got close enough, but a clean catch was out of the question. The ball deflected off my fingertips, before I kicked it safely over our dead-ball line.

If it had bounced back over my head, a St. George player would have grabbed it and scored.

The siren sounded. We had scored a big upset, 22–17. I was thrilled to bounce back from my disappointment and contribute.

The mood was positive afterwards as you'd expect, but I was still pissed off about being replaced. Not wanting to detract from the win, I didn't front Jones straight after the game. I decided to leave that for later.

The next morning, I picked up my copy of *The Sydney Morning Herald* (SMH) from the front lawn. Jones was quoted in the story about our win on why he replaced me. According to him, I had been too slow getting to that St. George clearing kick in the first half.

"That's nice," I thought. He's told all the journos but didn't have the courtesy to tell me.

That afternoon before training, I asked Jones for a chat. We went into a room under the grandstand at Leichhardt Oval. I closed the door behind us.

"Why'd you friggin' replace me?"

"Because you were too slow getting to the kick."

"Too slow? It was a good kick! It went over the sideline—big deal? It was a scrum 10 metres from the goal-line, our feed. You don't replace me for that."

"I've told you before that you need to be quicker getting to those kicks."

Later I challenged him about the *SMH* article.

"If you've got something to say about me Alan, I'd appreciate it if you tell me first. You've told the whole world before you told me. You don't do that to one of your players."

Jones is a hard bloke to beat in an argument. If the sky was cloudy, within a minute he could convince you it was sunny.

We went back and forth about me being hooked, but it finished in a stalemate.

In all my time playing rugby league, he's the only coach who ever accused me of being too slow getting to kicks.

The thing that had me scratching my head was Jones' comments on stage just two nights earlier at my testimonial dinner. That I should be considered for selection in the Australian team. How did he go from *that* to replacing me in the middle of a game?

I just couldn't work it out.

From then on, our relationship was very strained. We hardly spoke to each other. I kept my position in the team because I was playing some of my best football.

Barnesy was keeping a close eye on the situation. The last thing he wanted at the club was a repeat of the messy Freeman saga. He was very aware of how Whiz had gone from being unwanted by Jones, to killing it over at the Roosters. I told Keith, "He's trying to do the same thing to me."

That year, I had started a player agent company called *Football Management Services.* We recruited players to the firm and then helped them find a new club, if they so desired. We were the go-between. Our negotiations were far and wide, not just with the 16 Winfield Cup clubs.

English clubs were very much on the radar. Sheffield Eagles were a relatively new club, debuting in the 1984/85 season. Gary Hetherington was a former player who was now their owner and coach. He founded the club with his wife Kath.

I'd rung several English clubs to gauge their interest in a few Aussie boys by the time I got around to ringing Sheffield. Hetherington took the call.

"Actually, you've rung at a good time, Garry," he said.

"My wife, Kath, is over there in Australia right now looking for players. You should give her a call."

I took his advice and met Kath a couple of days later for a cup of tea at a Sydney hotel. After about 15 minutes, she stopped me in my tracks.

"I want to sign you, Garry. I want you to come and play for Sheffield."

I sat there, shocked. I had never considered the option of returning for another stint in England. I'd always imagined myself finishing my career at Balmain.

The more I thought about Kath's offer, the more I liked it. This might be just what I needed after the dramas of the past 18 months. What a great opportunity to get away and make a fresh start.

I had another cup of tea and told Kath I'd be in touch.

I spoke to Donna about it as soon as I got home. Kieren and Rhys were still only young at five and three respectively. We were all really excited by the thought of trying something new.

My old Tigers' teammate Bruce McGuire had played for Sheffield a couple of years earlier and had a great time. He told me he was keen to get back over there.

After a week, my mind was made up. I would be leaving Balmain at the end of the season to play in England.

The first person at the Tigers I told was Barnesy. It was tough telling him I wanted to leave. Golden Boots had been so good to me over the years, like a second father. But he knew the reasons behind my move.

My relationship with Jones hadn't improved and the Tigers had committed to him for the 1993 season. I couldn't work with him anymore. Another 12 months would have been impossible.

I also wanted to leave Tigers' fans with the best possible memories.

Despite my dramas with the coach, I was voted the number one fullback in the game by my peers in the annual *Rugby League Week* (RLW) player poll. I played all 22 games that season.

I announced my decision at a packed press conference at Balmain Leagues Club.

My goodbye to the fans came on Sunday, August 23. Balmain's biggest crowd of the season—17,365—crammed into Leichhardt to farewell myself and two of my longest-serving teammates.

Steve Roach was retiring, and David Brooks was finishing his career in the bush. It meant a great deal to me to have these two Balmain greats alongside me as we played our final home game.

We'd been through a lot together, including the pain of grand final defeats. Between us, we played more than 600 first-grade games for the Tigers.

This was it. Our last game at Leichhardt, a place filled with so many special memories—and people.

But just like what happened two years earlier in Wayne Pearce's farewell game, the opposition didn't get the memo. I scored a late try under the posts to give us a chance, but St. George hung on to spoil the party with a 20–14 win.

The three of us then took a long walk around Leichhardt at fulltime, waving to the fans and soaking up the love. There were plenty of tears. Donna let Kieren onto the field and seeing the little guy run towards me was such a beautiful moment. He joined us for the rest of our slow walk back to the change rooms. We were eventually chaired from the field by our teammates.

Our last game came the following Sunday, a 14–all draw with the Bears at a half-empty North Sydney Oval.

My time as a Balmain Tiger was over.

The number one movie that year was *Robin Hood: Prince of Thieves*, which featured the hit song from Bryan Adams, *Everything I Do*. The chorus is, "Everything I do, I do it for you." Those lyrics resonated with me. It's how I felt about my beloved Balmain Tigers.

It still makes me emotional thinking about it.

In the lead-up to that game against Norths, I decided to do something I believed was very important for the club. I wrote an open letter highlighting the negative impact of Alan Jones on the Balmain Tigers.

It was to be published in RLW after we had finished our commitments for the year against Norths.

It was completely my own doing. I had no input from anyone else. I said things I felt needed to be said. I wanted fans to know what it had been like for the past couple of years and how frustrating it had been for me as a player.

I wrote that Balmain was stagnating under Jones. For example, he hadn't changed our tap moves or scrum moves in 18 months. He wasn't concerned about defence. He just wanted to throw the ball from sideline to sideline.

My letter wasn't about me trying to get Jones sacked. But I wanted people to know what it was like playing under him.

In my opinion, the Tigers—a club I loved dearly—was going down the wrong path with Jones as coach for another year.

By the time the letter was published in RLW I was already in England, preparing for the season ahead with Sheffield. I received a lot of positive feedback from Balmain fans back home.

I continued my strong form for the Eagles and by the end of the season I was named at fullback in English magazine *Open Rugby's* 1992 World Team of the Year.

I'll admit it was a bit cheeky, but I sent a framed copy of the magazine to Jones back home in Australia. On the page which showed my name in the Team of the Year, I wrote him a little message.

"Dear Alan—thanks for all your support and inspiration. Regards, Jimmy Jack."

Apparently, the frame arrived at Alan's house with the glass cracked—very symbolic of our relationship.

That chapter was over. I was enjoying my footy again.

CHAPTER 47

THE ASSAULT

OUR halfback Brian Smith launched a bomb high into the sky above Leichhardt Oval and I chased hard like always. Alongside me was teammate Tim Brasher. In our sights was Sea Eagles' fullback Matthew Ridge.

The halftime siren was sounding as Smith kicked the footy. Ridge was in good position and caught the ball in his own quarter just before we reached him.

It was the last play of the first half, so Brash and I hit Ridge hard. There was no real plan, other than hoping he dropped the ball and we could pick up the scraps and score.

It was June 23, 1991, a date I'll never forget.

The big home crowd roared with delight as Brash and I tackled the Kiwi Test fullback. Ridge was the sort of bloke who didn't like getting tackled. He didn't like the rough stuff but was good at dishing it out.

On this occasion, as he battled to keep his feet in the tackle, Ridge resented being driven backwards. He used his free hand to grab my collar and 'jumper punch' me under the chin. I thought, "well, that's a cheap shot", so I threw a looping right hand at him that didn't even make contact.

That's when things exploded.

Manly centre Darrell Williams came flying in and ripped me away from Ridge. As Williams grappled with me, I was grabbed by someone else from my right-hand side. His left arm had come over my shoulder and neck area. He pulled me in tight and had me pinned.

It was Ian Roberts.

Roberts was a specimen, standing well over six foot and weighing more than 100 kilos. He was much larger than me.

With Williams still holding me, Roberts launched a series of uppercuts with his right hand at my unprotected head.

By this stage, Cliff Lyons had also joined Williams in holding me. Both my arms were restrained. I was pinned and helpless. My face was pointing towards the ground. Roberts had pulled me in tight with his left arm, the perfect method for throwing uppercuts with his right.

He unloaded on me. It was a frenzy. He clearly had a boxing background.

I was helpless against this thrashing machine. The only guy in a position to assist me was Tim Brasher, until he was pulled away by Sea Eagles' hooker Matt Dunford.

I was trying desperately to hang on and avoid the blows. My only hope was to cover up and that was difficult because my arms were being held by Williams and, to a lesser extent, Lyons.

This was completely foreign territory for me. I'm not a fighter. I'd never been in this situation before—it was a street brawl.

Finally, Roberts stopped the assault for a split second. Then I made the mistake of throwing one punch back at him.

I should never have done that.

He immediately threw two more uppercuts. Bang. Bang. He split me just above my right eye and under my left eye.

We both ended up on the ground in the Manly in-goal. Roberts was eventually pulled off me.

My battered head was beginning to pound as referee Graeme West blew his whistle and called both of us over. We were walking towards the referee when Roberts looked at me and said, "I got you Jack, I got you."

It was such a bizarre thing to say.

I shot back with, "You f&^%en 'got' me? Have a look at me! Have a look at what you did!"

Roberts was sent to the sin-bin for the offence of third-man in.

A few seconds later, I was also sin-binned for the punch I threw at Ridge.

I couldn't believe West had given us the same punishment.

My more immediate concern came as I jogged towards the change rooms. I could see the huge frame of Roberts ahead of me, just about to reach the tunnel. After his strange comment a minute or so earlier, I started to wonder if we were about to have round 2.

Thankfully, he wasn't waiting for me.

In the rooms, our team medico Dr David Clifford worked overtime stitching up both wounds. All up, I needed 14 stitches to two wounds. He spread Vaseline over the top for some extra protection. My eye was closing, but I had to get back out on the field.

"Just strap me up, I'm okay to go back!"

I was in pain. My head was throbbing. But we needed the win after a poor start to the season.

Roberts and I came together just once after we returned from the sin-bin. I tackled him and not a word was said from either of us.

We ended up winning the game 24–8, not that I was in any condition to celebrate just our fourth win of the season.

I emerged from the sheds all battered, bloodied and bruised. Donna was waiting in the back car park as she did after every home game. She looked at me with a mix of horror and disbelief.

"What the hell happened out there?!"

"I don't know. I didn't even start it," I replied.

Donna's experience as a trained nurse kicked in and she did everything possible to make me comfortable. She was worried about the effects of concussion and kept watch over me all night.

The next morning was a nightmare as I looked in the mirror.

My eyes were virtually closed. All the stitching was straining under the pressure of the swelling. My head felt like there was a jackhammer inside. It was the worst pain I'd ever endured.

At training that night, Keith Barnes was the first person I saw. He couldn't believe it. I looked like the Elephant Man.

The 'Marrickville Mauler', boxer Jeff Fenech, had fought a world title fight on the same weekend, and I looked more bashed up than the guy he beat.

The ferocity of the punches came as no surprise to legendary boxing trainer Johnny Lewis, who once trained Roberts.

He was once asked who the hardest puncher in rugby league is.

"Ian Roberts, just ask Garry Jack."

Lewis went on to say, "Roberts hit harder than any other rugby league player he'd trained."

I nearly fell off my lounge when I saw that interview on television. Lewis had trained Jeff Fenech and other boxing champions. He knew what he was talking about.

I guess I was lucky in some sense—it could have been way worse. I kept all my teeth, my nose wasn't broken, and there was no damage to my eyes.

All those outcomes are possible when you have a powerful puncher throwing uppercuts from such close range. He threw at least 10. Maybe more. And that's when the other bloke isn't throwing anything back. Why keep going? That's what I could never understand.

Even Ridge was taken aback. In his autobiography *Take No Prisoners,* Ridge wrote: "I've never seen him (Roberts) do anything like this before. It's ugly, Garry Jack's a mess. He looks like he's just been beaten up by a gang."

I'll never forget the empty look on Roberts' face while he was assaulting me.

No expression. No emotion. It was a poor act. To run in and target someone and attack them like that.

There was a State of Origin match where I ran in and grabbed my opposite number, Colin Scott. But that was one-on-one. Scott wasn't being held by other players.

I don't think the whole thing would have happened if Paul Sironen and Steve

Roach were playing that afternoon. There were no Balmain players physically strong enough to stop him once the fight started.

Blocker would never have let that beating happen.

I should also make the point I'm not dirty on Darrell or Cliffy for their role. They were holding me, but I honestly don't believe it was to help Roberts.

I was dirty on Ridge though, the guy who kicked it all off. He was quoted afterwards saying, "Garry Jack got his just rewards. He threw a punch at me first and didn't miss."

I was no fan of referee West either after his comments to the press.

"To be honest, I don't think the brawl was any worse than what you see at other games during the year," West told rugby league journalist Phil Rothfield.

"It's unfortunate that a player like Garry Jack was hurt. But he did start the fight. Nothing would have happened if he didn't hit Matthew Ridge in the first place."

Extraordinary comments from a referee. Even if I did start it—which I didn't—does that justify such a brutal retaliation?

West and his touch judges obviously missed Ridge's jumper-punch to my chin. West didn't even include the attack in his match report.

I'm not sure who made the phone call, but the Tigers didn't want this issue being swept under the rug. *The Daily Telegraph-Mirror* was tipped off about my appearance and they sent a photographer to my home in Cherrybrook.

When a photo of my swollen, battered face appeared in the newspaper on Tuesday morning, that's when the story really took off.

All the television stations were ringing. The phone wouldn't stop. I conducted some interviews at home, which wasn't pretty viewing. My left eye had totally closed, and my right one was halfway shut.

By that night I was in a bad way.

I told Donna my face felt like it was burning. We contacted the Tigers, and they arranged for me to attend Petersham Private Hospital in the morning.

I spent the next three days there on a drip. Doctors were worried my wounds would become infected. If that happened, it could spread to my brain.

I remained in hospital until Friday. We had a game that weekend against St. George—my 200th in first grade for Balmain. It was to be played in Adelaide of all places, but I was clearly in no condition to play, so I pulled out.

While I was in hospital, another savage blow was delivered—this time by NSWRL general manager John Quayle.

He decided Roberts wouldn't be cited, because the referee acted at the time when he sent both of us to the sin-bin.

The people who ran the game had decided a 10-minute stint in the sin-bin was sufficient punishment for a player throwing a dozen punches and putting another player in hospital.

What a joke.

Just imagine if Steve Roach did the same thing to Matthew Ridge? I bet you Blocker wouldn't have been able to play the next week.

The papers were scathing.

'Buzz' Rothfield wrote in *The Sunday Telegraph*, "League's image suffered a worse battering than Garry Jack's face from Quayle's non-action on one of the most brutal and sickening incidents for years."

John Quayle, as NSWRL general manager, had the sole power to cite Roberts for his acts but did nothing.

If the NSWRL gave Roberts a suspension of two to four weeks, I would have accepted that. But they did nothing.

Even after I returned home from hospital, I still had headaches and dizzy spells. These could last up to 15 seconds at a time. I was often woken from my sleep by flashbacks of that moment at Leichhardt. I would see Roberts' fist coming through and hitting me in the face.

I also found it difficult to breathe through my nose, something that stayed with me for the rest of my career.

The media stayed on the story for days. I gave an interview saying the game was entering dangerous territory by allowing players to escape punishment for such an act.

I had a very low opinion of Roberts because of what he did to me. I also believe he was being protected. Something just didn't add up.

They couldn't suspend Blocker quick enough whenever he put so much as a toe out of line. But they gave Roberts a green light for punching the tripe out of me.

Former judiciary chairman Jim Comans—the man hired to clean up the game in the early '80s—told *The Sunday Telegraph*: "If it could be shown that Ian Roberts was guilty, he would have received nothing less than 12 weeks (on my watch). To see the battered face of Garry Jack on television this week made me feel quite ill. You don't see boxers looking that bad."

He added that it didn't matter who started the fight, it's not up to Roberts to appoint himself "judge, jury, and executioner".

But incredibly, some people didn't see it that way.

Don Furner, my coach on the 1986 Kangaroo Tour, was quoted in *The Northern Star* newspaper, saying: "Garry Jack got what he deserved, because he started it."

What a shameful comment. Don Furner had been my Australian coach for three years. I respected Don, but he was way off the mark.

If I wanted justice, I had to do it myself. I decided to take Roberts to court. I had no other choice. Balmain and Keith Barnes supported my decision.

You go out there to play footy. You don't expect to be part of a jailhouse brawl.

Rugby league is a tough sport, I realise that. You might get hurt.

But you shouldn't get your face beaten to a pulp. I felt like I had to take a stand.

If this sort of behaviour was considered normal, then pretty soon it would be anarchy in rugby league.

I couldn't stand idle when there was no accountability from the NSWRL and no remorse from Ian Roberts. In taking legal action, I was essentially saying the game had failed me. The powerbrokers would not be pleased.

I knew by taking Roberts to court I was killing off one of my last remaining career goals: to once again wear the green and gold.

CHAPTER 48

THE RUMOUR THAT ROCKED ME

IAN Roberts was more than just an elite footballer. In 1994, he also became the first male rugby league player to come out as being gay.

In his own words, Roberts admitted his sexuality was "the worst kept secret in rugby league".

Although times were changing, it was considered a brave step back in those days for Roberts to reveal he was homosexual while still playing. I commend him for it, and I admire all the hard work he has done for the LGBTQI community.

That's why I was sickened by a rumour that took off in the aftermath of the incident at Leichhardt Oval in 1991.

That I *deserved* the beating he gave me because I had called Roberts a 'poof' or a 'faggot'.

I had supposedly provoked this Sea Eagles giant into giving me a flogging by crudely sledging him based on his sexual identity.

I want to set the record straight. I never vilified Ian Roberts.

The rumours caused so much distress to my young family. Donna was very upset. Kieren and Rhys heard people say their dad "got what he deserved".

The rumour was clearly started by someone trying to justify what had happened.

The fact is I didn't say anything to Ian Roberts.

To hear those rumours and know that the people I love were hearing them as well, was incredibly painful for me. I found it despicable.

Look at the video of the incident. I never even knew Roberts was there until he started launching uppercuts. Roberts snapped. What he did far outweighed anything I did. I was in the wrong place at the wrong time.

I was the victim, not him.

I couldn't have cared less about Ian Roberts being gay.

My legal action against him finally made it to court in February of 1999. The case would be heard at The District Court of New South Wales in Goulburn Street.

I wasn't the first player to take an opponent to court.

Darryl Brohman sued Les Boyd for breaking his jaw during a State of Origin game in 1983.

Two years later, Steve Rogers took action against Mark Bugden, also for a high shot that left him with a busted jaw.

I wasn't doing it for money, as suggested by Roberts' old Manly coach Graham Lowe.

I hired well-known Sydney lawyer Chris Murphy, who filed a $100,000 lawsuit against Roberts.

That figure was for damages for the shock I had suffered, the traumatic injuries, headaches and numbness, and the embarrassment of scarring to my face.

If I had sexually vilified Roberts by calling him those awful names, then it would have come out in court.

Matthew Ridge gave evidence and so did referee Graeme West—two men in the thick of the action that afternoon.

Not once did they mention anything about me directing a vile slur at Roberts.

When I took the stand, I told the court the incident had been an ongoing source of humiliation and embarrassment.

I owned a sports store in Burwood at the time—Garry Jack's Sports Scene. Customers would often ask me about being "bashed up" by Roberts. Some would even shadow box in front of me.

I told the court I had never been punched so hard in my life and it felt like I was being hit with a hammer.

Outside the courtroom one day, Roberts walked near Donna, but didn't know who she was.

Donna said: "I want to know why you bashed my husband."

Roberts said sorry, but Donna wasn't finished.

"I don't want to hear you're sorry. I want to know why you did it."

I could see what was happening and came over and told Roberts to go away. He looked at me and said he was sorry. I suggested the only reason he was sorry was because he was going to be next on the stand.

After four days in court, the judge asked the prosecution for Roberts to take the stand. But he never took the stand. They wanted to settle.

If I had vilified Roberts, that was his chance to tell everyone, and perhaps try and justify his actions.

We agreed to his legal team's offer to settle.

It wasn't the $100,000 in damages that I had been seeking, but like I said, it was never about the money. It was about proving that:

I didn't start it, nor did I vilify him.

This type of thuggery on the rugby league field must NEVER be accepted as normal by the game's officials and players.

I believe Matthew Ridge's testimony was the defence's biggest downfall.

His evidence was inconsistent with what he wrote in his autobiography, which was released a year earlier. I don't think Ridge was aware that my legal team had looked over his book.

My lawyer would say, "Well, that's different to what you said in your book, Mr Ridge!"

It was four hours of testimony that I enjoyed listening to, sitting just a few metres away from him, watching him squirm.

Ridge kept saying he had to get his flight back to Auckland, but he was going nowhere.

One passage from his book said Ridge spoke to Roberts after the game and asked, "What was going on out there?"

He wrote that Roberts replied, "I've been pissed off with Garry Jack for some time."

It was suggested it was something to do with a business venture that went sour.

That's not true. We had never been in business together. It was just another excuse for what he did.

The only thing that came close was when I sold life insurance and superannuation for a business at Bondi Junction, run by a guy who wanted to work with footy players. He recruited Roberts not long after bringing me on board and we worked together for a while.

But there were never any problems.

My only regret after accepting the settlement is I didn't seek a public acknowledgement from Roberts that I did nothing to deserve being assaulted.

Thankfully, Roberts has done this himself in public forums.

In 2016 he was interviewed by Peter Sterling on his *On The Couch* program on Fox League. Asked about his attack on me, Roberts revealed he was going through a troubled stage of his career because of serious issues in his personal life.

He went on to say: "It wouldn't have bothered me then—and I don't say this with any pride—if I'd have killed someone on the field. But there was a lot going on in my personal life then. I've apologised to Garry and I've spoken to Garry since that. He bore the brunt of my frustration. I'm truly sorry for that situation. That was totally irresponsible and totally not acceptable, ever."

In Daniel Pain's book *Rugby League's Heroes of Yesterday,* released in 2023, Roberts said: "I look back now and really regret it. He had every right to sue me."

I am pleased Ian has made these comments and acknowledged that I wasn't to blame for what happened to me.

He's admitted that he was in the wrong.

I bumped into him at a function about 20 years after it happened, and we shook hands.

Ian said, "I'm sorry." I accepted his apology.

I forgive Ian for what happened. But I can never erase the memories.

Roberts went to town on me when I couldn't defend myself and he made a mess of me.

He tried to humiliate me.

Rugby league's code of conduct can only work if all parties buy in. It's the only way we can ensure a safe environment, regardless of age, gender and ability.

The game's administrators from this era failed. They failed terribly. It was their job to protect its players from these acts of thuggery. All I wanted was justice to be done, but the NSWRL chief executive, John Quayle, refused to cite Roberts, despite a heap of pressure from the media.

This is why the court transcripts are so important for me. The facts are there for all to see. But sadly, mud sticks.

Instead of people talking about the great things I did in my career, they bring up the Roberts incident instead. It was 10 seconds of my career—and I didn't even start it.

It frustrates me that people still say, "What did you say to Ian Roberts?"

I still carry some baggage from that day. I've got to learn to let it go.

Hopefully this will help.

CHAPTER 49

STABBED IN THE BACK

I DIDN'T realise it at the time, but I took for granted the good times I enjoyed while playing for Balmain.

Being in a group of like-minded players, whose bond and friendship is still strong now.

Unfortunately, it isn't like this at all clubs. I was naïve to think it would be.

After leaving the Tigers at the end of '92, I played a year at the Sheffield Eagles under Gary Hetherington who was coach, manager and owner.

Reinvigorated, I played 33 games straight and scored eight tries. Even in my twilight years at 32, I felt mentally and physically fit.

I was involved in a bit of history in a Yorkshire Cup semi-final against Hull at Don Valley Stadium on October 6, 1992—the fastest try to start a game. Unfortunately, I was on the wrong side of this historic moment.

It came a week before we were due to play the touring Kangaroos, and I was thrilled to see a lot of them in the grandstand.

Hull kicked off and I caught the ball on our 10-metre line, with the intention of kicking it back into Hull's territory. But as I kicked the footy, their hooker Lee Jackson raced up at me and charged it down. The ball bounced back into our in-goal and Jackson pounced on it to score.

He had scored the opening try after just nine seconds!

At the time, it was the fastest try in either league or rugby union. I felt terrible, not only because it came from my kick, but because the Australian side was there to watch.

It was very embarrassing.

Luckily for me, we fought back and won the game 12–8. But we lost the Yorkshire Cup final to Wakefield Trinity 29–12.

Playing against the touring Australian side as part of their preparation for the World Cup final against Great Britain at Wembley was a tremendous honour.

I was captain of Sheffield, so I tossed the coin with my rival skipper—Allan Langer! That was such a surreal experience. I won the toss and 'Alfie' cheekily fired back, "Best of three!"

I joined an exclusive club of former Australian players to captain an English club team against the touring Aussies. This includes Chris Anderson, who did it at Halifax, and John Dorahy at Hull Kingston Rovers.

In the opposition were a couple of old Tigers' mates, Tim Brasher at fullback and Paul Sironen in the forwards.

Brasher scored two tries in the first half. When he crossed for his second, I pictured Alan Jones sitting smugly in Sydney, thinking how he should have put Brasher to fullback instead of me earlier.

Brash was racing away for a third try late in the first half. I showed him the sideline, and he went for it. I hit him low and tackled him into touch just before the corner post. Brash thought he stayed in and was blowing up. I told him to look at the touch judge's flag: "You're out Tim!"

The old 'show 'em the sideline' routine had worked again.

It didn't bother the Aussies though—they led 30-nil at halftime. Brash was given a rest in the second half and on came second-string fullback Brad Godden, a rookie who had burst onto the scene at Newcastle.

To say I was surprised to see him in the Australian squad would be an understatement. I had made myself available for selection while playing for Balmain and felt like I should have been selected.

The annual *Rugby League Week* Player Poll had named me as the game's top fullback. I was also named fullback in a 'World Team' voted on by the game's leading media commentators.

But it wasn't enough for the selectors. Brasher got the nod as their main man, and Godden was his deputy.

So, going up against the Knights' rookie, I was motivated to show the kid a thing or two.

Well, to be brutally honest, I didn't need to do much. Godden couldn't catch a cold that day. Every time we put a bomb up, he'd drop it. I beat him to the corner to score a try. He had a shocker and handed Brash his Test jersey. Godden never played representative footy again.

We 'won' the second half 22–20, the only time Australia was outscored in a half by a club team on that tour.

I was voted Sheffield's man of the match and received a silver pewter mug with my name engraved on it—still one of my cherished pieces of memorabilia.

The Eagles wanted me to play another season, but I told them I needed to have a think about it.

Back in Australia at my father-in-law's farm in Bowral in the NSW southern highlands, I received an overseas phone call. Salford secretary Graham McCarty had tracked me down. He asked if I would be their captain-coach for the next two seasons.

Graham was a good friend going back to my earlier stint with Salford in 1987/88.

We had always joked about me coming back and he knew of my interest in coaching.

The timing was perfect. I had come to realise my career in the NSWRL was over and our two boys Kieren (six) and Rhys (four) were still young enough to take overseas without disrupting their lives.

I signed a two-year deal as captain-coach of Salford. In the second season, I would move into a non-playing coach role.

A few months into the season, we learned that former Great Britain halfback Andy Gregory might be available after he fell out of favour at Leeds. I had played against Gregory many times at Test level and knew he was a quality player, even now in his later years.

We had made a slow start to the season, winning just two of our first 10 games. I needed a spark.

Leeds' coach Doug Laughton warned us about Gregory. He reckoned he would turn against us after the first year. But we pushed on regardless and signed him for two years.

To his credit, Gregory came across and played some really good football. He slotted straight into our team.

Gregory's first game with us was against Hull Kingston Rovers (HKR) on a bitterly cold day at Craven Park, in Hull.

During the game, a HKR attacker was hit by three Salford defenders. Gregory was one of them. He launched himself into the tackle and hit this poor bloke with everything he had. The HKR player was out cold. The referee and touch judges saw nothing.

On the bus ride home, I asked Gregory what happened in the tackle, because I was two metres away and also saw nothing untoward.

In his broad, distinct Widnes accent, Gregory said: "Ahh Jimmy, I hit him with me little persuader." He then raised his fist and cocked his forearm.

We won that game and went on to win seven of our next nine. I was working well with my new signing.

Our next game was against St Helens. Gregory pulled out injured on the day of the game, so I replaced him with Shaun Brown. We won 34–2. It was a record win for Salford over the Saints.

I put Gregory back into the side for the next game. We lost five in a row with him at halfback. I felt our relationship beginning to strain. I was becoming aware of little games he would play with me.

Gregory used to big-note himself about his time at glamour club Wigan. He reckoned when coach John Monie sent messages out to the team, he'd tell his teammates that it doesn't matter what Monie says because "everything has to go through me".

Despite all this, I was confident we could still work together.

After we dropped out of the top eight, I had a big decision to make. Do I stick with Andy Gregory, one of Great Britain's greatest halfbacks? Or make a change to save our season?

Gregory made it easy for me. He pulled out injured for our next game against Halifax. I brought Shaun Brown back into the team and guess what? We won 34–14.

Gregory recovered from his injury, so I put him back at halfback. We lost our next two games. That meant we had lost the last seven games with Gregory in the team.

I felt at times that he wasn't focused on the game and would even feign injuries when it suited him.

I believed this was his way of ensuring Salford didn't make it to the finals, because he wanted to take my job (which I was to find out later). The run of losses saw us finish in 12th position, well out of the finals.

As we prepared for the 1994/95 season, with me now a non-playing coach, it was put to me by someone at the club that if Gregory had an interest in becoming my assistant, it would bring out the best in him. That he would lead by example and set himself up to take over when I eventually returned to Australia.

Gregory was an extremely complex character, the life of the party. He loved to tell jokes. He could lead the team to success on the field, but he could also act like a spoilt kid.

I took him out for lunch in Monton and asked him to be my assistant coach, in addition to his playing duties. I made it crystal clear that I would be coaching the team, and he would be assisting me.

I was stunned by his response. Instead of thanking me for the opportunity, he told me he wanted to be head coach instead! Gregory suggested I would be better in a football manager type of role.

I told him that wasn't an option. He eventually agreed to be my assistant, but our 'partnership' had become a car wreck.

Gregory wouldn't show up for training sessions. He wouldn't even call to let me know.

We would go a week without speaking. Before a game against Warrington, I told him he wasn't in the team. I was fed up with his antics. I also told him to stay away from the players.

"You haven't contributed anything to the team in the past two weeks, so don't bother contributing to the team tomorrow," I told him. "I don't want to see you in the dressing sheds before the game."

Gregory just laughed.

I continued: "You think you can come and go as you please, well you can't. Your attitude is shithouse and has been for weeks. If you want to play in my team, you play by my rules. If you don't, then find somewhere else to play."

Gregory responded: "Your team?"

"Yeah—my team. And remember—I don't want to see your face in the dressing sheds before the game."

I couldn't help but think of Doug Laughton's warning. My relationship with Gregory was toxic and beyond repair. I also suspected he was trying to turn players against me.

I dropped our winger Tex Evans, someone I really liked, after he had a poor game with his hands.

I later heard that Tex had said something about me behind my back, so I fronted him at training. Suddenly, he unloads on me in front of the whole playing squad.

"You're a fuckin' c*&%—everyone here knows it; they all hate you! And you'll be gone soon!"

Another player, Richard Webster, called me an "Aussie bastard" and wanted to fight me in the coach's room when I dropped him from the team.

Throughout this saga, I was thankful I had our captain David Young in my corner. He knew about all the shit that was going on. He always supported me, and that's probably the only reason we managed to stay competitive on the pitch.

In his autobiography, *The Young One*, he accused Gregory of contributing to my downfall.

"It was always in my mind that Gregory might do anything to get his own way," Young wrote. "I had a great deal of respect for Garry Jack and did not wish to see him fall into a trap. But he was so naive. Gregory became very active behind the scenes and the writing was soon on the wall. Gregory was very clever—he started by winning the players' favour."

Along with David, I also had a great relationship with Steve Blakeley, Scott Naylor, Bobby Marsden, Craig Randall, Cliff Eccles and Nathan McEvoy. We signed former GB forward Mike Gregory (no relation) for that season. He was nothing like his namesake. A thorough professional and a gentleman. All those guys I mentioned supported me and tried hard every week.

My official demise at Salford began after a Monday evening training session in early March of 1995.

At 6.45 p.m., I was at a local bar called The Vault. Andy Gregory comes over and says the players have just approached him, and they want him to call the chairman John Wilkinson and get him down here.

"Do you know what it's about?" I asked.

"No Jimmy, I haven't a clue," he said.

I didn't believe him.

Earlier, I had overheard a conversation between two players when I was in the gents before training at 5.15 p.m. One of the players said, "I'll call the chairman at 6.45 p.m. and he'll be here at 7 p.m."

I asked Gregory if his was the voice I heard. I looked him straight in the eyes. He denied it but couldn't look at me.

Wilkinson arrived and spoke to the players. I phoned him later that night and he told me the players were not happy with the way I spoke to them, or my team selections.

It all came to a head when we played Castleford the following weekend at our home ground, The Willows. We were thumped 48–16.

Straight after the final siren, I heard a chant break out among Salford supporters.

"We want Garry Jack out!"

"Garry Jack go home!"

"Sack Jack!"

Here I was making my way down from the grandstand to speak with my players in the dressing shed, and I had to listen to this abuse. There were about 200 people there.

I'd never experienced anything like it in my 15 years at the top level of rugby league.

It was like a posse getting ready for a public hanging. It was intimidating and frightening. I had to push through them to get to the sheds.

I asked one of those doing the chanting, "What's all this about, mate?"

"We have to get rid of Garry Jack as coach," he replied.

He had no idea he was talking to the bloke he was supposedly desperate to see fired. I was even wearing my Salford blazer. That bloke had been brought in to make up the numbers. It was all set up. I had Kieren and Rhys with me as they screeched for my sacking.

It was terrible for my wife and two boys to have to put up with that abuse. Two days later, those fans got their wish.

Graham phoned at 7 p.m. to say Wilkinson wanted to see me at the club that night.

"Don't tell me you're sacking me?" I asked.

"You need to speak to the chairman, Jimmy."

I knew straight away I was gone.

Graham, a good friend in a difficult situation, met me in the lobby and took me to the boardroom. Wilkinson was already inside.

He said it was a "very difficult decision", but the club was terminating my contract. He refused to listen to my defence.

Wilkinson knew about all the trouble Gregory was causing with the players. But I was wasting my time. It was obvious a deal had been done.

I asked Wilkinson who was taking over as coach. He told me Steve O'Neill, the second-grade coach.

Two weeks later, Andy Gregory was appointed coach.

Salford won just two of their last eight games to be relegated to second division. I learned a lot about coaching during my time at Salford.

It reminded me of what Warren Ryan had once told me. "The number one rule to being a successful coach... keep the three players that hate you away from the 10 who aren't sure."

I was sacked on my 34th birthday. But you know what they say, one door shuts and another one opens.

We were heading back home.

CHAPTER 50

ONE FOR THE ROAD

I DIDN'T want my time in rugby league to end on such an ugly note at Salford.

It was a low point of my career, and I owed it to myself to finish on my own terms.

I decided to pull on the boots again.

Even though I was 34, I felt physically fresh. I hadn't played for a year. It's not like I was trying to come back from a serious injury.

Back home in Australia, I trained hard and waited to see if there was any interest.

Since I last played with Balmain in 1992, there were four new teams in the competition, now known as the Australian Rugby League (ARL).

The North Queensland Cowboys, Auckland Warriors, Western Reds and South Queensland Crushers had been admitted for the '95 season. That meant more opportunities, although a return to the Tigers was my preferred option.

Just as I was getting ready to spread the word on my comeback, a crazy thing happened.

The start of the Super League war.

On April 1, Rupert Murdoch's News Limited began a bold plan to begin a breakaway competition for the purpose of supplying sports content to its pay-TV arm, Foxtel.

The fight between News Limited and the ARL—supported by Kerry Packer—would become an extremely costly and damaging period for the game, which is well-documented.

Huge cheques were being thrown around by both parties. I thought to myself, *"Shit, I could make a comeback AND make a bit of money!"*

I put my head down and got myself in peak condition. I rang John Chalk at the Tigers to see if they were looking for a fullback. Chalky said he would speak to Junior—who had taken over from Alan Jones as head coach the previous year.

It wasn't just the coach that had changed since I'd been away. The team was no longer the 'Balmain' Tigers. They had been renamed the 'Sydney' Tigers.

The marketing geniuses reckoned it would help broaden the club's appeal (it lasted two years).

The jersey was now black and gold hoops, with some purple and white thrown in as well. Their home was Parramatta Stadium—not Leichhardt Oval.

None of it felt right to me. The club was losing its identity. But I was still keen to play.

Chalky came back with good news. They hadn't won many games, so he said Junior was keen to have me back.

I was pumped! I thought I'd never play in Australia again.

I agreed to an incentive-based contract of $3,000 per game. It wasn't about the money. Even though the Super League war had kicked-off, they could have offered me nothing and I would have said yes. I just wanted to play again. I knew I still had the ability to compete at that level and could help the team, which was still recovering from three years of Alan Jones.

My only motivation was to finish my career on the right note.

I returned in round 10 against the lowly Gold Coast Seagulls at Parramatta Stadium. We won 16–14 in front of a crowd of just 3,045. It was a far cry from winning a State of Origin series decider, but I was happy all the same.

We won a few more games, before falling in a heap. We lost eight of our last nine games.

Our only win in that time was against Parramatta, who finished second-last. I beat four defenders to score a 60-metre try in the 26–16 win. I loved the feeling of getting out in open spaces again.

Even though we were miles away from playing in the finals, it was great to play with blokes like Sirro and Brash again.

I played 13 games straight. I felt like my years of experience had helped some of our younger players. I called Chalky and asked him about going around again in '96.

A day later, Junior was on the phone.

"Hi Jimmy," he started... "It's a difficult decision to have to make, but I'd rather finish you a year too early than a year too late."

That's a nice way of saying I was gone.

One of my great mates, a guy I played Origins, Tests and grand finals with, had punted me over the phone. It was an extremely awkward conversation for both of us.

I respected Junior's decision and thanked him for giving me a chance to come back and play. But I was also disappointed because I felt I had more to offer.

To rub salt in the wounds, fellow 34-year-olds—Terry Lamb (Bulldogs), Des Hasler and Cliff Lyons (both Sea Eagles)—were all getting ready to play another season!

But I was being told I was too old.

My relationship with Junior is fine these days—we just don't talk about that particular stage of my career!

I had arrived at a point in my career that I hoped would never happen. I was going to pursue the option of playing for a rival club. It was either that or retire.

The ARL was frantically trying to sign as many players as possible to prevent Super

League from getting its rebel competition off the ground. I liked my chances of getting a contract.

It was common knowledge among players that the ARL was offering $50,000 upfront to stay loyal and not sign with Super League. Word was, if you hesitated, they'd increase it to $100,000!

That's what it was like for players during that crazy time. Christmas on steroids.

I didn't have a manager, so I picked up the phone and rang John Quayle. He was doing most of the recruitment for the ARL.

His response was blunt.

"We're not interested in signing 34-year-old fullbacks at the ARL."

"Really?"

"No, we're not interested."

That's what Quayle said to me. I gave my all to club, State and country, and that's how he put it to me. My loyalty to the ARL meant nothing. It was very disappointing to hear.

I believe Quayle's stance went all the way back to 1987 when I refused to travel to Los Angeles for that exhibition State of Origin match. Also, from when I criticised his decision not to cite Ian Roberts for what he did to me in 1991.

There was history there.

Quayle seemed to have forgotten the ARL had signed fellow veterans Hasler and Lyons to loyalty contracts. They also recruited my old Tigers' teammate Ellery Hanley—he was born in the same month as me!

He came back from England to play with the Tigers in the 1996 and 1997 seasons, earning a stack of cash in the process.

The ARL could have worked something out for me as well, but it was Quayle's way or no way.

I made the decision to call it a day. I never spoke to Super League. I didn't want to play for them because of the way they had gone about things. I also felt a sense of loyalty to the ARL, despite Quayle's arrogance.

I told Donna I was done and that was it.

I am eternally grateful that I was welcomed back to the Tigers by Junior, Chalky, and Barnesy.

I was very lucky to have had the career I had.

I played over 13 seasons with Balmain and Western Suburbs. I'd played with some players at the Tigers who were among the greatest to lace on a boot for the black and gold: Wayne Pearce, Steve Road, Ben Elias and Paul Sironen.

It was time to hang up the boots and be a good father and husband. No regrets.

CHAPTER 51

SECRETS OF MY SUCCESS

IN the mid-1970s, John Peard was terrorising opposition fullbacks with his towering punt kick, dubbed "the "bomb".

It was a new tactic and earned Peard the nickname 'Bomber' during his time with Easts and Parramatta.

About the same time as Bomber was wreaking havoc, I made the switch to fullback after spending most of my junior football in the forwards.

The ability to catch 'bombs' was now a huge part of being a good fullback. I took this part of the job very seriously.

We had four pine trees in the front yard of our family home in Cordeaux Road, Figtree. Every day, I headed outside and launched punt kicks into the air, making sure they didn't hit the trees, so I could get a clean catch.

I rode my bike down to Figtree High School and kicked bombs to myself for hours. I would aim to take 20 catches in a row. If I dropped one, my punishment was I had to start again.

I was fanatical about it.

It's one thing catching a bomb down at the local park or in the front yard. It's completely different during a game.

There are defenders chasing the kick, looking to smash you as soon as you catch it. Sometimes they're yelling at you… anything to distract you.

During games, I tried to imagine that it was just me and the four pines at home. I'd tell myself, *"Just watch the ball all the way into your arms."*

Greg Brentnall from Canterbury was the best fullback I saw under the high ball. I learned a lot from watching him as I was coming through the grades.

My technique was simple. I would bring my hands in tight to catch the ball on my chest. My knee would come up as added protection.

I would never take my eyes off the footy—that was the most important part. If it was a punt kick—like most of them were—I could comfortably predict where the ball would come down.

The torpedo bombs they launch these days are harder to pick. They can veer away and make you look silly.

I never worried about being creamed by the defence. As soon as that enters your head as a fullback, it means you're not fully focused. There's a very good chance you'll drop the ball.

My first priority of every game was to get my defence right for the first 10 minutes. My attack would come later, it was as simple as that. In my mind, it was better to save tries than to score them.

I put that down to playing as a lock forward in my minor league days and copying the cover-tackle technique of the great Ron Coote. He always tackled around the legs and that's what I modelled my game on.

I was too young to see the other legendary lock Johnny Raper play, so Coote was my idol. I wanted to be like him and play for South Sydney.

I proudly wore my Souths jersey with number 8 (that was the number for locks in those days) on the back.

Back in the late '60s early '70s, the lock forward was known as a 'sweeper'. In other words, the second line of defence from the third tackle onwards. So, moving to fullback wasn't that hard for me.

My preferred method of defence was 'showing' the sideline to the attacking player. This is when a line-break has been made, and it's just him and me. My tactic was to herd the attacker towards the sideline but give him enough space to think he had a chance of getting around me.

In a State of Origin game in 1988, Queensland winger Alan McIndoe burst down the sideline and I was coming across in cover defence.

McIndoe was a real speedster and had more pace than me. But in this instance, I knew I had him covered. The trick was, I didn't want him to know that.

As I moved closer to him, I slowed down a little to the point where he took me on and set sail for the corner. It was exactly what I wanted him to do. I then accelerated, tackled him around the legs and bundled him across the sideline.

Once McIndoe took the option of trying to burn me on the outside, it became a one-on-one where I could use the sideline to my advantage.

I'll admit it doesn't always work, though.

I once showed Great Britain winger Joe Lydon the sideline in a Test match at Old Trafford—not a very wise thing to do. In a split second he was gone and scoring a try down the other end.

After the game I was speaking to Tony Myler, the Great Britain five-eighth, and he told me that Lydon was the national 400-metre running champion.

"No one shows Joe the sideline—he gets quicker the further he has to run," Myler added.

Wish I'd known that a bit earlier!

Legendary St. George fullback Graeme 'Changa' Langlands taught me a different defensive technique.

If he was ever faced with an overlap, he wouldn't worry about waiting for the assistance of his teammates. Chang would run straight at the ball carrier and hit him as hard as he could—even if he'd already passed the ball!

He told me that even if the other team ended up scoring a try, the next time that same bloke breaks the line… "I'll be the first thing on his mind." He won't want to get smashed again, and that could see him rush a pass or a kick.

That approach worked many times for me. You take away their time and pressure them into a quick decision. It was a great lesson in fullback play and added some intimidation to my defensive arsenal.

But it backfired in a match against Wigan on the 1986 Kangaroo Tour when their captain Graeme West broke into open space.

I rushed at him like Changa said, but West was a monstrous 7-foot-tall Kiwi forward, so I had to jump off the ground to try and stop him.

Unfortunately, I got it wrong and hit him high. The referee sent me to the sin-bin!

Speaking of Langlands, he once tried to teach me how to goal-kick. It was in 1980 when I was still a rookie playing in Wollongong.

Changa kicked 648 goals for the Dragons and was a mentor to quite a few goalkickers.

Unfortunately, his coaching clinic didn't do the trick for me. I never became a goalkicker. And he wasn't impressed!

Before the second Test against Great Britain at Lang Park in 1984, we all went to the races on the Gold Coast on the Saturday. I wore my Australian team blazer and green-and-gold tie—I was proud as punch. Chang was there and we sat down for a beer.

He turned to me and said, "You were my greatest disappointment."

Having just played for Australia in a hard fought victory over the Poms, I was slightly confused. What was he talking about?

I asked him why.

"Because you can't goal-kick. You let me down."

Changa wasn't joking—he was deadly serious. I felt so deflated.

The fact is, goalkicking wasn't for me. I only kicked two goals during my entire career!

CHAPTER 52

LEGENDARY LAURIE NICHOLS

THE first time I laid eyes on Laurie Nichols, I thought he was mad.

It was my first time at a Balmain game, and I saw an old guy shadow boxing on the sidelines at a freezing Leichhardt Oval.

"Up the mighty Tiges!"

Laurie would yell this over and over as he unleashed a frenzy of left hooks and right crosses into the air.

Laurie Nichols was the Tigers' number one supporter for decades, stretching back to the 1960s.

His influence on fans—and footballers—was enormous. Balmain would allow Laurie special access onto the side of the field to help fire up the players during a game.

Laurie was famous not just for his shadow boxing, but also the chants he made up about Balmain's players (I'll get to these shortly).

I finally got the chance to meet Laurie Nichols face-to-face when I joined Balmain in 1982. Instead of the fruit loop I was expecting, I found Laurie to be a thoughtful, considerate, caring person.

Sure, he was a little bit 'out there'. But he had a great sense of humour and was as sharp as a tack.

He was fanatical about his Tigers.

I got to know Laurie very well. He lived at Springwood in the Blue Mountains and travelled down by train for each home game. He would get off at Central, catch the bus to Darling Street in Balmain, then walk the rest of the way to Leichhardt Oval. If I saw him walking, I'd pull over and give him a lift.

Laurie only ever wore a black and gold singlet and a pair of old-style trousers. I never saw him wear anything else.

Even when he went on a Kangaroo Tour during the middle of winter in England, he still trotted out in his beloved singlet.

Actually, I *did* see Laurie in a jacket once. It was at my Testimonial dinner when he wore a coat and tie. I almost didn't recognise him!

Even if you'd just played the worst game of your life, Laurie always had your back. He was incredibly loyal and that's why we adored him.

Our coach Cranky Franky Stanton knew how much the boys loved Laurie. One day, he invited him into the dressing room before a game against Souths to make a speech.

After Frank handed over to him, Laurie made a strong start. But then his passion for the beloved black and gold got the better of him.

Within two minutes, Laurie was a blubbering mess. I'm talking uncontrollable crying. He was so emotional about how much Balmain meant to him.

Watching on, we couldn't believe what we were seeing. A lot of us started to cry as well! Don't forget, this was an era where grown men were not meant to show emotion.

We went on to win the game, but I don't think Frank was impressed. He never again asked Laurie to make a pre-game speech.

Laurie's famous shadow boxing wasn't just for show, I can assure you. He could handle himself, even aged in his 60s.

Growing up in country NSW, Laurie did a lot of boxing training. He was taught how to fight in the old 'Sharman tents' that travelled from town to town. Punters could step inside and fight one of the Sharman boxers and have a bet on themselves to win.

Laurie told me that before the Sharmans accepted him as one of their fighters, he had to promise three things:

Only fight to defend yourself.

Train every day.

Never be the aggressor.

He lived by those principles every day. Whenever we went to Chinatown in the city for a feed after a game, Laurie would join us. But not in his usual role as no.1 fan. He would be our security.

There were always loudmouths around and some of them would have a crack at us—or Laurie. They thought of him as the mad, old Tigers' fan in the singlet. They would try and provoke him.

Laurie was good at shrugging it off. He'd heard it all before.

But one night, a couple of blokes just wouldn't leave it alone. They went too far—and soon discovered Laurie possessed a ripping uppercut.

Two punches were all it took. They were both on the ground. It was all over.

One of Laurie's other great gifts was coming up with catchcries for us players. He would sing them out during games. Eventually they became part of the vernacular for all Tigers' supporters.

My one was, "Jimmy Jack, world's best back."

There was a different one at the very start of my career, but it didn't last long.

"Garry Jack, leaves them on their back."

I could see what Laurie was getting at, but we decided it could possibly be misconstrued.

Laurie had a stack of good ones:

"Steve Roach, eats them on toast."

"Benny Elias, come and try us."

"Wayne Pearce, he's so fierce."

"Trevor Ryan, made of iron."

"Sound the alarm, it's Allan McMahon."

"Sirro, Sirro our hero."

"David Brooks destroys good looks."

His timing was always perfect. Laurie would know when to wind up the crowd. If we were struggling in a game, it wasn't long before we would hear Laurie revving them up in the grandstand.

During my playing career, I also featured in Aussie rhyming slang—and still do, apparently.

People will ask, "How's your Garry Jack?" In other words, "How's your back?"

I bumped into Test batsman Usman Khawaja at a function, and he told me all the cricketers still use that expression. We both had a laugh and deep down, I was a little bit proud.

My favourite Laurie Nichols story was when he stayed overnight at my unit in Five Dock, which I was sharing with teammate Bill Kain. It was April 1983, after we'd been to Chinatown one Saturday night.

Dad had been to the races at Randwick, so he came back to our joint as well. It wasn't long before we realised the sleeping arrangements were an issue. We had no spare beds, just two bean bags.

No problem. Laurie and Dad plonked themselves down and they talked and talked and talked. Dad had a great night.

Next time I saw Laurie, he said, "How is old Bean Bag going?"

"Who?"

"Your old man, Bean Bag."

Dad had a new nickname, courtesy of a night with Laurie Nichols.

Laurie would ask after 'Bean Bag' every time I saw him. I told Dad and he loved it.

Laurie was very influential with the Balmain supporter base.

In 1998/99 when the Tigers were exploring the possibility of a joint venture with the Magpies, Laurie didn't want a bar of it. He was a Balmain boy through and through.

This was a problem for the Tigers, who were cash-strapped and needing to merge to survive. If Laurie went public with his opposition, the vote was no chance of getting up.

After lots of talking, John Chalk and Keith Barnes eventually convinced Laurie to support the proposal.

The loss of Balmain as a single entity at NRL level broke Laurie's heart.

On the Wednesday before the new Wests Tigers were scheduled to play their inaugural game, Laurie died from an ulcer rupture in his stomach.

He was 81.

Some said it was fate. Like he couldn't bring himself to watch Balmain join a rival club.

I was very sad when I heard the news.

Laurie Nichols was just as much Balmain as any of us players. Fans would come to watch us—and Laurie.

He was never paid to entertain the crowd or pump up the players, and he never asked.

A genuine Tigers' legend. Laurie did it for his love of the Tigers.

And I loved Laurie.

CHAPTER 53

PORTALOO LESSON

THERE were lots of loyal people involved with the Balmain Tigers during my time at the club. Even though they didn't have the high profile of Laurie Nichols, they equally would do anything for us players.

Dickie, one of the team's 'rubbers' (masseuses), was one of those such people.

During the 1988 season we were taking on the Newcastle Knights at their home ground of Marathon Stadium. It was their first year in the competition and there was a big crowd.

Right from kick-off, I was copping it from a Knights' fan on the eastern side of the ground, which was a big, grassy hill back in those days.

This guy had a real problem with me.

He was screaming out that I was "hopeless", and that I was a "cat". There were other colourful adjectives as well.

Dickie had a reputation at our club for calling out bad behaviour from fans. He just wouldn't cop it. And he heard every single word from this loudmouth. So, Dickie marched straight over to where this clown was sitting.

"You can't speak about the Australian fullback that way," he said.

This bloke wouldn't back down. He again called me hopeless.

"I'm sorry, but you can't say that about the Australian fullback," Dickie repeated.

Full of ink, old mate then trekked up to use one of the temporary Portaloos that were lined up along the top of the hill.

For a bit of context, the hill at Marathon was a pretty decent size. Not quite the Himalayas, but it was a fair way up.

Anyway, this bloke went inside the Portaloo to do his business—and that's when Dickie struck.

Defending my honour, he gave the Portaloo a big shove from behind and sent it hurtling down the hill with old mate still inside!

It tumbled about 30 metres down the hill before coming to rest just inside the fence, near the playing surface.

The door flung open, and this bloke lurched out covered in filth, wondering what on earth happened. We never heard another word out of him for the rest of the day.

Thank you, Dickie!

CHAPTER 54

SCRUBBER, YOU BLOODY LEGEND

RUGBY league is full of characters who can give you a laugh and, when needed, remind you it's only just a game.

A man very close to my heart was Greg Brazier. He was my second cousin but was far more than that. He was a mate.

Better known as 'Scrubber', he was a legend of the Wests Red Devils. Along with Ian 'Chook' Neil, he ensured all our juniors had an opportunity to play at the highest level.

He was a character in the 'rough diamond' mould. For years, Scrubber would party until 3 a.m., then dash home to do his father's Mt Keira milk run.

His liking for a schooner of Tooheys New sent brewery profits soaring.

Scrubber was called 'The Phantom Tackler' after his penchant for tackling VIPs. Many were felled in comical circumstances due to this bizarre trait.

Wollongong Lord Mayor Frank Arkell, cricket legends Viv Richards and Dennis Lillee, tennis great John Newcombe and rugby league Immortal Johnny Raper all fell victim to The Phantom Tackler.

His mates once had to talk him out of tackling the Duke of Edinburgh at a Sydney function!

Whereas another person would have been off to the lock-up for similar actions, everyone laughed it off. They were just notches on the belt for Scrubber.

He was on a cruise ship once with a bunch of mates when they were kicked-off at Hong Kong. An elderly couple had complained about Scrubber's conduct.

No sooner had Scrubber's crew been dumped on the wharf than every other passenger walked off in protest! The only ones left on board were the whingeing old couple.

Another great story was when he played third-grade cricket for Mount Keira, who hadn't won a game all season.

At stumps, Scrubber rang through to the local radio station, 2WL, and gave announcer Sid Hayes the scores to read out in his sport report. The news was so good,

Hayes could hardly wait to tell his listeners.

"Mount Keira has finished day one at none for 385... with Greg Brazier 198 not out, including 10 sixes and 15 fours!"

There was only one problem. Mount Keira had been bowled out for double-figures and Greg Brazier barely troubled the scorers. Scrubber had made the whole thing up!

Sid never spoke to him again.

Scrubber was Australian through and through. As an Aussie, he would play 'Hoges' (Paul Hogan) off a break. He was the Crocodile Dundee of sports in the Illawarra.

He often told people there were two types of people in the world—Australians and those who would like to be Australians. And most of all he loved, admired and sang the praises of Illawarra and its sportsmen and women, wherever he went.

Scrubber's life took a turn after a melanoma was discovered on his back. Surgeons in Sydney performed a massive operation to try and prevent the cancer from spreading.

Scrubber took the operation in his stride, and it wasn't long before he was back at Western Suburbs Leagues Club and Coniston Pub, showing his mates the scars and grinning defiantly in the face of adversity.

For five years, the cancer lay dormant. Scrubber went on grabbing every day like an orange and squeezing every drop of pleasure out of it.

He never complained... even when the dreaded thing returned. He received care at his home, including from Donna.

Not long before he passed away on July 28, 1986, Scrubber had watched Blocker Roach collect the man-of-the-match award at the SCG as Australia thrashed New Zealand. A week earlier, I had won the same recognition after our victory in the first Test in Auckland.

Two Red Devils' players doing good. Scrubber was proud.

Steve and I were two of the pallbearers at his funeral at West Wollongong United Church. I'm not sure who said it, but there was a very apt line from the service.

"If you could bottle Scrubber Brazier's down-to-earth charisma and distribute it to the four corners of the world, all problems would be solved."

He was a one-off.

Scrubber was laid to rest next to his parents Harry and Gladys Brazier, and just down from his Uncle Jimmy (Pop) and my nan and the rest of our extended family at Lakeside Cemetery in Kanahooka.

Thanks Scrubber—I will never forget our time together.

CHAPTER 55
THE EIGHTH WONDER

LEICHHARDT Oval will forever be the spiritual home of the Balmain Tigers and the modern-day Wests Tigers.

Tucked away down Mary Street in Rozelle, it's hailed as "The Eighth Wonder of the World". There's nowhere else quite like it.

So, what is it about Leichhardt Oval that makes it so special to play there?

Well, when you go through the old turnstiles at the Mary Street end, your first look at the ground is from behind the goalposts. Immediately, you feel close to the players—and in the old days, to the incomparable Laurie Nicholls shadow boxing down on the sideline.

As a player, you could always feel the energy of the crowd. Didn't matter if there were 10,000 or 20,000 fans there, we always knew we could win.

In the Warren Ryan era of 1988–90, we won 34 of 39 games at Leichhardt Oval, at the impressive success rate of 87.17%. We lost five games at home in three years.

My first game in first grade there for Balmain came in round 5, 1982, against the highly fancied Rabbitohs. The roar of the crowd as we ran out of the tunnel was unbelievable.

We were fighting hard but trailed 8–7 with only 10 minutes remaining. It was then that Olsen Filipaina was unleashed from the bench by coach Frank Stanton.

The Big O absolutely smashed Souths captain Mitch Brennan to dislodge the ball, and John Davidson scored one tackle later to win us the game, 12–8.

The noise from the crowd after Olsen's tackle was like nothing I had ever heard before. There were just 9,443 fans there that day, but it sounded like 90,000.

The crowd—and Olsen—got us home.

My first ever visit to Leichhardt Oval came in 1978 with my cousin Scrubber. We were there to watch the Illawarra representative team play in the Amco Cup quarter-finals against Easts. I was hobbling around on crutches due to an ankle injury.

Another Wests Red Devils' old boy, the legendary Bob 'Bozo' Fulton, was playing for Easts that year but was out injured. Scrubber knew Bozo from their days in the 'Gong, so we managed to have a chat with him during the game.

While we were talking, Scrubber grabbed me and said to Fulton, "This kid is going to play for Australia one day."

Bozo sort of smiled and said he hoped so. It was a bit embarrassing at the time, but I appreciated Scrubber's confidence in me.

There's another standout memory from my first trip to Leichhardt.

On the way into the ground, we bought a hot dog from a vendor. It smelled that damn good we couldn't resist. To this very day, I swear I was served by a young Wayne Pearce, who would later become a great teammate of mine.

I looked at the ground that night and thought about how good it would be to play there.

A special part of Leichhardt for us players was 'Wimpy's Well'.

This was a private retreat for the players underneath the Keith Barnes Stand at the southern end of the ground.

It was set up by Ray 'Wimpy' Gerrie and his wife Merrell in 1984 as a place for the players to relax after training or a game. It was named the 'Well' from Bruce Springsteen's hit song, Glory Days, which includes the line:

"Think I'm going down to the well tonight, and I'm gonna drink 'til I get my fill."

I'll never underestimate the impact Wimpy's Well had on everyone at Balmain.

Our mateship and culture flourished in that small room under the grandstand.

Leichhardt also brought out the best in us in four-quarter football. Our home ground hosted much of the mid-week competition, because the light towers were the best in Sydney (outside the SCG).

We made the final four years in a row from 1985–88, winning it twice in '85 and '87. The Tigers won 14 out of 15 games at Leichhardt during the National Panasonic Cup.

Overall, I played 117 games there for Balmain, the same number as the great Benny Elias. I played another three with Wests, giving me a total of 120 appearances at The Eighth Wonder.

I'm proud to say that's more than anyone else. It's a mark unlikely to be topped, because these days the Wests Tigers only play three games a year at Leichhardt. If only the Winfield Cup grand finals were played at Leichhardt Oval, we would have won two or three premierships.

It was our very own *Field of Dreams*.

CHAPTER 56

BEST COACH BLOW-UP

I KNOW what you're thinking—this must be an anecdote about Warren Ryan, one of the most intimidating coaches of the modern era.

But surprisingly it *wasn't* The Wok who produced the biggest coaching blow-up I witnessed during my career.

Instead that distinction goes to Balmain's reserve grade coach of 1982, Laurie Freier.

Laurie was a bloke who liked to be in complete control. He was a big, strong bastard too.

We had a guy in our Balmain team called Wayne Innes. He was a halfback who played first grade the previous season.

He was a good guy. An ex-copper who was a bit of a pretty boy. His nickname was 'Mirrors' because he loved looking at his own reflection.

During a game, Wayne decided to try a chip-and-chase inside his own quarter just before halftime.

It's always a high-risk play and unfortunately for Wayne, it didn't come off. The other team picked up the bouncing ball and scored a try. The siren sounded and we trudged into the dressing room to hear from our coach.

Laurie wasn't happy. When he saw Wayne come in and take a seat, he gave him both barrels.

"You don't chip-and-chase in your own quarter!"

Wayne just sat there, motionless. He may have been absorbing the comments, I don't know. But to Laurie it looked like Wayne didn't give a shit about anything he was saying.

The coach was now steaming.

He flew over to where Wayne was sitting, picked him up, and shoved him backwards into the wall. The impact was so hard, a few tiles cracked and fell to the floor.

Laurie had lost it!

The rest of us were sitting around thinking, *"What the f#%@ is this?"*

These days, any coach who carried on like that would be out of the job the same afternoon, and probably unemployable.

But back then, we all just got on with it.

At our end-of-year awards night, Laurie was awarded the dubious title of "The Yahoo Flipping Idiot of the Year". And guess who came out and presented the award?

Yep, his old mate Wayne Innes.

To show that all was forgiven, Wayne even strapped a broken tile to the back of his dinner suit!

CHAPTER 57
HAVING A BLINDER

RUGBY league these days is cleaner than it's ever been.

When I was playing, spear tackles, high tackles and all-in brawls were part of the game.

There were also 'facials'.

This would happen in just about every tackle. Someone on the defensive team would shove their hand in your face and massage it in a very unfriendly manner.

The 'Christmas hold' was another.

This expression comes from the tradition of getting 'nuts' for Christmas. I don't think I need to explain that any further…other than to say there was one game against St. George where I feared I'd never be able to have any kids!

You might read this and ask why I didn't complain to the referee?

It would have been a waste of time. It was a tough sport, and the refs treated most of this stuff as part of the game. Because there were only a few cameras used in the television broadcast, it was very difficult to prove any on-field allegations.

There were plenty of sneaky tactics designed to put players off their game.

A popular one involved players secreting a blob of Dencorub or Tiger Balm into the top of their socks.

When they made a tackle, they would reach into their socks and smear the liniment across their opponent's face.

Let me assure you, their promotions are spot on when they boast "fast-acting". Within seconds, your eyes were burning. It was impossible to see, and you'd need a trainer to come out with a sponge before you could start playing again.

It would occasionally happen with grease too, which I could handle. But Tiger Balm was another story. People could be blinded by that stuff. It was incredibly reckless.

I was playing the Bulldogs once in the mid-80s and I ran the ball into one of their forwards. They were great defenders, but this tackle felt even harder than normal. Like I'd run into a reinforced concrete barrier.

Something felt wrong about it.

Anyway, it came out later that some Bulldogs' players of that era were using ice-hockey pads instead of conventional rugby league shoulder pads.

These things were big and bulky and full of fibreglass. Completely illegal in our game.

Before a game, players would put on their normal shoulder pads for the mandatory pre-game inspection. Then as soon as the touch judge left the room, they would swap them over for the ice-hockey pads.

I'm sure Canterbury wasn't the only club doing it. But the Dogs were eventually exposed, and thankfully, we never saw it again.

CHAPTER 58
YOU'VE BEEN SERVED

NOT all injuries in rugby league are because of foul play or blatant thuggery.

Sometimes they are simply the result of playing the most physical team sport in the world.

I can vouch for this after what happened to me following a tackle I made during the 1987 season.

We were playing a mid-week semi-final in the National Panasonic Cup against Eastern Suburbs at Belmore Sports Ground. I was backing up just 24 hours after playing for NSW in State of Origin I at Lang Park.

Roosters' second-rower John Mackay made a half-break and was preparing to pass the ball inside our quarter. It was a close game and things were looking dicey for us. It was my job to try and shut down this attacking raid.

As I got to Mackay, he swivelled to pass, and I hit him across the top of the shoulders in a wrapping motion with my right arm. I was trying to prevent him from offloading the footy to a teammate. It was a tackle I had made many times in my career.

Mackay managed to pass the ball, but he fell awkwardly with me on top of him. He let out a terrible groan as we both hit the ground.

I regained my feet and asked Mackay if he was okay. He didn't reply and just lay there. I could see his leg was at a strange angle.

My teammate Ross Conlon took one look at Mackay and said it was a dislocated hip. Rosco knew what he was talking about because the same thing happened to him a few years earlier.

Referee Kevin Roberts issued me with a caution and penalised me for a high tackle. In my opinion, it was the wrong call. I never hit him in the head. It was the way he fell that injured his hip.

We won the game 14–12 and then news came through that I had been cited by Easts.

NSWRL boss John Quayle looked at the footage and decided to take no further action.

The injury put Mackay out for the rest of the season, which was a shame. Thankfully, he was able to come back and play the following year with Easts.

My conscience was clear. It wasn't a dangerous tackle. It was just hard and aggressive. No one likes to see another player injured, but I had done nothing wrong.

Mackay dislocated his hip after falling awkwardly. He didn't suffer a broken jaw or a fractured cheekbone. His injury was not caused by any high contact.

A couple of months later, I had just finished training with the Tigers when a guy came up to me behind the Leichhardt Oval grandstand.

"You Garry Jack?"

"Yeah—why?"

"This is for you. You've been served."

He then stuck a court summons in my hand. John Mackay was suing me for damages to the tune of $100,000.

I engaged high-profile solicitor Chris Murphy to represent me. We took another look at the footage and there was no contact with the head. It was a ball-and-all tackle.

There was talk Mackay's legal team was happy to settle the issue out of court. I asked Chris about this, and he said it would be cheaper to settle than run the case in court, even if I was completely innocent of any wrongdoing.

A settlement figure was reached and accepted by Mackay.

Throughout it all, the Tigers were backing me the whole way. Bill Anderson—our coach in '87—was very supportive and we met regularly.

Bill and the club knew I wasn't a dirty player. It was an accident. And that's the thing in rugby league—accidents happen.

As traumatic as it was for Mackay, the whole experience was a traumatic time for my family as well.

I never saw him again.

CHAPTER 59

RUGBY LEAGUE'S TIGHTEST MAN

I WAS taught the value of money from a very young age.

Mum and Dad had a favourite expression: "A penny saved is a penny earned."

It really resonated with me... and led to me gaining a reputation as rugby league's biggest tight-arse.

In my time at Balmain, I won the 'Big Spender' award at the end-of-year presentation on no less than 10 occasions. The boys would throw coins at me while I was on stage getting my award. I'd bend down and scoop them all up. Thanks boys!

They used to call me 'Diamond Jimmy Jack—the Tightest Man in the World'. Apparently, I hung on to two-dollar coins so tightly the Queen would wince!

I'm not going to deny all the stories about me. Most are true. Like the one with the toll collector.

We had finished training early one night at Leichhardt Oval at about 5.30 p.m. A lot of guys headed for their cars to go home. Others went to Wimpy's Well, under the old grandstand, for a feed and a Coke.

I stayed out in the middle of Leichhardt for some more practice under the high ball. I went for another hour or so on my own before heading into Wimpy's.

The first bloke I ran into was Bruce McGuire.

"Geez you're committed Jimmy," he gushed. "You're out there kicking and catching the ball when everyone else has gone home. I reckon that's amazing."

It was nice to hear. But Bruce didn't know the full story.

I was still living in Wollongong at that stage of my career. The main route to and from Sydney was via the old F6. Back in those days, you had to pay a toll of 40 cents at Waterfall.

Because I was making the trip so regularly, I got to know one of the guys who worked as a toll collector. He was a mad footy fan and recognised me. We occasionally had a quick chat as I fumbled around for my 40 cents.

One day, he saw me approaching and waved me through. Just like that. No charge! Happy days.

I made sure I remembered what he looked like. Each trip, I would slow down as I approached the toll booths so I could pick out which lane he was in.

If I went in his lane, he'd let me through for nothing every time.

I was very grateful to this legend. On one trip, I had a box of fruit with me, so I gave him some grapes as a thank you.

The only catch was—his shift started at 8 p.m.

I worked out that it was roughly a 45-minute drive from Leichhardt to Waterfall, so I couldn't leave training before 7.15 p.m. Otherwise, I'd arrive too early and my mate wouldn't have bundied on.

I had to fess up to Bruce. I couldn't sit there any longer and accept his praise under false pretences.

"Mate, I can't leave early otherwise I've got to pay the 40 cents in tolls."

It wasn't long before my secret was out, and my reputation grew.

I wasn't the only Tigers' player who occasionally skipped the toll.

In those early days, I used to drive up from Wollongong with Blocker Roach for training.

We had an arrangement: if it was my turn to drive, Block would have to pay the 40 cents. And vice-versa.

We were approaching the tollgates one day when I noticed Block rummaging through his pockets. He was looking for coins because it was his turn to pay. Blocker stopped and looked over at me.

"Sorry Jimmy—I've forgotten my wallet mate. I haven't got any money."

I had left my wallet at home too because I figured I didn't need it.

"Well, I don't have any money either!" I snapped. "What are we going to do?"

After a moment or two of silence, Block came up with a plan.

"Don't worry Jimmy. If he doesn't let us through ... I'll f&%$en bash him!"

We arrived at the tollgates and I tried to explain our situation to the gentleman in the booth.

"Look, we come here every day, we're young blokes, and we don't have any money today."

He just looked at us, saying nothing. I was getting nowhere. Blocker suddenly leaned across me, coming into the toll collector's view. I tried a different tack.

"Look, if you don't let us through, this bloke is going to rip your arms off."

Blocker then let out an almighty growl like a hungry grizzly bear. The bloke shit himself and waved us through!

Another famous story was on the 1986 Kangaroo Tour.

I kept all my spare change in a glass in my hotel room in Leeds just in case I wanted to buy a snack or a newspaper. At one stage, it was up to 40 quid.

Then suddenly, it was gone. Nothing left. I asked my roommate Gary Belcher about it, and he eventually confessed to 'borrowing' it.

There are different versions of this story, depending on who's doing the talking.

In Paul Sironen's autobiography, *Sirro! Tales from Tiger Town*, the big fella wrote: "Belcher rolled back into their room at about 3 a.m. on the morning of the third Test.

"As Belch tiptoed across the room in a valiant attempt not to disturb Jimmy's slumber, he just about crapped his 'dacks' when Jimmy suddenly rolled over and boomed in his foghorn voice, 'Badge, I'm missing three quid from my glass. Did you take it?'

"That was so much like my mate Jimmy—despite the fact he had an international to play, he spent the entire night tossing and turning because he was determined to get to the bottom of the missing money."

Hey Sirro—it was more than three quid, mate!

On the final leg of that tour, each player was rewarded with a slab of XXXX, courtesy of our major sponsor, Castlemaine Perkins brewery.

It's quite cold in France during winter, so I put my beers on the windowsill in my hotel room to keep them chilled.

One night, I was drinking at the hotel bar with Mal, Badge, Bert and a few of the other boys. When it came time for my shout, I ran upstairs to my room and grabbed a nice, cool six-pack of XXXX. I returned to the bar and handed them out.

Didn't the boys blow up! They were filthy that I'd used the free beers for my shout instead of paying at the bar.

I don't know what they were so unhappy about—XXXX was better quality beer than what they were serving us. And I saved myself 50 bucks!

I never minded being the butt of jokes for being thrifty.

But let me say this—I ain't the only one who was careful with a dollar.

Des Hasler and Terry Lamb would give me a run for my money—pardon the pun —in the tight-arse stakes. I learned stuff off those two guys I didn't even know was possible.

We were staying at the Dragonara Hotel in Leeds on the 'Roo Tour when I spotted Des and Baa having a cup of tea together.

"Hey fellas, mind if I join you?"

My friendly query was ignored. They just sat there in silence. Didn't say a word to me. I started to think about what I must have done to upset these blokes.

After about five minutes of awkwardness, Baa said, "Unless you buy us a cup of tea, we aren't going to talk to you."

So, I bought them a cup of tea and we chatted away. That's how they saved some cash.

Somehow, I don't think I was their only victim.

There are plenty of stories and we could go on forever. Bruce McGuire often reminds me of one from our time playing together at Sheffield.

We had a round of golf at Royal Lindrick, but Bruce kept losing his balls in the drink. I had no spares, so he asked me to get some more off the kid who was selling them on the other side of the fairway.

I bought three from the kid, then caught up with Bruce and handed them over.

"That's three for five quid," I told him. He handed over the cash and we kept playing.

Unfortunately, Bruce's form never improved and he lost all three balls with two holes still to play.

He wanted to finish the round, so he found the kid and gave him five quid for three more balls. Bruce thanked him and then walked off.

"Oi," yelled the kid from behind. "You forgot your change."

Bruce headed back and was given three quid. "It's three for two quid, mate," said the kid.

"How long have they been at that price?"

"They've always been that price, mate."

Bruce pondered this for a second, then screamed in my direction. "JIMMMMMMMY—YOU BASTAAAAAARD!!!!"

Everyone has a Jimmy Jack story. I didn't mind people having a good time at my expense. That's what rugby league is all about—having a laugh with your mates!

CHAPTER 60

A MOMENT I WILL NEVER FORGET

FOR our 30th wedding anniversary on 2 November 2015, Donna and I decided to do something that would change our lives. There was no lying on the sand in Fiji or climbing the Eiffel Tower for a kiss. We walked the Kokoda Track.

Our son Rhys joined us as we retraced the 1942 footsteps of the Australian Army/militia who pushed the Japanese Army back over the Owen Stanley Range and away from Port Moresby. Four months of strength and sacrifice from our troops ultimately led to the defeat of Japan and stopped their plan to invade Australia.

It was a time of reflection for all of us, especially Donna, as her pop Albert Felix Verhaeghe was a heavy vehicle driver for the militia during the conflict. Donna had his war medals in her backpack as we walked. We often talked about Albert and what it must have been like for him.

Charlie Lynn, who fought in the Vietnam War, was our travel guide. He had done the 96-kilometre trek an incredible 82 times! At the age of 71, he was a genuine character and an inspiration. He was a tough bastard but a great leader and friend to all.

Donna, Rhys and I trained for six months in the lead-up to our trek. Every weekend, we would walk two to three hours around either Cherrybrook, Manly or the Blue Mountains with our backpacks on. But even that didn't adequately prepare us for how tough the walk was going to be as we traversed the rugged mountains and dense rainforest of Papua New Guinea along a muddy, steep track.

It's very dangerous terrain, but we were in great hands with Charlie. His 'entourage' included 'Big Joe'—an old PNG rugby league player weighing 110 kilos and standing around six foot four. He was in charge and kept us safe along the trek.

What strikes you straight away is the landscape and the mountains that go on forever and ever. We walked to the small village of Menari where we found kids selling packets of Twisties and cans of Fanta and Coke, which we gratefully purchased.

Charlie talked us through the battles that raged around these parts more than 70 years earlier and how the local Fuzzy Wuzzy Angels helped carry injured Australian soldiers to safety.

Pretty soon, it started bucketing down with rain, which set the tone for the week. Everything we were carrying was completely saturated, but at least it meant we didn't have to take our boots off while crossing the river. They couldn't get any wetter! And even though there was plenty of rain, we still managed to enjoy stunning sunsets every day.

Templeton's Crossing and Brigade Hill are significant historical battleground areas along the Kokoda Track where the Japanese were forced back. We had our first look at trenches dug by Aussies.

We sat around the fire at night, having a rum with Charlie and hanging off his every word. That also gave us time to dry out our clothes and socks!

We reached the village of Efogi after four days of walking, which always began nice and early at 4.30 a.m. There is no going back from that point. You're in the middle of nowhere. If I had my cardiac arrest on the Kokoda Track, I would have been history.

All the boys in the village (about 10) were out in a paddock playing rugby league when we came walking through. Interestingly, they were using a Sherrin AFL ball. But they weren't playing Aussie Rules. Rugby league is a religion in PNG, and they were all doing their best Benji Marshall sidesteps. For an old footy guy like me, it was great to see.

As they were having fun with their mates, I couldn't resist joining in. But it didn't take long for my body to remind me I was 54 years old. There was no magic from me!

That night, the villagers played some traditional PNG music and had a small choir sing for us, which made us feel very welcome.

The Isurava Memorial was the highlight of our trek for me. The Battle of Isurava was the first major battle of the campaign. The site now serves as a place of remembrance and reflection for those who fought, including the young soldiers of the 39th Battalion.

There are four granite pillars erected to commemorate Papua New Guinea and Australian soldiers who fought and died during the Kokoda Track campaign in World War II. The Battle of Isurava shattered the myth of Japanese invincibility and demonstrated the resilience of the Australian forces.

Inscribed on each granite pillar, standing 10 feet tall and weighing 3.5 tonnes, are the words "Courage", "Endurance", "Mateship" and "Sacrifice". They represent the core values of the soldiers who fought and died along the track.

The three of us stood there, holding Donna's grandfather's war medals, very proud of what Albert Felix Verhaeghe had done for his adopted country after relocating from Belgium following the end of World War I. We now understood a lot more about the sacrifices Albert and the previous generation had made for us.

It was an incredibly powerful moment for our family and one I will never forget. As I looked across the magnificent valley adorned by spectacular mountain peaks, I whispered, "Thank you."

Lest we forget.

CHAPTER 61

DONNA JACK

THERE are so many moments from Garry's career that fill me with pride.

His debut for Australia in 1984 is one that stands out.

Garry wanted to wear the green and gold so badly. I was his girlfriend at the time, and I couldn't wait to get to the SCG and cheer him on from the grandstand.

There was just one problem. I had a double-booking.

Saturday, June 9, was also the wedding date for my best friend. And I was in the bridal party!

It was an early afternoon wedding, so once the formalities were over, I said my goodbyes and raced to the SCG to grab my seat in the Members' Stand. I was still in my bridesmaid's dress and heels as Garry ran out for the kick-off!

But that's the life of being married to a professional sportsman. You never know what's around the corner.

The first time I met Garry, I was taken by his rugged good looks, mop of blond hair, beautiful blue eyes and muscly arms (no, Garry didn't write this for me!).

On our first date, the big thing I learned was how much he loved his family. For me, that was the biggest tick of all.

As I was a relatively accomplished sportswoman at a young age (nothing compared to Garry though), we had much in common.

I knew the game of rugby league well because my father had a very successful career for Bowral and the Mittagong Lions during the 1960s. I watched footy every weekend with Dad (not that I EVER envisaged marrying a footballer).

When we first started talking about getting married, I had just become a registered nurse at the Royal North Shore Hospital. I decided it would be a good time for me to take a holiday and really think if this was the life I truly wanted.

I trekked to California to stay with a friend of my mum's for a few weeks. When I arrived back to Sydney Airport, Garry was waiting for me with roses and a ring.

As they say, the rest is history.

Cathy (Roach), Terri (Pearce) and I all wedded at the end of the 1985 season within six weeks of each other. Balmain was a very close-knit club!

Then came the babies. We all had our first children at around the same time. You can imagine what it was like at the club.

We would all sit up the back of the main stand at Leichhardt Oval, breastfeeding our babies, while trying our hardest to be discreet and not offend anyone (different times then).

After the arrival of many more babies, Keith Barnes organised an area in the old grandstand for us all to sit instead. Maybe Keith had received complaints about too many flashes of breasts.

Whatever the reason, it was nice to get away from Mr Elias' (Benny's dad's) cigar smoke!

Life was incredibly busy. I remember one of the girls saying, "Even though they (our husbands) are home, they are not at home."

This was so very true. I think the downtime for Garry was when he was at work. Yes, they did work in those days, on top of the footy.

I was full of admiration for Garry's 100 percent commitment to any of the teams he played for, whether that be his beloved Tigers, NSW or Australia.

I loved his loyalty to Balmain, which had so much to do with the late, great Keith Barnes. And of course, his teammates like Block, Junior, Benny, Sirro, Brash, Bruce, Brooksy… I could go on and on.

To this day, it is just so nice to see them all together when we go to functions. Nothing has changed, just a few more pounds, grey hairs and wrinkles—although some may dispute this!

My proudest memories of Garry have been with our three sons—Kieren, Rhys and Brandon.

I remember having long days with a very active Kieren and baby Rhys. Then Garry would come home from training and take over. He would go straight up to see Rhys and pat him off to sleep, then play with Kieren until it was his bedtime.

The boys came to every game with me in Sydney, even the away games. As long as they had snacks, books and pencils, they were happy.

After every game, they would go into the dressing sheds to see their dad. I think they just liked to go for the bottles of Coke that Mum wasn't supposed to know about!

Brandon came along whilst Garry was coaching in England, which meant he had more time to be around.

The three boys were the apple of their father's eye and still are to this day.

They have each grown into amazing, talented young men, of which we are so proud.

Kieren and his wife Charlotte have given us a beautiful little grandson, Alfie, as well as twins Clara and Hugo.

He brings so much love and laughter to us all. We are so grateful to be making many memories to cherish as the years go by.

Yes, there is life after football.

GARRY JACK PLAYING RECORD[1]

AUSTRALIAN CLUB CAREER

Western Suburbs (1981)

5 matches, 1 try.

Balmain/Sydney Tigers (1982–1992, 1995)

244 matches, 60 tries, 1 goal, 1 field goal.

2 Mid-week cup final wins.

22 pre-season and mid-season games.

ENGLISH CLUB CAREER

Salford (1987, 1993)

50 matches, 13 tries.

Sheffield (1992)

32 matches, 7 tries, 1 field goal.

1 tour game vs Australia, 1 try.

REPRESENTATIVE CAREER

Australia (1984–1988)

22 Tests, 11 tries.

5 Test series wins, 3 Ashes series wins, 1 World Cup final win.

12 tour games, 9 tries.

New South Wales (1984–1989)

17 matches, 1 try.

2 State of Origin series wins.

City Firsts (1984–1985)

2 matches.

Country Firsts (1986–1987)

2 matches.

1 https://www.rugbyleagueproject.org/players/garry-jack/summary.html

TOTAL CAREER

412 games
103 tries
2 goals
1 field goal

MAJOR AWARDS

Dally M Fullback of the Year (1985)
Dally M Representative Player of the Year (1985)
National Panasonic Try of the Year (1985)
Dally M Fullback of the Year (1986)
Golden Boot Award (1986)
Dally M Fullback of the Year (1988)
Australian Sports Medal for services to rugby league (2000).

MORE REALLY GOOD SPORTS BOOKS FROM FAIR PLAY PUBLISHING

Riding Shotgun
Andy Bernal

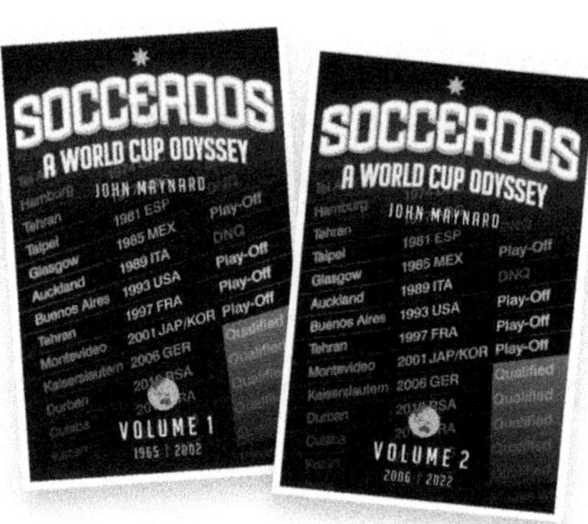

Socceroos – A World Cup Odyssey,
1965 to 2022 Volumes 1 and 2

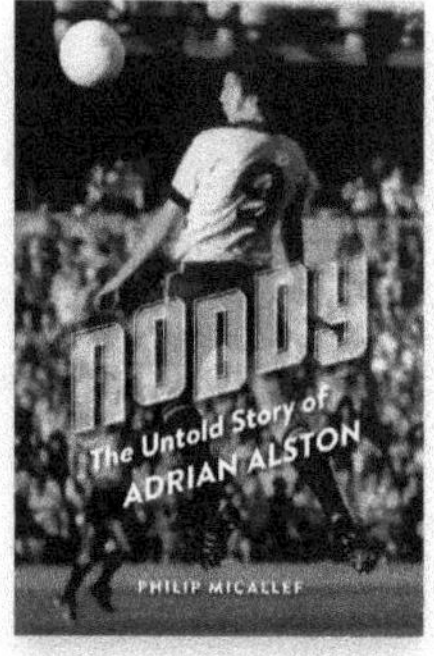

Noddy, The Untold Story
of Adrian Alston

Hell for Leather
The World of a
Sporting Journalist

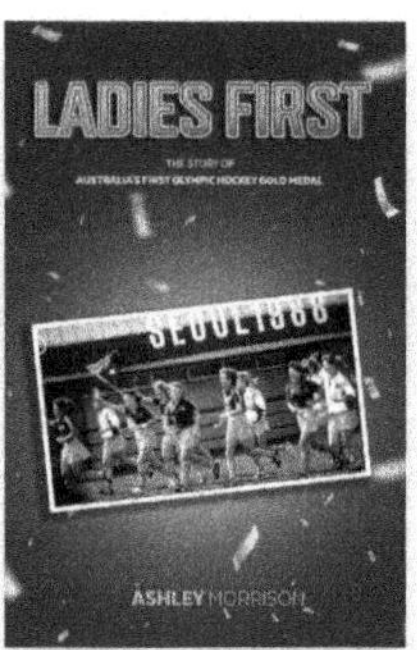

Ladies First
The Story of Australia's
First Olympic Hockey
Gold Medal

Michelle Ford
Olympic Champion
Turning The Tide

Richard 'Dick' Thornett
The Natural

Available from
fairplaypublishing.com.au/shop
and all good bookstores

www.fairplaypublishing.com.au

www.ingramcontent.com/pod-product-compliance
Ingram Content Group UK Ltd.
Pitfield, Milton Keynes, MK11 3LW, UK
UKHW021834270726
14058UKWH00001B/136

9 781923 236394